American University Studies

Series VII
Theology and Religion
Vol. 166

PETER LANG
New York • Washington, D.C./Baltimore • San Francisco
Bern • Frankfurt am Main • Berlin • Vienna • Paris

Albion and Ariel

Douglas J. Culver

Albion and Ariel

British Puritanism
and the Birth
of Political Zionism

PETER LANG
New York • Washington, D.C./Baltimore • San Francisco
Bern • Frankfurt am Main • Berlin • Vienna • Paris

Library of Congress Cataloging-in-Publication Data

Culver, Douglas J.
    Albion and Ariel: British Puritanism and the birth of political Zionism /
Douglas J. Culver.
      p.   cm. — (American university studies. Series VII, Theology and
religion; vol. 166)
    Includes bibliographical references and index.
    1. Christian Zionism—Great Britain—History. 2. Puritans—England—
Doctrines—History. 3. Jews—Restoration—History of doctrines.
4. Palestine in Christianity—History of doctrines. I. Title. II. Series.
DS149.C79   320.5'4'0956940941—dc20   94-16473
ISBN 0-8204-2303-3
ISSN 0740-0446

Die Deutsche Bibliothek-CIP-Einheitsaufnahme

Culver, Douglas J.:
Albion and Ariel: British Puritanism and the birth of political Zionism /
Douglas J. Culver. - New York; Washington, D.C./Baltimore; San Francisco;
Bern; Frankfurt am Main; Berlin; Vienna; Paris: Lang.
    (American university studies: Ser. 7, Theology and religion; Vol. 166)
    ISBN 0-8204-2303-3
NE: American university studies / 07

The paper in this book meets the guidelines for permanence and durability of
the Committee on Production Guidelines for Book Longevity of the
Council on Library Resources.

Contents

Acknowledgements

No task like this is ever done without the constructive criticisms, useful suggestions and most of all the encouragement of others. In this regard special thanks are due Mr. Richard Pachella, Rare Books Librarian at the Union Theological Seminary, New York City, Dr. David Rudavsky, Institute of Hebrew Studies, New York University; my father, Dr. Robert Duncan Culver, longtime Chairman of the Department of Systematic Theology and Christian Thought, Trinity Evangelical Divinity School, Deerfield, Illinois, and my wife Lyrle whose abiding love sustained me.

Chapter I

Prolegomena

This study has been undertaken because of the writer's particular interest in the following circumstances and forces now at play in the world of scholarship.

In General

Growing Interest in Things Eschatological and Prophetic

Beginning with the world crises wrought in World War I, continuing through succeeding decades and especially prominent since the 1954 Evanston meetings of the World Council of Churches there has been an increasing emphasis in Christian thought on General Eschatology[1] and within this division of theology specifically on questions relating to the future of Israel, the Jewish Messianic hope, the Jewish Church[2] and so on. These studies have necessitated some tentative probings of Protestant source materials having to do with biblical Prophetic passages.[3]

Growing Interest in State of Israel

Growing theological interest in the State of Israel since its establishment in 1948 has been manifest in reexamination of Christian interpretation of the biblical passages which refer to a national restoration.[4] The theological issue of the Jewish people as an integral aspect of Christian doctrine is being intensively restudied by some who, prior to the events of 1948, had entirely dismissed the validity of the idea from any point of view, biblical or otherwise.[5]

Recent Availability of Tools of Research in the Field
Bibliographical tools and collections of primary data are now
available that permit scrutiny to some depth at the historical
vortex of forces which cycling backward, eddy and meet in the
place, period, principles of this investigation. That is to say,
theological interest in things Jewish and concomitant interest
in the present reality of the nation of Israel find their point of
origin in Reformation events, persons and thought (for us
here, in Great Britain).[6] This facet of the investigation is relatively new territory to scholarship,[7] with some aspects achiev-
ing researchability to the non-peripatetic scholar only in the
last two decades.[8]

Challenge of a Unique Literature
The challenge inherent within the nature of the study simply
to identify and isolate the germane source material was a point
of attraction. From the perspective of the level of sophistica-
tion, ubiquitous presence and penetration into almost every
facet of life by the printing trade today, the state of the art was
in the first half of the seventeenth century yet in relative
infancy. But it was, nonetheless, already flourishing and
became daily more economically profitable.[9] It has already
eclipsed the method of public, personal confrontation in
debate and speech-making as the best means to gain an opti-
mum exposure for one's ideas.[10] It was readily recognized as a
most effective means of mass communication and propagan-
dizing and was to remain so right down to the margins of our
own time.[11] The printed word, from sonorous debates in parliament to simple homilies by village parsons, recorded by
scriveners, soon found its way to the stationers' stalls. And the
booksellers, enterprising Englishmen that they were, did not
scruple at blindness when it came to works officially, by royal,
or later, parliamentary decree, proscribed from the publication and sale.[12] Indeed, as any schoolboy will testify, what is
censored or suppressed, if that fact is properly advertised, is all
the more likely to achieve wide distribution and to turn a
handsome profit in the bargain.[13] Hence the quantity of
materials from this epoch is embarrassingly rich, especially in

matters religious and theological, the master passions of the age.[14]

Successfully to plow the field and discern in which furrows to find the pertinent materials must be accomplished somewhat the same way a farm boy locates the fattest fishworms in a field of freshly turned sod—watch where the crows settle. The trick was systematically to check and cross-check in the bibliographic tools to the literature where a given title on the subject and/or author was listed first by one or the other, then year by year through the period with an eye cocked for allied ideas, men, events, doctrines, Scripture passages. The terms "Kingdom of God/Christ," "Second Coming," "Millennium," "New Jerusalem," "Reign of the Saints," "Jacob's Household," "Zion," "Fifth Monarchy," and so on were usually a dead giveaway leading frequently to something immediately fruitful or pointing to something bibliographically cousin to it farther down the line that was. The *McAlpin Collection* (q.v., Appendix II) which organizes and lists by full title under the year, and having an author-title index as well, was especially fertile and produced the greatest number of useful items. The *Dr. William's Library of Early Nonconfirmity 1566-1800* was a close second by virtue of its mutually exclusive, cross-indexed author, title and chronological volumes, twelve in all. In addition, the tendency of scholarship of that day to give lengthy titles to works which in truth turned out to be propositional outlines of a book's contents was, and is, in this regard at least, a distinct advantage. Response to published polemic would often include the name of the man, or men, whose work(s) was to be answered, and sometimes the title of the work itself, as, e.g., Thomas Hayne's *Christ's Kingdom on Earth, Opened according to the Scriptures: Herein is examined what Mr. Th. Brightman, Dr. J. Alsted, Mr. I. Mede, Mr. H. Archer, The Glympse of Sions Glory, and such as concurre in opinion with them, hold concerning the thousand years of the Saints Reign with Christ, and of Satan's binding: Herein also their arguments are answered* (1645). Perhaps a more apt, if also painful illustration may be had in the books of Robert Maton and Alexander Petrie, respectively, on both sides of the millennial question. Maton's first book on the topic is entitled: *Israel's Redemption, Or, the Jewes Generall and*

Miraculous conversion to the faith of the Gospel: and return into their owne Land: And our Saviours personall Reigne on Earth, cleerly proved out of many plaine Prophecies of the Old and New Testaments (1642).   To this work Petrie issues his rebuttal: *Chiliasto-Mastix, Or the Prophecies in the Old and New Testament Concerning the Kingdome of Our Saviour Jesus Christ Vindicated from the Misrepresentations of the Millenaries and Specially of Mr. Maton in his book called Israel's Redemption etc.* (1644).   And Maton replies: *Israel's Redemption Redeemed, Or, the Jewes generall and miraculous Conversion to the faith of the Gospel: and returne into their owne Land: And our Saviours personall Reigne on Earth, cleerly proved out of many plaine Prophecies of the Old and New Testaments and the chiefe Arguments that can be alleged against these Truths, fully answered: Of Purpose to satisfie all gainsayers; and in particular Mr. Alexander Petrie, Minister of the Scottish Church in Roterdam.   By Robert Maton, the Author of Israel's Redemption etc., Divided into two Parts, whereof the first concernes the Jewes Restauration into a visible Kingdome in Judea: And the second, our Saviours visible Reigne over them, and all other nations at his next appearing, whereunto are annexed the Authors Reasons, for the literall and proper sense of the plagues contain'd under the Trumpets and Vialls* (1646).[15]

By the time each of the reference bibliographies has been searched in this manner, checked against the very useful *British Museum Library Catalogue* and cross-checked against one another, there is reasonable certainty that all *available* data has in fact been identified.[16] Happy, confirming helps along the way come occasionally in checking through the sources and scholars quoted in later works. For one instance, Edward Bickersteth's mid-nineteenth century solid, scholarly works entitled *Guide to the Prophecies, Restoration of the Jews* and *Signs of the Times* (London: Seelys, 1852) were particularly useful.

In this connection, though one of the factors attracting the present writer to the task, no claim is made that the result is exhaustive in any absolute sense. The nature of the case is such that it is almost certain more materials do exist in private collections and libraries, especially in Great Britain. Doubtless, pamphlets, sermons, tracts, miscellaneous longhand manuscripts, perhaps even a bound volume or two, which, initially suppressed by the authorities or withheld from publication precisely because of the suppression of earlier similar works, or for unknown reasons, never have come to public knowledge, would shed further light on the topic. From time to time, with the upset of war, sale of estates, bequests to universities, antiquarian societies, etc., further resources do rise to the surface and are made available to scholars.[17]

The reader is again referred to Appendix II for a complete list of the printed catalogues of collections, reference bibliographies, and other bibliographic tools used in this investigation. The distinctive function of each can be quickly ascertained from the compass of the work and other details outlined therein.

Contribution of Recent Old Testament Scholarship
Such recognized Old Testament theologians and scholars, to name but a few, as H. H. Rowley, G. E. Wright, M. F. Albright, R. H. Pfeiffer, R. deVaux, M. North, C. H. Gordon, G. R. Driver, M. Burrows, T. J. Meek, A. Alt, S. Mowinchel, S. Moscati, O. Eissfeldt, G. von Rad, E. G. Kraeling, John Bright, N. Glueck, Y. Yadin, A. Dupont-Sommers, K. Schubert, *et al.* have contributed vastly to the discussion of related topics from the biblical standpoint, solidly underlaid by linguistic, historical and archaelogical confirmation. Matters of biblical introduction are fairly well agreed upon and need not be an undue variable in such a study as the present one,[18] so that attention can be spent on interpretative history.

Particular Reasons for Undertaking the Study

The Relation Between a Biblically Versed Public and Jewish Hopes in Britain
It seems from the perspective of the present day that the verdict of history has demonstrated an intimate connection between the steeping of the people of Great Britain in the Bible on the one hand and the realization of Jewish hopes on the other. Theodor Herzl himself wrote in his diary,

From the first moment I entered the Zionist movement, my eyes were attracted towards England because I saw that by reason of the general situation there, it was the Archimedian point where the lever could be applied.[19]

And again in an address in London to the Fourth Zionist Congress in August of 1900 he said,

England, mighty England, free England, with its world embracing outlook will understand us and our aspirations.[20]

Herzl seemed to have an unerring instinct. It is no mere happenstance that his only son was by his own wish brought up in an English school and English university.[21]

Norman Bentwich expresses this same fact in its more practical implications:

Throughout the nineteenth century the English were the people continuously concerned with the movement of the return of the Jews to the Holy Land. That was so partly because more than others they were a Protestant Bible-reading people, and a large section had a belief in the fulfillment of Hebrew prophecy; and partly because England, as a world-power, had a permanent interest in the Middle East which commanded the route to India.

That interest became greater still after the construction of the Suez Canal and the British occupation of Egypt in 1881. But long before that, English statesmen and English divines and writers had been concerned with the Jewish return to the Bible Land.[22]

In this same connection it is instructive that in the article "Zionism" in the widely esteemed *Encyclopaedia Brittanica*, Lucien Wolf alludes specifically to the Christian millennial doctrines of seventeenth century English Nonconformists that sustained and "gave fresh impetus," as he puts it, to the Jewish restoration idea.[23] But Mr. Wolf elaborates no further.

Thus in at least adumbrate fashion there has been general acknowledgement of the theme here in view. There has been, however, no thorough documentation of the central thesis of Jewish restoration as it is contained and developed in the literature and the period this study will examine and treat. The problem for us here is simply to answer this question: What are the origins and content of the idea of Jewish return as a nation to Palestine as developed in the biblical and theological exposition of British Nonconformity 1585—1640?

Dimensions of the Study

As to Chronological Limits of the Investigation

A *terminus a quo* of 1584 is adopted because this is the date of the first work in Great Britain which treats in some discernibly germane way the idea of a national restoration for the Jews. Many incidental references to Jews and things Jewish can be found in earlier theological literature:[24] Duns Scotus, William of Occam, John Wycliffe, the sixteenth century reformers, Cranmer, Latimer, Ridley and so on, but no systematic treatment, however brief, really no recognition in any sense, of the biblical-eschatological centrality of this idea. It begins its appearance in the Nonconformity[25] rising after the Elizabethan Settlement.[26] Francis Kett's *The Glorious and Beautiful Garland of Man's Glorification Containing the Godly Misterie of Heavenly Jerusalem* (1585) is the first work with what appears to be deliberate discussion of the idea.[27]

A *terminus ad quem* of 1640 is adopted because it marks a definite end to the period of pioneer development with which the present writer is concerned. By this date the originators and initial advocates had passed from the scene[28] without first hand disciples to carry on the idea as they envisioned it. Beyond 1640 a new generation of protagonists arose who brought with them the influences of the new moment in history, hence new emphases and uses for the idea.[29] Significantly, however, among the second generation of expositors there can be found nothing essentially new. Innovation did not brand their stage of development of the idea but rather they began by reissuing the works of the pioneers, beginning in 1641. This was accomplished by posthumously publishing several works that had not been put into print by the real authors for reasons of political discretion, i.e., personal safety.[30]

Following 1640, development of the notion of Jewish national restoration is marked, and muddied for a time, by the angry currents of the rush and flow of historical and political events. Precisely in this year the tide turned in favor of parliamentary interests and began its inexorable swell as the members of the Long Parliament sat to begin and ultimately to consumate their intense struggle against Stuart despotism by turning to force of arms and regicide in the Great Rebellion.[31] And the tide did not ebb, much less reverse, for nearly two full decades (1658) when English sentiment over-ran reason and rashly invited back Stuart rule in the person of Charles II. Be this as it may, the instructive point is that expectations and demands of the many parties to the fray following 1640, Fifth Monarchy Men, Ranters, Levellers, Diggers, Independents, Baptists, Separatists, even to some degree the quietistic Quakers, and myriad lesser parties, most of them literate and all vocal—from the radical, rabble-rousing Lilburne to the highly urbane, sophisticated genius of John Milton, plus the newly recognized utility of the printing trade, combined to fill stationers' stalls to overflowing with pamphlets and tracts arguing variations on the common prophetic themes of imminent apocalyptic events, pending divine judgment, cataclysmic, millennial advent, onset of the Kingdom of Christ (with Zion restored, Jerusalem resplendent, Jews returned, and converted) intermixed to favorable advantage with the position and views of one's own faction in the scramble for power. Neither the multiplicity of materials nor the complexity of the situation, especially of the ten year period immediately following 1640, can be exaggerated. The epoch from seating of the Long Parliament to accession of Charles II to the throne, approximately 1640-1658, provides material enough for several dozen theses in each of half a hundred categories related to the topic under investigation.[32]

Hence the year 1640 is put forward to serve as a limit to the study. It is a watershed division, widely used and recognized.[33]

Historical-Critical Scope of the Investigation

The goal here is historical and critical in nature with the overall purpose of exposing the ongoing stream and flow of development.[34] It is historical in so far as it is descriptive; it is critical in so far as it is synthetic. That is, the task is not to assess the validity of a given writer, notion, movement, school or system of thought but accurately to report, describe and synthesize. Analysis, rather than propaganda or value judgment, is the purpose.

Hence, also, no definitions of what constitutes one a Jew, therefore theoretically qualified to take part in the contemplated restoration to Palestine, will be attempted on the part of the investigator nor extrapolated from the literature under examination. This issue, however interesting, is related by way of parallel rather than truly touching the question under treatment.

Presuppositions

The most rudimentary element is the idea of a Jewish restoration to Palestine and the existence of the Jewish people as an ethnic and religious entity was as a matter of interest and theological comment in the period 1585-1640.[35]

A second presupposition is that theological statements of the period evince notions of a Jewish restoration and role for the Jewish people in some distinct sense other than preparation for Christianity. Rather, Jewish national restoration was an organic component of Christian doctrinal system.[36]

A final presupposition is that the body of theological literature of the period yields sufficient material on the topic to be valid for collection and treatment of the problem.[37]

Nature of the Contribution

From the facts above, it appears that the time is ripe for a full investigation of this stream of thought and feeling where it was originally conceived and the process of gestation began, namely, in the theological tracts rising out of English Nonconformity in the period 1585-1640. We will see that theological and biblical controversy was the seminal precursor of what later[38] gained separate identity of its own among the frank protagonists of Jewish restoration,[39] and which, in time, took political form in Zionism.[40] Zionism in Britain did not spring suddenly full grown into being like Athene from the head of Zeus, but was built from blocks resting logically and emotion-

ally on foundations laid in this period. As Israel Zangwill so
aptly put it:

> Seldom, indeed, has a coming event cast so obvious and lengthy a
> shadow before as the intervention of Britain on behalf of a Jewish
> Palestine.[41]

Something must prepare the way for so momentous a series
of events.[42] For every effect there must be a sufficient cause.
This investigation, then, will scrutinize that time of embryonic
conception and the period of early gestation of the idea which
grew through the century and became, at length, the robust
child of the eighteenth and nineteenth century in England.
By the final decades of the latter we find a people openly and
habitually concerned with the movement of the return of the
Jews to the Holy Land and a Protestant Bible-reading people,[43] believing in the literal fulfillment of Hebrew
prophecy.[44]

Several things are evident at this point: (1) the materials
are available in the quantity and quality necessary to an adequate scholarly inquiry. (2) Competent scholars have been
active in several related aspects of the topic. (3) A thorough,
cogent treatment of the specific materials, period and issue
involved is timely.

Hopefully, therefore, results from this investigation will
make a unique contribution to understanding the origins,
early content and initial development of the idea of Jewish
restoration to a national homeland in Palestine as it came to
birth and developed in Great Britain. It will help clarify at
germinal points the place of the Jewish people and of Jewish
national restoration in the history of succeeding Protestant
Christian theological and doctrinal discussion. It will help to
show the relevance and interplay of the development of Christian doctrine in history. And again it will demonstrate Victor
Hugo's axiom that nothing can stop an idea whose time has
come.

While projected as a limited topic for investigation, the end
product should not be of narrow parochial interest and importance only, but may also have ramifications and applications in

the broadening ecclesiastic and ecumenic conversations of our day.

Notes

1 This term, as used here, is to be sharply distinguished from the fashionable uses of it in popular circles to suggest a hankering after whatever lies "out there" beyond, i.e., of things mystical — albeit while employing the vocabulary of interests genuinely belonging to the spiritual dimensions of human life. Things mystic, often smacking of the merely occult, have become objects to conjure with. Any and everything that is sweetly unreasonable or piquantly obscure is welcomed and exalted to the dignity of a more or less esoteric cult. Flirting with psychedelic drugs, explosion in narcotics use and the marginal cultures each engenders — is it too much to be hoped? — represent a deep hunger and thirst after eternal verities of the spirit.

Among recent treatments of bonafide Eschatology are the following: R. H. Charles, *A Critical History of the Doctrine of a Future Life*; S. D. F. Salmond, *The Christian Doctrine of Immortality*; Rudolph Otto, *The Kingdom of God and the Son of Man*; E. F. Sutcliffe, *The Old Testament and the Future Life*; Oscar Cullmann, *Christ and Time*; G. E. Ladd, *Crucial Questions about the Kingdom of God and The Blessed Hope*; G. R. Beasley-Murray, *Jesus and the Future*; H. Quistorp, *Calvin's Doctrine of the Last Things*; D. Daube and W. D. Davies (eds.), *The Background of the New Testament and its Eschatology*.

2 One of the better known is Jean Danielou's *The Theology of Jewish Christianity*, translated by John A. Baker (Chicago: Henry Regnery Company, 1964). Of particular interest here is the chapter on millennarianism and the twelve pages of bibliography at the end of the volume.

3 D. Daube, *The New Testament and Rabbinic Judaism*. M. O. E. Oesterly, *The Jewish Background of the Christian Liturgy*; H. Britenhard, *The Millennial Hope of the Early Church*; B. W. Newton, *The Millennium and Israel's Future*; Notes in the *New Scofield Bible*; O. T. Allis, *Prophecy and the Church*; pre-eminently the exhaustive, monumental five volume work of Hermann L. Strack and Paul Billerbeck, *Kommentar zum Neuen Testament aus Talmud und Midrasch* (München: Ch. Back'sche Verlags Buchandlung Oskarbeck, 1922-28).

4 Robert D. Culver, *Daniel and the Latter Days* (Westwood, New Jersey: Fleming H. Revell, 1954), pp. 213ff. gives a lengthy selected bibliography. More recently yet, Wilbur M. Smith, *Arab/Israeli Conflict and the Bible* (Glendale, California: Regal Books, 1967), is an excellent primer on the topic, together with bibliographical leads for further study.

5 Albertus Pieters, a representative, highly esteemed, conservative spokesman in Reformed theological circles, Professor at the Western Theological Seminary of the Reformed Church in America, says bluntly in his widely read *The Seed of Abraham* (Grand Rapids, Michigan: Wm. B. Eerdmans Publishing Co., 1950), that the present people who refer to themselves and who are known as Jews are not in any way to be identified with the "Seed of Abraham" spoken of in Scripture. The Jews, according to Dr. Pieters are no more than the present day followers of Talmudic tradition begun in Jamnia by Jochanan ben Zakkai. This people, says Dr. Pieters, hasn't the remotest connection with the Israel of the Old Testament. Moreover, the modern political extension of the ongoing tradition begun in Jamnia, styled as Zionism and now consumated in the state of Israel is interesting politically as a kind of historical-political anomaly but has no reference to Biblical prophecy. *Vide* Chapter VIII, "What of the Jews," pp. 132-148 of Pieter's work *supra.* Here is a contemporary scholar whose piety and expository, theological and hermeneutic qualifications are recognized and highly regarded in serious circles. Wilbur M. Smith, perhaps the leading, evangelical theological bibliographer notes the same attitude (not his own) that runs through Protestant theology in his *Israeli/Arab Conflict and the Bible* (Glendale, California: Regal Books, 1967), pp. 6-7, when he says,

> There has always been a marked difference of opinion in the Christian Church regarding many of the problems which this crisis raises. Indeed, among many reformed theologians, and many others also, there is the strange conviction that there really is no future for the Jew as a nation on this earth. For many years the idea that the Jews would ever repossess Palestine was ridiculed. Since 1948 the attitude has changed by such to one of condemnation, affirming that the state of Israel is all a mistake on the part of the Jews.

A little later (pp. 35-38) Dr. Smith outlines the four modes of interpreting out of existence the knotty difficulty posed to this school of thought by the present reality of the state of Israel and the corresponding biblical ligatures which bind the two together.

6 The data of the study itself will steadily confirm this.

7 E.g., One of the major research tools became available only in the winter of (1968), viz., the twelve quarto size volumes of the *Dr. Williams Library Collection of Early Nonconformity 1566-1800. Vide* Appendix V for description of this and other bibliographical tools used. Moreover, scrutiny of the titles of the bibliography of secondary sources treating the period under study will reveal them, as very recent.

8 Micro-filming of incunabula and rare printed materials through such facilities as University Microfilms, Ann Arbor, Michigan, and The Folger Shakespeare Library, Washington, D.C., has only lately been fully functional in the literature of this area of research. Donald Wing's

Short-Title Catalogue of English History and Theology Printed in England, Scotland, Ireland, Wales and British America and of English Books Printed in Other Countries, 1641-1700 (1946) and Pollard and Redgrave's *Short-Title, Catalogue of Books Printed in England, Scotland and Ireland, and of English Books Printed Abroad, 1475-1640* (1944) especially, but also M. M. *Bishop's Checklist of American Copies of Short-Title Catalogue Books* (1950), the 1964 republication of an updated *British Museum Library Catalogue* and the already mentioned *Dr. Williams Library Catalogue* (1968) have been responsible for considerable increase in accessibility of materials, hence also of scholarly productivity.

9 William Haller, *The Rise of Puritanism* (New York: Columbia University Press, 1947), pp. 232, 250, 370ff.

10 *Ibid.*

11 *Ibid.* Noteworthy in this connection is the rather important fact this period was without qualification the most brilliant age of *belles lettres* in western civilization. Nothing yet has managed to approach Shakespeare, Marlowe, Milton, Bunyan, etc.

12 William Haller, *op. cit.*, p. 377. The Stationer's Company in London exercised authority over the license to print. It maintained in its offices what was known as *Stationer's Register*. Royal and Parliamentary ordinances required that nothing be printed unless entered therein. Of course, since most of the materials here under study were revolutionary in character for that day, certainly inimical to royal prerogatives and later to parliamentary strictures, they were not thus entered.

13 William Haller, *op. cit.*, p. 378.

14 If this period was anything, it was an age of intense, explosive, religious excitement and biblical study. To the relative exclusion of most other disciplines of human thought and endeavor — and ultimately to its own hurt — theology carried the day at the very apogee of public interest and discussion. The Reformation doctrine of the priesthood of the individual believer had made every man into a theologian, for good or ill.

15 Unfortunately, works from this period seldom have indices or other topical aids. Page by page is the only feasible method of travel to one's destination in surveying content.

16 Laying hands on this material for personal scrutiny is yet another problem. Rare book and special collections librarians are understandably chary of subjecting these frail, time worn, irreplaceable works in their care to overmuch handling. Flattery, cajolery and other specious maneuverings help, but usually quick reference to Bishop's Checklist, a letter of request, a check to covery photoduplication costs and time (!) is necessary. Eight to ten weeks wait, often more, is a source of consider-

able frustration because of the breaks of continuity in writing and documentation thus caused.

17 E.g. The *McAlpin Collection and Catalogue*, has, since the 1926 publication of its five volume index, added several thousand more titles. No published index is yet available for this newer material but accessibility is possible via a supplementary card catalogue to the general catalogue of the library holdings on the Union Theological Seminary premises in New York City. The *Dr. Williams Library* alluded to above began as a kind of special theological antiquarian repository, only in 1968 finally getting a catalogue of its holdings into print. Supplements of various related collections irregularly, but frequently, do make it into print announcing recent acquisitions.

18 This should not imply there is no gulf between conservative and more critical views. It does mean that the lines thus drawn are quite well defined and, with minor adjustments, established firmly enough in viable hypothesis and fact to support an historical investigation of the uses to which the interpretations thus derived have been put.

19 Theodor Herzl, *Complete Diaries*, edited by Raphael Patai, translated by Harry Zohn (New York: Herzl Press and Thomas Yoseloff, 1960), volume V, p. 1364. Also, *vide* Norman Bentwich, *Early English Zionists* (Tel Aviv: Lion the Printer for the Zionist Organization, Youth Department, n.d.), pp. 5-6ff., for several germane comments from observations of Herzl and his coterie of associates.

20 "England, das grosse, England, das freie, England das über alle Meere blickt, wird uns und unsere Bestrebungen verstehen." World Zionist Organization, *Stenographisches Protokoll der verhandungen des IV. Zionisten Congresses London, 13, 14, 15, 16 August, 1900* (Wien: World Zionist Organization, 1900), p. 5. Also available in extracted and translated form in the "Progress Planning Kit" of the *Theodor Herzl Centenial*, published by the Theodor Herzl Institute, 515 Park Avenue, New York, New York 10022. These materials together with a large set of files of Herzl pamphlets, biography, diaries, etc., are held by the Jewish Agency Zionist Archives, 515 Park Avenue, New York, New York 10002.

21 Theodor Herzl, "Memorandum to Lord Landsdowne," *Diaries*, IV, p. 1367ff.

22 Norman Bentwich, *op. cit.*, pp. 5-6.

23 Lucien Wolf, "Zionism," *Encyclopaedia Brittanica*, XXVII (1911), p. 987.

24 *Vide* Henry Gouge, *A General Index to the Publications of the Parker Society* (Cambridge: University Press, 1855), pp. 420-422, for an exhaustive listing of references to Jews in the works of the primary British Reformers.

25 *Vide* Appendix II for an alphabetical listing of definitions of theological and historical terms used in this study, as, e.g., "Nonconformity."

26 The Thirty-Nine Articles (q.v. Appendix II) was that to which those known as nonconformists would not conform.

27 This must be qualified to the extent that it is limited to extant, printed materials originating in Great Britain. The section "Challenge of a Unique Literature" *supra*, sketches the methodology involved to isolate and secure them.

28 Several of the first advocates of the idea of Jewish restoration paid with their lives or goods or both for their temerity.

29 At this point it must be observed that in the literature under study the notion of Jewish restoration nowhere stands alone. Rather than being an autonomous idea it was basically a necessary element in the eschatology of pious men who approached the Bible, both Old and New Testaments, very seriously with a view to ascertaining there "those things which the Lord himself in his word commandeth" as "plainly set forth in the Scriptures for all to follow" (*An Admonistion to Parliament* [1572] cited in William Haller, *Elizabeth I and the Puritans*] Published for the Folger Shakespeare Library, Ithaca, New York: Cornell University Press, 1964], p. 1). We must remember, as well, that the doctrinal scheme which was in the forefront of the religious ferment in England in the seventeenth century was Calvinism, which stressed the systematic nature, i.e., logical continuity and coherence, of biblical truth. Eschatology fit, therefore, with Ecclesiology, Anthropology, Hamartiology, Christology, Soteriology, Theology Proper, etc., the other spokes of the wheel in the doctrinal expression of Christianity. The force which prevailed in the minds of men of such persuasion was, reduced to its most rudimentary elements, simply, to ascertain and do the will of God revealed in the Scriptures (Wm. Haller, *op. cit.*, p. 24). Hence a hermeneutic that accepted at full value whatever the Bible said and gave it the constraining power of absolute, binding truth found a prominent place for the future of the people of Israel as vividly painted in the Prophets as well as the Apocalyptic books of each Testament. To these deeply religious men, therefore, the notion of a restored Jewish nation in its divinely appointed promised home was part of the fiber of the whole fabric of biblical truth. It could be made useful, too, as was increasingly recognized, as an implement in the rapidly gathering, intense struggle against episcopacy and royal despotism. This latter aspect developed strength and became more and more visible in the two decades following 1640 through the period of the Long Parliament, Civil War, and Commonwealth to 1658, especially in the writings of the Fifth Monarchy men, John Archer's *The Personall Reigne of Christ Upon Earth* (London: Benjamin Allen, 1642), special case in point.

30 E.g., Giles Fletcher's *Israel Redux: Or the Restauration of Israel* was not published until as late as 1677—more than 50 years after Fletcher's

death in 1611—when all his works were collected and issued, bound with a current treatise on the same topic by Samuel Lee (London: S. Streater for John Hancock, 1677). Thomas Brightman's Latin treatise *Apoclypsis Apocalypseos* (1609) was translated into English in 1615 then reissued in 1641. A curious tract entitled *Brightman Redivivus: A Man Bright in Prophecy* appeared yet later in 1647 (London: Printed for Peter Cole, and are to be sold at the Sign of the Printing Presse in Cornhill neer the Royall-Exchange). A similar story is true for the works of Joseph Mede, Sir Henry Finch, and so on. Finch, in fact, received several pages of attention, however disfavorably, as late as 1650 at the hands of the historian Thomas Fuller in his *Pisgah-Sight of Palestine and Confines Thereof, with the History of the Old and New Testament Acted Thereon* (London: J. F. for John Williams, 1650), pp. 194-202.

31 Commonly known as the Civil War. The eminent British historian, J. R. Green thus refers to the victorious struggle against Stuart tyranny on the part of Puritan forces (at this point loosely embracing most of the nonconformist dissenting groups). J. R. Green, *Short History of the English People* (New York: Harper and Brothers, 1894), volume III, *passim.*

32 William Haller's three volume edition of *Tracts on Liberty in the Puritan Revolution 1638-1647* and his one volume edition *Leveller Tracts 1647-1653* alone comprise 2000 pages of raw material through which the topic of this investigation trails. In addition there are whole libraries given over to this area as, e.g., the *Dr. Williams Library (London) Collection*, which merely to catalogue requires twelve quarto volumes, the *McAlpin Collection* requiring five oversize volumes for cataloguing, the many multi-volume bibliographies for the period such as Donald Wing's six-volume *Short Title Catalogue*, and The British Museum *Thomason Collection* (Index is two volumes), etc. Moreover, this period of time was one of extreme religious and civil and historical restiveness. Even the Civil War which ensued, with emphatic military victory for the Parliamentary forces, did not resolve the burning issues of the day, which, indeed, continued to roil the waters to the century's end. Moreover, how to trace and assess the genius of a Milton or Bunyan, or Cromwell himself, through the literature from their hands alone, much less the huge numbers of documents preserved and written *about* them in the most elemental terms of their influence, their Puritanism, their personalities, or even on a fairly self limiting doctrinal point like the one in view here, is hopelessly vast. Hence we do well to stop before crossing the threshold of 1640 into the new epoch which lies beyond.

33 William Haller in his *Rise of Puritanism* (New York: Columbia University Press, 1938), thus terminates his study. J. R. Green in his *Short History of the English People* makes exactly the same determination of dates for reasons of the clear historical-political disjunction.

34 Some will object that the term "progress" should be used. Ideas are rather like living organisms, however. The medium in which the life of

an idea is lived out is history, with all its turns and twists, reverses, calamities. Moreover, things organic do die. While each of the two words is tarred with the same brush, "progress" smacks more strongly of the value-creating dogma of evolutionary theory. It will therefore be avoided. The requirement is indication of continuity, in a line only sometimes, and forward to consummation in fits, spurts, spiralings and occasional dyspepsia. A philosophy of history is not intended.

35 It is impossible to read far in any biblical or theological work of any generation in the Protestant era without somewhere encountering allusion to Jews and things Jewish in a variety of specific connections. E.g., see the index to such standard works as J. L. Neve's *History of Christian Thought* (Philadelphia: United Lutheran Publication House, 1943), or J. A. Dorner's *History of Protestant Theology*, Translated by G. Robson (Edinburgh: T. & T. Clark, 1908). Also, any general biblical and theological work in the attached bibliography will corroborate this point. But the particular richness and prominence of systematic reference in this period to Jews, Israel, Jerusalem, Zion and myriad Old Testament motifs is related directly to the pervasive influence of the Bible and the irresistible appeal it had to the imagination of the English people who saw there in the pages of Scripture

> . . . not an abstract systematic exposition of general principles and precepts but the richly imaginative representation of the life of a people recognizably like themselves—patriarchs, prophets, judges and kings; husbands, wives and their families, all involved in the common predicaments of personal, family and public life. And running through the whole, from Genesis to Revelation, was the saga of a people acutely conscious of their own identity as a people, believing themselves to have been singled out from the beginning and set apart from all others for a special purpose and testing by an inscrutable almight power who keeps them under His constant care and observation and may be expected to break in upon them at any time with His commands and judgments.

William Haller, *Elizabeth I and the Puritans* (Published for the Folger Shakespeare Library, Ithaca, New York: Cornell University Press, 1964), pp. 30, 31.

36 LeRoy Edwin Froom in volume II of his massive four volume *Prophetic Faith of Our Fathers* (Washington, D.C.: Review and Herald, 1946-54), connects allusions to Jews in exposition of the biblical book of Daniel in the Old Testament and Revelation in the New Testament with 108 Reformation writers from the time of Luther and the primary reformers to the end of the Reformation epoch on the continent with the Peace of Westphalia in 1648. There are many incidental references to Jews and things Jewish among the earliest writers of the English Reformation. Direct treatment in the manner examined here begins with Frances Kett in 1585.

37 In general, the Protestant Reformation, terminating on the Continent with the Peace of Westphalia in 1648 but not truly settled in England till the end of the seventeenth century, was in fact the period of theological and biblical study *par excellence* in Christian history. Nothing has approached it in sheer mass or overall quality of production in this field. *Vide* R. H. Bainton, *The Reformation of the Sixteenth Century* (Boston: Beacon Press, 1952). Cf. also Kenneth Scott Latourette, *A History of Christianity* (New York: Harper and Row, 1953). Roland Bainton is perhaps the leading scholar in Reformation Studies, especially of Luther and the German movement. He makes this specific point in the introductory pages of the above work. Kenneth Scott Latourette of Yale University was known as the most eminent Church historian of the day. His superb *Expansion* series and his *History*, cited above, are standard, recognized works. In particular the period of rising Puritanism in Great Britain produced prolifically on biblical topics especially those relating to the Second Coming of Christ and concomitant eschatological doctrines of Divine Judgment, the Millennium, reign of the saints, victory over Antichrist, restored Israel to a rejuvenated Zion with all its enemies subdued, etc. John Lord reports of Oliver Cromwell, e.g., in his *Beacon Lights of History* (New York: Fords, Howard and Hulbert, 1884): "His favorite doctrine was the second coming of Christ and the reign of His saints" (volume four, p. 99).

38 After 1640 the tide of history pressed the idea of Jewish national restoration into a more or less self contained category apart from its integral relation within Christian systematic theology and doctrine. Robert Maton's *Israel's Redemption etc.* (1641) is perhaps the earliest example, but from here on this pattern is the norm.

39 Oblique allusions to Israel's or Jewish restoration by the end of the Protectorate under Cromwell all but disappeared. It was no longer necessary to disguise the idea or to couch it in clever theological subterfuges. This can readily be observed in chronological fashion from the titles of the works on the topic. Especially from 1640 onward, a work on Jewish restoration can be quickly recognized as just that. Prior to this date such an overt declaration was risky. Cecil Roth's *Magna Bibliotheca Anglo Judaica*, is indicative of this phenomenon, as one example among the reference bibliographies. He records only one title prior to 1640, Thomas Draxe's *The World's Resurrection . . .* (1608) — note no direct allusions here and yet every other title of the 45 Roth lists to the publication date (1837) of the last work is perfectly transparent as to its contents.

40 Franz Kobler, *op. cit.*, p. 21 to the end of the work.

41 Israel Zangwill, *The Voice of Jerusalem* (New York: Macmillan, 1921), p. 297.

42 Amiel, the French thinker, says simply, "the decisive events of the world take place in the intellect." Morris Jastrow, *Zionism and the Future of Palestine* (New York: The Macmillen Co., 1919), p. 13.

43 Thomas Carlyle's remark "All of history is an inarticulate Bible" is a capsulized commentary on the impact the Bible had in English life and literature.

44 A broad Christian community which accepted the Old and New Testaments as the Word of God written and therefore authoritative and binding in every regard of its teaching is, of course, historically and logically a necessary antecedent of this position. The great evangelical revivals of John and Charles Wesley and later of D. L. Moody played a prominent part in reconfirming the Bible-reading habits and biblically informed outlook of the people. For a prime example of the thorough treatment of the doctrine of Jewish restoration received with full bibliographical support demonstrating the pervasiveness and penetration of this aspect of theology, see the exceptional mid-nineteenth century (1852) works of Edward Bickersteth, especially in his *Guide to the Prophecies, Restoration of the Jews* and *Signs of the Times,* published by Seelys of London. There was in this period unusual activity in things prophetic, and an intense popular interest. Section III of the Appendix in Bickersteth's *Restoration* is a revealing essay entitled "Personal Intercourse with the Jews." He also includes a long annotated bibliography.

Chapter II

Diaspora – Restoration:
Stark Reality – Splendid Hope

The Singular Nature of the Birth of the Modern State of Israel

Only one event since Titus' legions extinguished the last sparks of Jewish independence *circa* the year seventy of the Christian era has as radically affected the Jewish people, namely, the establishment of the State of Israel.[1] That this achievement was wrought at all under the circumstances which prevailed was, to say the least, an epic feat.[2] That it was accomplished under so crushing a series of nearly impossible obstacles and political anomalies is historically scarcely credible.[3] Far greater powers and vastly greater numbers have often failed in lesser undertakings.[4] But it did indeed take place.

Truly this watershed event may be correctly viewed as the single greatest accomplishment of Diaspora Jewry.[5] The sheer grit of the Jewish people has the modern State of Israel for its monument. Nothing, therefore, ought to be said or inferred to blunt the sharp image of the heroic dimension and indigenous quality of that long struggle.

There was, however, a non-Jewish element hidden in the Restoration of the Jews to their homeland in Palestine.[6] A most revealing and instructional passage to this effect in the framework of this investigation is a short paragraph in Cecil Roth's October 20, 1936, presidential address to the Jewish Historical Society of England. He says quite directly that,

> England and English theorists [i.e., Biblical expositors, originally and later political figures, poets, etc.], are *jointly* [italics mine] responsible

with Jews for the evolution of Zionism in its modern form. It is not a question of reversing the policy of the past twenty years, but that of the past three centuries. Such as association is not lightly to be broken. This is no mere Jewish enterprise, but *an enterprise in which England and the Jews are closely, inseparably, associated* [italics mine].[7]

Though not common knowledge, this supreme ideal of world Jewry has, in fact, been shared, nurtured and actively advocated by segments of several nations among whom the Jews from time to time have dwelt.[8]

The Contribution of Great Britain

The people of Great Britain stand out in distinct relief against the relatively quiescent background of the rest of the nations. The Balfour Declaration (November 2, 1917), for example, stands as a twentieth century "Decree of Cyrus" which pales other nations' patronage of the idea.[9] But such a proclamation of an overt protagonist as Sir Arthur James Balfour does not leap to maturity *ex nihilo*. Presumably only God can thus create matter and then life from a vacuum. Rather, it, like all other living things, must at some point in time be conceived, undergo gestation, be brought to birth in travail, be carefully nourished and cultivated, arriving only at length at maturity in that organic process we call history.[10] On this point in the same address to the Jewish Historical Society of England referred to above, Cecil Roth underscores this point at a time when Jewish very survival was looking, at best, shaky, and any kind of national resurgence or homecoming to a sovereign state of their own was at its nadir:

There is yet another point, of particular interest at the present time. In the new edition of the *Bibliotheca Anglo-Judaica*, published by our Society, there figured for the first time a section comprising what has been written in English by non-Jews advocating the restoration of the Jews to their ancient home in Palestine. Nahum Sokolow, in his monumental *History of Zionism*, made a preliminary survey of the ground; *but even those familiar with his researches must be amazed at the number, the continuity and the authority of the works in question, stretching back in unbroken sequence as far as the seventeenth century* [italics mine]. There can be no doubt that these publications played a considerable part in the evolution of the Zionist idea. The Jews, it is true, preserved the impulse; but these English theorists gave the question a certain degree of actuality, and pressed it from time to time upon the notice of the Western world. The interest in Zionism shown by Joseph Chamberlain and his successors was not, therefore, anything novel; it was a new expression, in perhaps more practical form, of an enthusiasm which had been familiar in England for some three centuries and which had been in no small measure responsible for the eagerness with which Herzl and his colleagues and forerunners looked to English sympathy and aid.

That enthusiasm reached its culmination in the Balfour Declaration of 1917, and its fulfillment on the Turkish debacle in the following year. Today, there are certain elements in this country who are working for a reversal of this policy. Looking at the matter in its historical perspective, it appears that this would be an unexampled tergiversation. England and English theorists, are jointly responsible with Jews for the evolution of Zionism in its modern form. It is not a question of reversing the policy of the past twenty years, but that of the past three centuries. Such an association is not lightly to be broken. This is no mere Jewish enterprise, but an enterprise in which England and the Jews are closely, inseparably associated. The comparative date and validity of agreements made during the present generation, under the stress of war, is insignificant by the side of this centuries-old-association. I trust that new research workers will be forthcoming who will enable us to demonstrate to the world that, if by the renunciation of Zion we Jews would lose much of our inheritance, England, too, would lose no small part of hers.[11]

Where does one look for the seminal idea later to be developed by such luminaries as John Milton, Percy Bysshe Shelley, Oliver Cromwell, Isaac Newton, Lord Byron and George Eliot into a frank and positive yearning for Jewish Restoration?[12] The answer to this rhetorical question is historically quite obvious. It is raised only to punctuate more sharply that nowhere more than in Britain was the idea of Jewish Restoration worked into doctrine that became, finally, an object alive not only in the realm of thought and discussion but also on the plane of political action.[13] Only among the people of England do we find ranking spokesmen of succeeding generations inspired and urged on by visions of a revived Israel.[14] Only in Great Britain has the creation of a homeland for world Jewry been a deliberate, constant and serious issue.[15]

Temporary Reversal of Britain's Policy

True, this whole matter has been tragically clouded by still vivid memory of the 1939 White Paper and by anti-Zionist acts of British Governments at the very terrible moments when tens of thousands of Jews were perishing at Dachau, Auswitz and other Nazi death camps.[16] These acts, particularly the stubborn restriction of Jewish immigration to Palestine in the very hours when remnants of East European Jewry were desperately fleeing to Palestine, even after the end of the war, were reprehensible.[17] While these certainly obscure the plain fact which over three centuries of idealism, sentiment and activity aimed directly at obtaining a homeland in Palestine for the Jews unequivocally proclaims, the idea of Israel's restoration, we will discover, is part of the very brickwork lying at the foundations of the British Commonwealth. It early became a rudimentary spiritual part of that people's personality, character and history — in spite of temporary abandonment.[18]

Studies to Date

Among those who have taken notice of the theological antecedents of what later became British Zionism there exists the tendency to belittle its significance and to treat its documents as a peculiar series of eccentric, sectarian theological treatises with particular axes to grind, as, e.g., the immediate political goals of the tracts issued by various champions of the Fifth Monarch Movement.[19] Most notably in this connection John Archer's *Personal Reign of Christ Upon Earth* (1642) is urged as a case in point which raises but incidentally the notion of the return of the Jews in a larger scheme of apocalyptic events supposedly scheduled to transpire in Britain at large.[20]

Fifty years have passed since Nahum Sokolow made the first and so far only attempt to outline the whole story of the idea of Jewish Restoration in his *History of Zionism* (1919). His treatment of the advocates of Israel's Restoration in Great Britain, which, significantly enough, constitutes the bulk of the work, pays little attention to the theological origins and implications of the pervasive influence such considerations had in English life. Moreover, the work was done at a time before several of the earliest documents now available had yet come to light.[21] Albert M. Hyamson's *British Projects for the Restoration of the Jews* (1917) is specifically political and concentrates on the nineteenth century with no attention to the foundational thought which always precedes action. Cecil Roth's all-embracing *Magna Bibliotheca Anglo-Judaica* (1937), one of the bibliographical bases for the primary materials treated in this study, has only one title in its listings for the restoration idea in the period under investigation. Since the 1965 edition of the *British Museum Catalogue*, the 1968 publication of the twelve volume *Williams Library Catalogue of Early Nonconformity 1566-1800* and the 1945 publication of Donald Wing's six volume *Short-Title Catalogue of Books printed in England, Scotland, Ireland, Wales and British America and of English Books printed in Other Countries, 1641-1700*, Cecil Roth's work needs updating to include a good number of source documents newly come to light. A brief paperback volume by Franz Kobler entitled *The Vision Was There* (1956) in the Popular Jewish Library series of the World Jewish Congress gives a quick historical survey of the British Zionist movement. While undocumented, it has a preliminary bibliography and is a good general introduction to the topic.

Scope of the Present Investigation

Introductory Considerations: Attachment to the Land

We should note at this point by way of introduction that the ligatures connecting the people of Israel with the land of Israel lie at the very origins of the Hebrew nation.[22] The Scriptures everywhere testify of the permanence and inseparability of this bond.[23] In this specific connection the comment of Nahum Sokolow on Genesis 13:14, 15 is a strong argument:

> It is impossible to understand how it can be said that this covenant will be remembered, if the Jewish people is to continue dispersed, and is to

be *forever* excluded from the land here spoken of. As to the return from Babylonian captivity, that will not answer the intention of the covenant at all. For to restore a small part of the Jewish people to its own land for a few generations, and afterwards disperse it among all nations for many times as long, without any hope of return, cannot be the meaning of giving that land to the seed of Abram forever.[24]

And again on Deuteronomy 30:1-5 Sokolow insists:

Here we have in plain words, simple and clear, the fundamental idea of Moses: the Jewish national future and the possession of the land for ever. This cannot be explained away by sophistry. In vain some Jews declare: We are not nationalist Jews. We are religious Jews! What is the Jewish religion if the Bible is not accepted as an Inspired Revelation? It is strange and sadly amusing that some Jews, adherents of the monotheistic principle, describe themselves as Germans, Magyars, and so on, 'of the persuasion of Moses.'[25] If this is not blasphemy, it is irony. The real Moses, the Moses of the Pentateuch, brands dispersion as a curse, and his whole religious conception, with all the laws, ceremonies, feasts, etc., is built up on the basis of the covenant with the ancestors a covenant immovable and unalterable. No matter whether Jews call themselves religious or nationalist: the Jewish religion cannot be separated from nationalism, unless another Bible is invented.

Judaism, or the Jewish religion is based first upon the teaching of Moses, and next upon that of the prophets, and it is a favourite claim of the modern school of Jewish reform that their Judaism is 'Prophetic Judaism' in opposition to the Judaism of orthodox Jews, who lay particular stress upon the Talmud. But what do the prophets teach?[26]

At this point Sokolow gives a nearly exhaustive catalogue of prophetic utterances regarding national restoration.

History, biblical exegesis and living Jewish testimony speak with one voice: the two entities, land and people, people and land, are of a single fabric. The people fail of authentic identity without the land and *vice versa*. We have just seen that beginning with the time of Abraham's call[27] all the way to the opposite pole of Old Testament chronology in the utterances of the last of the Prophets,[28] the pronouncements on this theme are the same: Canaan is the destination of the newly born nation delivered from bondage in Egypt;[29] Zion is the grand hope of the captives in Babylon.[30] "Next year in Jerusalem," while simply a customary Pesach greeting was at heart and origin the cry of every self-conscious Jew in the multiplied thousands of humble hamlets in the backwater communities of Eastern Europe.[31] Across the centuries this ideal has galvanized and sustained a harried, preyed-upon people.[32] No tyranny that moved across the scene,[33] often from horizon to horizon, no ensconcement in new found comforts in another land has ever been able to dislodge this fervent hope.[34] The cords of memory connecting people to land, land to people, it seems, were to prove impossible to sever, however strenuously alien powers and spirits might otherwise strive to sunder them. Rites,[35] takkanot,[36] prayers,[37] teaching,[38] poetry,[39] philosophy,[40] even death itself[41] like so many spokes of a wheel turned on the hub of this hope. When life became bestial, as often for long seasons it did, the flame of passion for the Promised Land burned the more hotly.[42] Spiritual longing seemed to increase in direct proportion to the degree of degredation faced in the stark realities and coercions of daily life.[43] No more powerful impulse for return to Palestine in the centuries of victimization in the Diaspora can be found than the dreadful traumas of actual physical expulsion, as, e.g., in 1492 took place in Spain and slightly later in Portugal. This took place after more than a dozen generations of the highest order of attainment and noble cultural contribution in those lands.[44]

Early Attempts at Return

As the centuries slowly unrolled, many thousands of Jews from every corner of the Diaspora found some way to get back to that Land, which, then, though naked and desolate,[45] remained on in their hearts as *The Land*, the Promised Land.[46] We discover that not long after being driven out of the Iberian peninsula organized efforts were beginning to take form for the sole purpose of returning to Palestine.[47] The colorful David Reubeni and his enthusiastic disciple, Solomon Molko, paid with their lives for the temerity of suggesting the notion of reconquest of the Holy Land by force for this purpose.[48] Their Messianic dreams, though they triggered ill consequence deeds, presaged activities and movements which followed on an unprecedented scale in the seventeenth century.[49]

Analogous Jewish and Christian Views

By the late 15th century, restoration ideas of distinctively Jewish origin are to be found in a common stream with Christian millennial expectations, albeit of a variant spiritual current.[50]   The analogous goals of the two are strikingly similar.[51]   A restored Holy Land and revivified Jerusalem of greater magnificence than her former glory is an essential aspect of both Jewish Messianism and Christian eschatological doctrine.[52]   This notion was developed in Christian thought by the earliest of the Patristic writers and is argued on the basis of the authority of Scripture.[53]   The main elements of this aspect of this division of Christian theology were derived chiefly from the twentieth chapter of the Revelation of St. John, the latter portions of Daniel, Romans 11, Isaiah 11, 12, 65, 66, Ezekiel 31, 37, 40ff., etc.[54]   The return of Jesus Christ, or the doctrine of the Second Advent, the great conflict with antichrist and the thousand years of reign with the saints constitute the central structure from which the rest is suspended and developed.[55]   Justin Martyr (c. 100-165),[56] Irenaeus (c. 130-202),[57] Tertullian (c. 160-290),[58] Lactantius (c. 250-330),[59] and a number of others[60] envisioned these phenomena as immediately pending with a resettled Holy Land and splendidly rebuilt Zion as the stage for this cosmic drama.[61]   Specific national resuscitation for the Jewish people in this scheme was rather incidental to the grand sweep, but it was there, and its manifest nature was analogous to Jewish Messianism.[62]

Dramatic Change in Medieval Christian View

Patristic viewpoint changed radically in the third century. This change is represented in full flower in the person of Origen (c. 185-254).[63]   He marks the advent of the allegorization of exegesis generally and spiritualization of millennial expectations in particular.[64]   His opposition to the older views was based on their character as "views come to by those who understand the Divine Scripture in a sort of Jewish sense."[65] This perspective became the prevailing one, lasting throughout the medieval period, systematized in St. Augustine's *The City of God* and has remained on as an integral feature of Roman Catholic theology.[66] Augustine taught that the Church itself is the Millennial Kingdom of God.[67] Christ rules it, through and by the Church's rule.[68] Scriptural statements suggesting a concrete nature of restored carnal glory in Palestine and to the Jews ought rather to be taken on a qualitatively higher level, i.e., spiritually, rather than in the woodenly literalistic fashion required by a real millennium, restored Israel, etc.[69] Thus Augustine's hermeneutic reduced Israel into a mundane prefiguring of some spiritual entity yet to come in the Divine plan of the ages, viz., the Church.[70] The Prophets, the writer of the Revelation etc. must be interpreted, according to Augustine, with the understanding that the ones therein being spoken of and addressed were yet spiritual children, unable and unprepared for the true, larger and nobler meaning possible only in Christ's spiritual kingdom—His Church.[71] Other conclusions, he argued, were inimical to the earthly authority and reign of the Church inasmuch as a separate Divine plan for the Jews and the ancient people of Israel, apart from Christ, was thus necessarily involved, whereas the nation of Israel had been but general preparation for the Church and a temporary repository of revelation. By their stiffnecked disavowal of Christ they were guilty of heinous revolt against the Son of God.[72]

Augustine succeeded in idealizing Rome as the Christian Zion.[73] With the spread and acceptance of these views, millennarian expectations in Christian eschatology faded and largely disappeared.[74]

Revival of Millennial Expectations and Concomitant Doctrine of Jewish National Return

Some seven hundred, plus, years later in the first decades of the twelfth century, the wane of the *ancien regime* of medievalism, accompanying corruption in the Church and popular disenchantment from the abuse of temporal papal authority, brought a resurgence of prophetic millennial belief, especially among the persecuted evangelical sects.[75] By the twelfth century an Italian monk, Joachim of Floris (c. 1130-1202),[76] was again winning a hearing for a kind of millennairian idea, though not strictly the literal thousand year kingdom with Jerusalem restored, Jews returned as a nation, etc.[77] But his disciples[78] believed the second advent of Christ and the institution of His earthly thousand year reign to be imminent, apparently borrowing liberally from Jewish sources in their calculations.[79] These doctrines are found in refined form, in pre-Reformation teaching.[80] The orthodox Anabaptist movements of the fifteenth and sixteenth centuries held strongly to them.[81] Though far from being any major emphasis, the Swiss and German Reformations also were not immune from these influences.[82] Even John Calvin at Geneva, with his aristocratic upbringing, demonstrated some affinity for an aspect of the millennarian teaching in that he was a theocrat,[83] though he rejected millennial notions.[84]

The Unique Situation in England

The Continent, however, was not to be the place where the newly revitalized millennialism was to blossom and flourish. It remained to the Isles of Britain to provide the seed bed and cultivation for full flower and ripe fruit. The situation there was unique. England enjoyed relative political and religious tranquility in contrast to continental Europe's constant series of wars, ruthless intrigue at the game of power politics, consequent economic distress and growing spiritual despair across the sixteenth and seventeenth centuries. None of the physical decimation nor moral anarchy that affected nearly every corner of the continent penetrated tellingly into England.[85]

Not only the wars of the period but especially the Counter-reformation observed taking place across the Channel strengthened in English minds the notion that the English people had a special position in the providential scheme of history. It was, to a people steeped in Scripture, analogous to that special place held by the ancient Israelites. This notion was eminently congruous with the prevailing Calvinism, which suggested the idea of Divine Election as belonging to the privileged and faithful nation. Above all, Englishmen found in the astonishing facts of their own recent history a reason for believing that they were under the special protection of the ALMIGHTY. Such an idea is repulsive to the modern mind, as savoring of an intolerable vanity, and generally indicative of a portentous ignorance. But neither vanity nor ignorance could be connected with it in that age.[86]

England had attained to such a pinnacle of prosperity and fame under Queen Elizabeth, that she was regarded with as much envy abroad as exultation at home. The Old Testament authenticated the belief that temporal blessings were proof of Divine Approbation.[87]

A contemporary book (1624) entitled *Thankful Remembrance of God's Mercy in an Historical Collection of the Great and Merciful Deliverances of the Church and State of England, Since the Gospel Began there to Flourish, from the Beginning of Queen Elizabeth,*[88] by Bishop Carlton of Chichester enlarges on the theme:

> . . . true religion bringeth a blessing and that religion that bringeth always a curse is to be suspected.[89]

Bishop Carlton continues,

> It is the privilege of the Church to enjoy miraculous protection and strange deliverance out of dangers.[90]

Then at the very end of the book he explains his entire thesis,

> My purpose in writing this book is to declare the great works of God in the defense of this Church of England since Religion was planted here by Queen Elizabeth.[91]

Mix with this general outlook the facts of the pervasive influence of the Bible, a rising nonconformity, a highly literate populace, the emergence of the most brilliant epoch of *belles lettres* in the English language, a burgeoning printer's trade, continuing economic expansion and prosperity, success in foreign affairs, Stuart despotism, Puritan determination to

> establish those things only which the Lord himself in his Word commandeth, what things how the government of the church should be constituted, how worship and discipline should be administered . . . as plainly set forth in Scripture for all to follow inasmuch as nothing in

this mortal life is more diligently to be sought for and carefully looked into than the restitution of religion and reformation in God's church . . . [on the ground that] nothing else and nothing less would suffice if God's will is to prevail in England.[92]

and we have all the ingredients of place, time, political climate, *dramatis personae*, intellectual and spiritual excitement and moral energy in which perfectly mulched soil the seeds of millennial expectation could germinate, sprout and begin to grow.

Notes

1   The latter event was an inverse result of the former. Salo Wittmayer Baron, *A Social and Religious History of the Jews,* volume I (New York: Columbia University Press, 1966), pp. vii-viii; Salo Wittmayer Baron, *op. cit.,* volume II, pp. 89-198. Baron's remark in two places of the Preface to volume one (pp. vii-ix) that the "third commonwealth" [i.e., the state of Israel] is "the fulfillment of a millenial hope, the rebirth of its nation on its ancestral soil" is suggestively similar language to that used in the literature of the period here in view from late Elizabethan and early Stuart England. Cf. also: 1) Two articles regarding the causes and effect of the Series of disasters under Roman hegemony: a) Elias J. Bickerman, "The Historical Foundations of Postbiblical Judaism," *The Jews, Their History, Culture and Religion,* volume I, ed. Louis Finkelstein (New York: Harper and Row Publishers, 1960), pp. 70-114; and b) Judah Goldin, "The Period of the Talmud, 135 B.C.E.-1035 C.E.," *op. cit.,* pp. 115-214. 2) Cecil Roth, *A History of the Jews* (New York: Schocken Books, Inc., 1966), 93-110, 385-424. 3) Bernard J. Bamberger, *The Story of Judaism* (New York: Schocken Books, Inc., 1967), pp. 94-106, 407-412. 4) Isidore Epstein, Judaism, *A Historical Presentation* (Baltimore: Penguin Books, 1966), pp. 111-120, 319-323. 5) Israel Goldberg and Samson Benderley, *Outline of Jewish Knowledge, The Second Commonwealth,* volume III (New York: Bureau of Jewish Education, 1931), pp. 583-686. 6) Max L. Margolis and Alexander Marx, *A History of the Jewish People* (New York: Harper Torchbooks, 1965), pp. 199-204. 7) Howard Morley Sachar, *The Course of Modern Jewish History* (New York: Dell Publishing Co., 1958), pp. 542-568.

2   The dimensions of this accomplishment, especially regarding establishment of a viable state out of the chaos of war, snarled foreign entanglements, knotty religious intrigues, economic crisis, exploding immigration, (population doubled in first three years) agonizing practical problems of water and food supply, housing, medical aid etc. is dramatically outlined in chapter XXV of Howard Morely Sachar, *op. cit.,* pp. 542-568.

3   *Ibid.*

4   With reference to Palestine itself, what the might of Rome or the Turks could not do in centuries, or, in our day, even the British Empire was not able to accomplish, the Jewish people has accomplished — not just in a political or territorial sense but in terms of a reintroduction of a wholesome and flourishing ecology for man rather than a dying one. Agriculture, manufacture, education, the arts and humanities, social

well-being have revived to an astonishing level for which there is no historical antecedent or parallel. *Vide* especially Isidore Epstein, *Judaism* (Baltimore: Penguin Books, 1966), p. 319.

5 *Ibid.*

6 Compelling evidence to this effect is available in the lengthy appendices of documents in Nahum Sokolow, *History of Zionism 1600-1918* (London: Longmans, Green and Co., 1919), volume two, pp. 161-401. Particularly suggestive in this regard are chapters one through four in volume one of the same work treating specifically the origins of Zionism in England and the continuously prominent, if not leading role, played by that nation right up to 1948 and the momentous events of that year.

7 Cecil Roth, "The Challenge to Jewish History," *Transactions of the Jewish Historical Society of England* 1935-1938, Volume XIV, p. 20. (Presidential Addresses delivered before the Jewish Historical Society of England, October 20, 1936 and January 11, 1938.) The non-Jewish element in Zionism as we know it today was, well before the birth of the state of Israel, an acknowledged, earnestly sought after requirement to the success of the movement. Herzl's *Diary* is a massive documentation of this desire and necessity. This writer was singularly impressed with the passion with which Dr. Herzl sought to enlist non-Jews in his cause. *Vide* the fine five volume *Complete Diaries of Theodor Herzl*, edited by Raphael Patai, translated by Harry Zohn (New York: Herzl Press and Thomas Yoseloff, 1960).

8 E.g., among persecuted evangelical sects, millennial ideas and the parallel theme of Israel's redemption (return as a nation to a revivified Palestine) was present and advocated by the Cathari or Albigenses and the Waldenses or Vaudois as early as the eleventh and twelfth centuries in France and among the disciples and followers of Jan Hus in the fifteenth century, in what is now Czechoslovakia. It is instructive that this theme was a favorite also of Wycliffe in the early part of the fifteenth century in England, and that Hus and Wycliffe knew of and influenced one another. *Vide* Kenneth Scott Latourette, *History of Christianity* (New York: Harper and Row, 1953), pp. 451-55, 666-69. *Vide* also the fine article by Johann Jakob Herzog, "Waldenses," *The Schaff-Herzog Encyclopaedia of Religious Knowledge*, Volume four (New York: Funk and Wagnalls, 1891), pp. 2470-2477, and the article by Carl Wilhelm Adolf Schmidt, "Albigenses," *op. cit.*, volume one, pp. 46-47.

9 Nahum Sokolow's *History of Zionism* gives well over fifty percent of his treatment specifically to following the course of Zionism in Great Britain, the persons attached thereto, the events, institutions, societies, and so on. In addition, the work has an introduction by none other than Lord Arthur James Balfour himself and volume two has a lengthy tribute to Sir Mark Sykes plus over two hundred pages of appendices consisting of source documents drawn straight from seminal British Zionism. One is led to the inevitable conclusion from this and many

parallel evidences which *en masse* show *prima facie* that Albion (Great Britain) and Ariel (Jerusalem) in this instance at least, are cut of a common cloth. Cecil Roth's long article outlines the three century's association, the implications thereof for present and future British policy, and the practical manifestations of the same produced in the intervening history. By far, the lion's share of theory and practice leading up to the consummation of affairs in 1948 derives from Great Britain.

10 Cecil Roth, *op. cit.*, p. 19.

11 *Ibid.*, pp. 19, 20.

12 The history of Zionism literally bristles with the names of eminent English *literati*, clergymen, statesmen and other public figures. Sokolow's *History of Zionism* catalogues several dozens. *Vide* especially the several appendices in volume two.

13 Nahum Sokolow, *op. cit.*, volume two, pp. xxxvii-xliv. *Vide* also Bernard J. Bamberger, *The Story of Judaism* (New York: Schocken Books, 1967), pp. 341-346.

14 Cecil Roth, *op. cit.*, p. 19.

15 *Ibid.*, p. 20.

16 Great Britain, *Parliamentary Papers*, "Palestine Statement of Policy" (London: His Majesty's Stationery Office, 1939), 12 pp. This is the so-called "White Paper of 1939," which confined Jewish immigration into Palestine to 75,000 persons within the ensuing five years, with continuance of Jewish immigration at the expiration of that period to depend on Arab consent. This policy, transparently enough, was tantamount to liquidation of all hopes for the establishment of a Jewish state in Palestine. Joseph Badi, *The Government of the State of Israel* (New York: Twayne Publishers, 1963), pp. 9-16.

17 For a good commentary on British moral culpability in this specific connection Bernard J. Bamberger, *The Story of Judaism* (New York: Schocken, 1967), chapter fifty-seven, is brief but balanced.

18 Nahum Sokolow, *op. cit.*, pp. 1-5.

19 This aspect of millennarian thought and activity is treated in Michael Fixler, *Milton and the Kingdoms of God* (London: Faber and Faber, 1964). It seems that multitudes of sects sprang up in this revolutionary epoch, each claiming to have a corner on truth and a privileged method to usher in the *regnum Christi.* One example often cited as representative of the excesses of the age, is that of Hannah Trapnel, a Fifth Monarchist prophetess whose remarkable visionary ravings were directed against the newly founded Protectorate under Cromwell. The millennarian sectories thought her inspired and coupled her prophecies of certain

omens of doom, all of which indicated a sure, Divine displeasure with the new regime, and promised its destruction. *Vide* Michael Fixler, *op. cit.*, chapter five, "Liberty, Power and Faith," pp. 172-220; also p. 86.

20 Norman Cohn, *The Pursuit of the Millennium* (New York: Harper and Brothers, 1961), pp. 321-376. This section of Mr. Cohn's work is an appendix entitled "The 'Free Spirit' in Cromwell's England: The Ranters and their literature." It is an attempt at showing that moral license, political radicalism, general antinomianism and hankering after anarchy was characteristic of these so-called sectarians.

21 Sokolow's first chapter, "England and the Bible," consisting of four and a half pages, gives in adumbrate form a tracing of the influence of the Bible in the formative periods of England's early self-consciousness. It is undocumented, exceedingly broad, and therefore sketchy. A sermon preached by the Reverend Paul Knell (1615-1664) on April 16, 1648 entitled "Israel and England Paralleled" serves as an ideological starting point in the history of the idea. The Reverend Knell saw Israel as Israel (i.e., as a people distinct, having ethnic identity uniquely their own and not co-extensive with a spiritual Israel otherwise construed as preparation for, or type of, the New Testament Church), and then as a nation answering to and upon whom the biblical prophecies of restoration are to be performed. The date of Knell's sermon is well past the *terminus ad quem* of the present study. A good deal of ground lies between it (1648, the date of Knell's sermon) and the *terminus a quo* (1585) the starting point for this investigation in which to ferret out the germs of the idea as well as considerable development. Sokolow's treatment of this early epoch may be capsulized in the following quotation from page three:

> The indebtedness of English literature to the Bible is immeasurable. The Bible has inspired the highest and most ennobling books in the English language. No other book has been so universally read or so carefully studied. The Bible has been an active force in English literature for over twelve hundred years, and during that whole period it has been moulding the diction of representative English thinkers and literary men.

Not until the days of Johanna and Ebenezer Cartwright and their petition (January 5, 1649) on behalf of repeal of Jewish banishment from England, the ensuing public debate and the efforts of Manasseh ben Israel does Mr. Sokolow really warm to his subject—though for some unexplained reason he does include, in the nearly 250 pages of appendices, two excerpts from early works, viz., the anonymous tract *Newes from Rome* (1607), pages 190-205 of volume two, and Sir Henry Finch's *The World's Great Restoration* (1621), pages 207, 208 of volume two. Also, a curious letter from the eminent biblical scholar Reverend Joseph Mede (1586-1638) to Sir Martin Stuteville alluding with approval to Finch's book is appended to the short quotation therefrom on the same pages.

22 "And the Lord said unto Abram, . . . 'Lift up now thine eyes, and look from the place where thou art, northward and southward and eastward and westward; for all the land which thou seest, to thee will I give it, and to thy seed for ever'" (Genesis 13:14, 15).

23 The earliest is from none less than the Law-giver Moses:

> And I will bring the land into desolation; and your enemies that dwell therein shall be astonished at it. And you will I scatter among the nations, and I will draw out the sword after you; and your land shall be a desolation, and your cities shall be a waste. . . . And yet for all that, when they are in the land of their enemies, I will not reject them, neither will I abhor them, to destroy them utterly, and to break my covenant with them; for I am the Lord their God. But I will for their sakes remember the covenant of their ancestors, whom I brought forth out of the land of Egypt in the sight of the nations, that I might be their God: I am the Lord (Leviticus 26:32-33, 44-45).

Again, later in the Pentateuch (Deuteronomy 30:1-5) the same theme is found. The prophet Joel also echoes the idea:

> Then was the Lord jealous for His land, and had pity on His people. And the Lord answered and said unto His people: Behold, I will send you corn and wine, and oil. And ye shall be satisfied therewith; And I will no more make you a reproach among the nations; . . . For, behold in those days, and in that time, when I shall bring back the captivity of Judah and Jerusalem, . . . So shall ye know that I am the Lord your God, dwelling in Zion my holy mountain; Then shall Jerusalem be holy, . . . But Judah shall be inhabited forever, And Jerusalem from generation to generation (Joel 2:18, 19; 4:1, 17, 20).

Amos, especially 9:14, 15 is emphatic on the idea. Hosea underscores the notion of return in 3:4, 5. Micah in 2:12, 4:6, 7, 7:20 sounds the return. Zephaniah in 3:20 is very clear. Jeremiah in 3:18, 23:6, 31:35, 36, 33:24-26, 46:27 can not be understood in any other way. Ezekiel discloses close circumstantial detail that is impossible to allegorize in 37:26, the whole of chapters 38 and 39. Obadaiah speaks of the return of the captive to Zion in 1:17 and 20, 8:13, 10:10. But none surpasses the certainty and utterly lucid declarations of Isaiah. His prophecies alone, are sufficiently definite with regard to a second restoration of Israel (*vide* especially 11:11) as to authenticate the idea if none other reference were to be found. A recent Christian writer expresses the same judgment of the weight of this passage in saying, "Most writers of every school rightfully regard this as the strongest single text in the entire Old Testament supporting the Premillennial doctrine of the restoration of Israel". Robert D. Culver, *Daniel and the Latter Days* (Westwood, New Jersey: Fleming H. Revell Company, 1954), p. 81.

And it shall come to pass in that day, that the Lord will set His hand again the second time to recover the remnant of His people, that shall remain from Assyria, and from Egypt, and from Pathros, and from Cush, and from Elam, and from Shinar, and from Kainath, and from the islands of the sea. And he will set up an ensign for the nations, and will assemble the dispersed of Israel, and gather together the scattered of Judah from the four corners of the earth. The envy also of Ephraim shall depart, and they that harass Judah shall be cut off; Ephraim shall not envy Judah, and Judah not vex Ephraim (Isaiah 11:11-13).

And in the so-called second Isaiah this theme is recorded in lyrical motif:

Lift up thine eyes round about, and see: They are all gathered together, and come to thee; Thy sons come from far, and thy daughters are borne on the side. . . . Who are these that fly as a cloud, and as the doves to their cotes? Surely the isles shall wait for me, and the ships of Tarshish first, to bring thy sons from far, Their silver and their gold with them, For the name of the Lord thy God, and for the Holy One of Israel, because He hath glorified thee (Isaiah 60:4, 8, 9).

For as the new heavens the new earth, which I will make, shall remain before me, said the Lord, so shall your seed and your name remain (Isaiah 66:22).

24 Nahum Sokolow, *op. cit.*, p. 161.

25 The self-description of "Germans, Magyars [or Frenchmen, Russians, etc.] of the Mosaic persuasion" derives from the answers of the Assembly of Notables of leading Jews called by Napoleon to answer to twelve specific questions in order to decide Jewish status. Abraham Furtado served as spokesman for his co-religionists. The Assembly of Notables was later to be transformed, more or less, by Napoleon into a reconstituted Sanhedrin of sorts in order to give the aura of binding authority to the formulations thus to be delivered. The reply of this "Sanhedrin" to the thrust of questions four, five and six regarding Jewish attitudes toward France as their country and non-Jewish Christian Frenchmen was in Furtado's words:

We no longer form a nation within a nation. France is our country. Jews, such today is your status: your obligations are outlined, your happiness is waiting.

(Howard Morely Sacher, *op. cit.*, p. 63). *The Twelve Answers*, this one most importantly, provided a rationale, as Howard Morely Sacher puts it:

. . . for 'salon Jews' and *Kaiserjuden*; for Germans, Frenchmen, and Americans of the 'Israelitish' or 'Mosaic' persuasion; for Jews in a hurry to assume the protective coloration of their Christian neighbors. The ultimate significance of the Paris Sanhedrin, therefore, was not its rejection of corporate Jewish autonomy, but rather the sanction it provided for some Western Jews to reject Jewish civilization in its wider ethnic and cultural implications.

Ibid. Cf. Chapter III "Emancipation in the West," pp. 53-71 for an excellent recounting of the background of Western Jewish 'emancipation' in the ideals of the French Revolution and the consequences thereof.

26 Nahum Sokolow, *op. cit.*, p. 162.

27 Genesis 13:14, 15.

28 If the critics' conclusions are accepted, perhaps Daniel ought to stand here, if not, then perhaps Malachi. In either case—or others, depending on the systems of dates one accepts—their sentiments are equally clear on the matter. *Vide* Daniel 2:44, 7:27, 12:1, Daniel's eloquent prayer for his people and land in Chapter 9, with Malachi 3:12, 23.

29 Exodus 15:15-17; Deuteronomy 1:19-21; Numbers 13:2, 17.

30 Ezekiel 36, 37, 38.

31 Pesach itself, as the festival of redemption, literally exudes the sentiment of return to the land. Every feature of the celebration is an aspect of this theme. Hayyim Schauss, *Guide to Jewish Holy Days* (New York: Schocken Books, 1965), pp. 38-85. Schauss summarizes this very well when he says (p. 47): "So Pesach became the festival of the second as well as the first redemption."

32 In just about every instance of pogrom, persecution, ghettoization, libel, humiliation, massacre and hosts of other disabilities visited upon Jews and Jewry to the present hour, hope against hope in divine Messianic intervention, miraculous deliverance and restoration to their former land and glories has been a basic characteristic that seems to have inured Jews to pain, loss and death. In their last minutes, e.g., with only the blackest of reasonable expectations the zealot defenders of the Temple mount in Jerusalem against Titus' steadily advancing forces fought with unbelievable valor. Cf. Cecil Roth, *History of the Jews* (New York: Schocken Books, 1966), p. 110. The same thoughts carried through the disaster of 1648 among Eastern Jewry who were butchered and maimed in the barbarous sweep of Bogdan Chmielnicki across the Ukraine. The enormity of these atrocities is difficult to exaggerate. Cf. David Rudovsky, *Emancipation and Adjustment* (Diplomatic Press, 1967), pp. 116-121, especially in connection with the comments about the emotional and educational climate thus created for pseudo-messiahs (as Shabbetai Zevi and Jacob Frank) of that epoch in such intense periods

of suffering that could only be construed in the hearts of the sufferers as the *Hevlei Mashiach*, the pangs that were to herald His coming.

33   Cecil Roth, *History of the Jews*, pp. 109ff; David Rudovsky, *Emancipation and Adjustment*, pp. 115ff.

34   Even in relative ease and comfort the theme of return to the soil of Zion rises to the surface. During the lengthy and flourishing "golden age" of Jewry in Iberia, e.g., there were passionate expressions of yearning for Zion. And in the case of Judah HaLevi and many others, the yearning ultimately had to be expressed in deed — by actual pilgrimage to the Holy Land. The exalted passion of HaLevi's love songs to Zion are worth an example here:

> "Beautiful height! Oh joy! the whole world's gladness!
> A great King's city, mountain blest!
> My soul is yearning unto thee — is yearning
>   From limits of the west.

> "The torrents heave from depths of mine heart's passion
>   At memory of thine olden state,
> The glory of thee borne away to exile
>   Thy dwelling desolate.

> "And who shall grant me, on the wings of eagles,
>   To rise and seek thee through the years,
> Until I mingle with thy dust beloved
>   The waters of my tears?"

Cf. Bernard J. Bamberger, *op. cit.*, pp. 156-157, also Baron, *op. cit.*, I, p. 157ff.

35   The significance of the breaking of the goblet or glass in the Jewish wedding ceremony is a forcible reminder. Hayyim Schauss, *The Lifetime of a Jew* (New York: Union of American Hebrew Congregations, 1965), pp. 193, 194.

36   For one example, the curious ordinance enacted by early Babylonian teachers proclaiming the legal fiction of possession of four ells of Palestinian soil to Jewish business men in order for them to do business. According to Talmudic law, one could issue to an agent a letter of authorization to collect funds from a debtor or depository only if it was accompanied by the transfer of a parcel of land to the agent. Since few Jews owned land this action was necessary to facilitate the proper conduct of trade and business in the far-flung transactions in which Jews were engaged. As a Gaon explained it, "the land may have been occupied [i.e., by Gentiles] for many generations, but we have the old legal maxim that [ownership of] land is never lost by illegal seizure, and hence Israel still holds title to it [i.e., the Palestinian land]." Assaf's edition of *Teshubat Hageonim*, 1928, p. 31, No. 78. Cf. Baron, V, pp. 27ff.

37 Note the content of the Kaddish prayer. It is very significant that Ezekiel 38:23 is prominently included. The long and magnificent passage terminates in the notion of theodicy. Ezekiel outlines, from chapter 36 onward, the re-establishment of a glorified nation of Israel amidst the dismay and fall of surrounding enemies, the end to the old and terribly acrimonious jealousy between Judah and Ephraim and so on. Note also the Rabbinic admonition that "those who pray abroad shall direct their hearts toward Palestine, those who pray in Palestine shall turn their hearts toward Jerusalem . . . so that all Israel will be found praying toward the same spot" (T. Berakhot III 16). Drawn from Daniel 6:11? Cf. also Salo Wittmayer Baron, *op. cit.*, VI, p. 14 and VIII, p. 211.

38 *Mishnah Pesachim* X, 6. Note the elements of the Pesach Seder—all geared to the theme of deliverance, in a specific regard hoping to live long enough to celebrate Pesach in a new, free Jerusalem. Cf. Hayyim Schauss, *Guide to Jewish Holy Days*, p. 56. Beside many incidental allusions, as "and build Jerusalem, the sacred city, speedily in our days," etc., several traditional sections concluding with "next year in Jerusalem" are especially to the point of the argument here. These references are taken from E. D. Goldschmidt, *The Passover Haggadah* (New York: Schocken Books, 1969), pp. 82-85.

39 Yehuda HaLevi's *Libbi be-mizrah* (My heart is in the East) is perhaps the best known and archetype of thousands of imitations and translations. Baron, VII, p. 300, note 46, records, two original Hebrew versions, eight English translations, seventeen German, six Yiddish, five French, four Russian and miscellaneous other renditions. It is worth reproducing a portion here in one of its English translations:

> My heart is in the East, and I in the far West,
> How can I savor food, and find in it delight?
> How shall I pay my vows and self-denying oaths?
> When Zion bows to Edom, and I to Arab might?
> I find it easy to leave all the bounty of Spain,
> And to cherish instead the dust on the Temple's site.

Cf. the pertinent comments of Heinrich Graetz, *History of the Jews* (Philadelphia: Jewish Publication Society of America, 1893), Volume III, pp. 336-338.

40 Note especially Maimonides' views in *Mishneh Torah*: "The Book of Judges," Treatise V, 12:5.

41 Baron (*A Social and Religious History of the Jews*, Volume II, p. 289) tells us of the deeply entrenched tradition regarding burial in the Holy Land: "Since the sacred oil of Palestine held out the promise of immediate resurrection at the end of days, pious Jews from all over the world, including some exilarchs, made arrangements to be buried there [i.e., in Palestine]."

42 Baron's statement (VII, p. 169) in relation to Zionide poetry, that yearning for return "inspired many would-be pilgrims to the Holy Land, and gave an emotional lift to the entire people in its darkest hours" is to say less than more about the centrality of the restoration hope. Unfortunately, this yearning also created the kind of climate into which a clever charlatan could, and often did, easily win a hearing and following. *Vide* David Rudavsky, *op. cit.*, pp. 116-121, for an unusually succinct explanation of the circumstances, psychology and consequences involved in arousing Messianic expectations in the instance of the dreadful pogroms unleashed *ad seriatim* at the hand Cossack raiders, furious Russian troops, fanatical Polish Roman clergy, Papal blood accusations, fiscal failure in the *Kahal* due to wholesale dissemination of the Jewish community, ransom demands, exhorbitant interest rates on borrowed money, arbitrary poll taxes, and other excessive exactions of the middle decades of the seventeenth century in the Ukraine and Poland. Small wonder Shabbatai Zevi and Jacob Frank were so immediately successful or the disaster of the debacle wrought through them so dreadful. Cf. Jacob R. Marcus, *The Jew in the Medieval World* (New York: Harper and Row, 1965), pp. 261-262, 279-283.

43 Salo Wittmayer Baron, *op. cit.*, V, p. 185. "Never absent from the innermost yearnings of Diaspora Jewry, love for Palestine was constantly reactivated in periods of great stress or epochal transformations." Hayyim Nachman Bialik, the best known of recent Hebrew poets, poignantly capsulizes the whole range of emotions in many poems which personify and idealize his love of Zion.

44 Cecil Roth, *History of the Jews*, pp. 218-232. This section of Roth's work regarding the events leading up to the expulsion from Spain in 1492 is significantly and appropriately entitled, "The Crowning Tragedy." For an excellent treatment of all aspects of Jewish attainment, perhaps the best overall picture can be had from Salo Wittmayer Baron, *op. cit.*, VI, 227, 284f.; VII, 146ff.; VIII, 199f.; VI, 188; VII, 136ff.; VIII, 263; III, 156; IV, 158ff.; II, 210; III, 27-43, 33ff., 108f., IV, 44ff., 148; Vi, 51, 58; VIII, 248; IV, 3ff, 39, 162, 179f.; VIII, 39, 63f., 135, 298, 311; III, 33ff., 44; 155ff., 169; VI, 46, 208, 262; VII, 47, 54f. For a recital of the events of expulsion, Margolis and Marx, *A History of the Jews*, pp. 470-476 is a good summary especially of its barbaric and bestial dimensions.

45 The rape of nearly everything to which the Ottoman suzerains put their hand is a commonplace. It remains on in literature and in life from the revolution in Turkey at the end of World War II as a by-word to us in the form of "terrible turk." Palestine was plucked clean of everything of value, including human life, via outright piracy, rapine and iron-fisted taxation. The latter consisted of levies even against trees, a fact which denuded the countryside and further impoverished it.

46 A not untypical example is that of Joseph Nasi who moved by gradual stages from his native Portugal to Turkey and thence to Tiberias, which in due course the ruins thereof he secured permission from Sultan

Selim II to rebuild. *Vide* Jacob R. Marcus, *The Jew In the Medieval World*, pp. 320-322. Max L. Margolis and Alexander Marx, *A History of the Jewish People*, pp. 487, 491, 503, 514-518. Chapter sixty-nine entitled simply "Palestine" (pp. 515-525) of Margolis and Marx's work is particularly instructive in this regard. Cf. also Heinrich Graetz, *History of the Jews* (Philadelphia: Jewish Publication Society of America, 1894), Volume IV, pp. 572-628.

47 Margolis and Marx, *op. cit.*, pp. 470-478, 505ff. Cf. Graetz, *op. cit.*, *Index volume*, pp. 447-449 for extensive historical documentation.

48 A first hand description is available in Joseph HaKohen, *Emek HaBaka*, ed. by Letteris (Cracok: n.p. 1895), pp. 113-117. It is reproduced in Jacob R. Marcus, *The Jew in the Medieval World* (New York: Harper and Row, 1965), pp. 251-255. Cf. also Cecil Roth, *History of the Jews*, pp. 241-242. Graetz, *op. cit.*, IV, 499ff.

49 A general statement is in Baron, VII, p. 169. For pseudo-Messianic—national restoration schemes *vide* particularly Jacob R. Marcus, *op. cit.*, pp. 261-262, 279-283; *The Jewish Encyclopaedia*, "Pseudo-Messiahs;" *The Hastings Encylopaedia of Religion and Ethics*, "Messiahs (Pseudo-)." For more comprehensive coverage *vide* especially Baron, V, 184-191. Cf. also Abba Hillel Silver, *A History of Messianic Speculation in Israel from the First Through the Seventeenth Centuries* (New York: The Macmillan Co., 1927); Joseph Sarachek, *The Doctrine of the Messiah in Medieval Jewish Literature* (New York: Jewish Theological Seminary, 1932); Graetz, *Index Volume*, pp. 447-449.

50 Margolis and Marx, *op. cit.*, pp. 489-494. The episode of Manasseh ben Israel's intercession for Jewish readmission into England is a remarkable case in point.

51 *Ibid.*, p. 490. Cf., also among first hand sources, the striking similarities, e.g., between Manesseh's *Hope of Israel* (London: R. I. for Hannah Allen, 1650) and Sir Henry Finch's *The Calling of the Jews* (London: Edward Griffin for William Bladen, 1621) or Giles Fletcher's *Israel Redux* (London: S. Streater for John Hancock, 1677).

52 In this connection, Jewish views and Christian alike appeal to Scripture. E.g., Ezekiel chapter 40ff. where the grand vision of city and temple is painted in heroic dimensions and splendid colors. Cf. Manasseh's *Apology for the Honourable Nation of the Jews* (London: John Field, 1648), and notably his *Precious Stone or the Image of Nebuchadnezzar, or the Fifth Monarchy* (London: n.p., 1655) with Fifth Monarch Man John Archer's *Personall Reigne of Christ upon the Earth* (London: Benjamin Allen, 1642) or Johann Heinrich Alsted's *The Beloved City* (London: n.p., 1643). Cf. also Graetz, V, pp. 23ff.

53 For comprehensive documentation and bibliography consult LeRoy Edwin Froom's massive four volume *Prophetic Faith of our Fathers* (Washington, D.C.: Review and Herald, 1950-1954). Related literature

may be found in the selective bibliography of Robert D. Culver's *Daniel and the Latter Days* (Westwood, New Jersey: Fleming H. Revell, 1954), pp. 213-221.

54 The so-called apocalyptic portions of Daniel and Revelation are dismissed by many as entirely unintelligible except in some vaguely figurative sense or as simply peripheral.

55 Froom, *op. cit.*, I, pp. 24, 25, expresses his view that the notion of a restored nation of Israel in Palestine is merely a "by product" of biblical prophecy and relates it specifically to the period and literature here under study, referring specifically to the Fifth Monarchy movement, Lord Protector Cromwell and Manesseh ben Israel. Culver, *op. cit.*, pp. 76-90 and 161-176 sees the Jewish people as *dramatis personae*.

56 Justin Martyr, *Dialogue with Trypho the Jew*, volume five, p. 160ff. *Ante-Nicene Fathers. Translations of the Writings of the Fathers Down to A.D. 325.* Ten Volumes. New York: Charles Scribner's Sons, 1899-1926.

57 Irenaeus, *Against Heresies*, p. 526ff. of Book V, volume one of *Ante-Nicene Fathers. Translations of the Writings of the Fathers Down to A.D. 325.* Ten Volumes. New York: Charles Scribner's Sons, 1899-1926.

58 Tertullian, *Against Marcion*, Book III, chapter three, volume three, pp. 342ff. of *Ante-Nicene Fathers, etc.*, and *An Answer to the Jews, loc. cit.*, pp. 158ff.

59 Lactantius, *Epitome*, chapter 72 in *Ante-Nicene Fathers, etc.*, volume VII, p. 254ff.; also *Institutes*, book seven, chapters 24, 26, pp. 219ff.

60 Hippolytus (d.c. 236), Julius Africanus (c. 150-220) perhaps Cyprian (c. 200-258), *et al.* An excellent overview is in Froom, *op. cit.*, pp. 283-308. Of particular instructive value is Froom's comment that in the early church through the second century and into the third, the teaching of the millennial hope, of which doctrine Israel's restoration is a necessary, endemic concomitant, was very strong—so much so that St. Jerome (c. 340-420) was later led to comment on the idea as a "Jewish dream" (Froom, I, p. 307, from *Commentaria in Danielem*, chapter 7, in Migne, *Patristica Latina*, vol. 25; and *Commentaria in Ezechielem* in Migne, *Patristica Latina*, vol. 25).

61 It is the loss of this supreme hope early in the fourth century that leads Philip Schaff to comment: "The Christian life of the Nicene and post-Nicene age reveals a mass of worldliness within the church; and entire abatement of chiliasm with its longing after the return of Christ and his glorious reign [millennium], and in its stead an easy repose in the present order of things" (*History of the Christian Church*, seven volumes, New York: Charles Scribner's Sons, 1882-1910), volume 2, p. 619. Froom (*op. cit.*, I, p. 307) explains that this "abandonment of millenarianism [and hence also personal piety in his view] was made

possible because of the changed status of the church in the world of the fourth century. After Constantine had suddenly lifted Christianity out of persecution into popularity, and not only the wealth but the multitudes of the Gentiles had begun to flow into it, the Church came to think less of the personal coming of Christ and more of its own increasing influence in this present world." Adolph Harnack, *History of Dogma* translated from the third German edition by Neil Buchanan (Boston: Little, Brown and Company, 1895-99), p. 480, expresses the same view.

62 An honest perusal and weighing of the literature requires this conclusion. It is not so much a question of quantity of material on the topic but of emphasis.

63 Origen was probably born in Alexandria, Egypt, likely of Greek parentage. He brought Neo-Platonism to his faith and injected his encyclopedic knowledge of philosophy, Greek literature and philology as well as his vast learning in theology and Scripture into it. He is known as the most brilliant scholar of his day, especially for his work in the field of textual criticism.

His *Hexapla* — the Old Testament in six parallel columns, two Hebrew, four Greek: (1) Hebrew text, (2) Hebrew text transliterated into Greek alphabet, (3) version of Aquila, (4) version of Symmachus (5) the Septuagint, (6) version of Theodotian — requiring 28 years of labor, is the monument to his genius. Froom. *op. cit.*, I, pp. 310-315.

64 Frederic W. Farrar, *History of Interpretation* (London: Macmillan and Co., 1886), pp. 129, 130ff. Origen sought "inner meaning" on a "higher, nobler level" than that available through historical-grammatical exegesis. His hermeneutic knew no restraint other than the limits of imagination. Johann Heinrich Kurtz, *Church History* (New York: Funk and Wagnalls, 1889-90), volume I, p. 155.

65 Franz Kobler, *The Vision Was There* (London: Lincolns Prager, Ltd., 1956), p. 11.

66 Kenneth Scott Latourette, *History of Christianity* (New York: Harper and Row, 1953), pp. 175, 176. This is only to be expected for in the person and work of St. Augustine we have capsulized what is "most characteristic of medieval Roman Catholicism." Williston Walker, *A History of Christianity* (New York: Charles Scribner's Sons, 1959), p. 160.

67 Etienne Gilson, "Foreward" in the Image Book edition of Saint Augustine's *The City of God* (Garden City: Doubleday, 1962), pp. 13-35. Also pp. 507ff in the text itself have to do with the eternal city. Full text is available in Augustine, *The City of God*, Book one, *Nicene and Post Nicene Fathers*, 14 volumes, edited by Philip Schaff (New York: Charles Scribner's Sons, 1905-1917), volume VII.

68   Augustine, *The City of God*, Book one, Preface, in *Nicene and Post Nicene Fathers*, 14 volumes, edited by Philip Schaff (New York: Charles Scribner's Sons, 1905-1917), volume VII, p. 429ff.

69   Augustine, it is reported, was repelled by the straightforward historico-grammatical exegesis of Scripture.   He is reported to have adopted the Philonic (rabbinical?) rule that everything which appears unorthodox must be interpreted mystically, allegorically or figuratively.   He quotes and uses with approval, to the point of "seeming an echo," the hermeneutic of a certain Tichonius.   Tichonius' *Book of Rules*, says Farrar (*op. cit.*, pp. 235-236, 467), are "as baseless as Philos's, and even more so than Hillel's."   In any case, Augustine's concept here is couched in the language of Tichonius' "Fifth Rule."   Augustine, *op. cit.*, chapter 7 entirety, and especially pp. 427ff.   See also Edward Elliott, *Horae Apocalyptical*, four vols. (London: Jackson and Halliday, 1862), vol. I, pp. 395; also volume IV, p. 137; and note 3, p. 325.

70   Specifically in Augustine's thought, the Kingdom of God in Christ is idealized in the city of Rome.   This is the raw lumber from which the medieval theory and policy of the religio-political state church was constructed.   Rome became in literature and life the New Jerusalem.   *Vide* especially Augustine's opening remarks in the Preface to the *City of God* (vol. II, p. 1ff. of the *Nicene and Post Nicene Fathers*).

71   Augustine, *op. cit.*, Book XX, chapter 7.

72   *Ibid.*, Book XVII, Book XVIII, chapter 46.

73   *Ibid.*, Book XVII, p. 436f.

74   Alexander Clarence Flick, *The Rise of the Medieval Church* (New York: G. P. Putnam's Sons, 1909), p. 83ff.

75   The Albigenses (or Cathari) in the twelfth century and the Waldensians, thus named from Peter Waldo (in the twelfth century onward to modern times) are outstanding examples.   Froom I, 808-811, 829-886.   There were a number of similar but lesser groups, as the Humiliati, the Vaudois, the Paulicians and so on.

76   Joachim is one of the least known but most powerfully influential of the figures in the pre-Reformation epoch.   His major emphases echo and re-echo through the works of Wycliffe, Nicholas of Cusa, Hus, Luther, Calvin and even in so diverse a figure as Dante. Johann J. Dollinger, *Prophecies and the Prophetic Spirit in the Christian Era* (London: Rivingtons, 1873), p. 106.   His conversion and call to "prophetic exposition," to use his own words, are traced, significantly, to a pilgrimage to the Holy Land which he took as a young man.   Edmund G. Gardner, "Joachim of Flora," *Catholic Encyclopedia*, volume VIII, p. 406.

77 Joachim, *Exposito Magni Prophete Abbatis Joachim in Apocalyssim* (Ventijs: In Edibus Francisci Bindoni ac Maphei Pasini Socii, 1527), folios 16v, cols. 1, 2; folios 7v, col. 1, and folios 209v.-211r.

78 There is some dispute whether the so-called Joachimites were really disciples, i.e., spiritual descendants of Joachim, or rather an entirely separate group who merely happened to have had access to the same materials Joachim had, viz., Jewish cabalism. Borrowing is evident in their literature particularly from the writings of Eleazar ben Judah Kalonymus (c. 1176-1238). Alfred-Felix Vaucher, *Lacunziana: Essais sur les propheties bibliques* (Collongeseous-Saleve, Haute-Savoie: Imprimerie Fides, 1949), p. 60. Froom, *op. cit.*, II, 184-219 gives a nearly exhaustive listing of other Jewish writers, contemporary with and antedating Joachim, knowledge of whom it is very possible Joachim had. It is suggestive to recall that this age produced the public disputations between the Jewish renegade Pablo Christiani and Nahmanides before King James of Aragon. Sarachek (*op. cit.*, pp. 176-182) reports the occasion, stating that four days were consumed on the Messianic question. Incidentally, the king judged Nahmanides the winner, awarding him gold dinars worth about $12,000.00 today, and royal protection for the homeward journey.

79 Froom, I, 719.

80 Among them the best remembered are probably Hus, Wycliffe and Savanarola. The important thing, however, is not always *what* they said but the serious handling of the Scriptures in respect for historico-grammatical exegesis. It seems that such an approach led them to common conclusions in this aspect of Christian theology—and still does. *Per contra*, eisegesis is an extraordinary danger and has a uniform history of vascilating opinion. *Vide* Willis J. Beecher, *The Prophets and the Promise* (Grand Rapids, Michigan: Baker Book House, 1963), pp. 3-15, for a brief treatment of the principles involved. The best recent, overall statement of this hermeneutic can be found in Bernard Ramm, *Protestant Biblical Interpretation* (Boston: W. A. Wilde Company, 1956). The central principle is in regarding the Bible as *sola fidei regula* and not *prima fidei regula*.

81 Again, on the basis of an historico-grammatical hermeneutic. The same exegesis that led to stubborn persistence in the biblical practice of immersion of believers only, re-immersion in the case of converts from groups practicing paedobaptism, led also to acceptance of the idea of literal Jewish national return to Palestine rather than spiritualizing the evidence of these passages. Conrad Hübel and Felix Manz, young scions of prominent Zurich families were martyred for their stand. Manz was "baptized" to death, i.e., executed by drowning. The Mennonites (from Menno Simos), Hutterites (from Jacob Hutter), the Amish (from Jacob Amman) were persecuted terribly by Roman Catholic and Protestant alike. They fled to Holland, to South Russia, and later to America. Their industry and thrift have made them gen-

erally welcome, but their piety is generally scorned. The principles of most present day Baptist denominations are traceable back to this movement to make every effort truly to follow the New Testament teaching in faith and life. *Vide* Kenneth Scott Latourette, *op. cit.*, pp. 778-787.

82 Luther alludes to the return of the Jews in his *Ein trostliche predigt von der zukunft Christi und den vorgehenden zeichen des Jüngesten Tags* (Wittenberg: Hans Luft, 1532, unpaged). Cf. Froom, II, 280, on Luther in this specific aspect of his eschatology.

83 Hence Calvin's emphasis in making Geneva a center of ideal social order in the here and now. Interestingly, Servetus, was a passionate millennialist, believing the Messianic age imminent. Kenneth Scott Latourette, *op. cit.*, pp. 757-760. Also Froom, II, 439.

84 Calvin's outlook on this point was basically Augustinian (q.v. *supra*). A typical statement from his commentary on Isaiah 11:11 where the prophet speaks of a "second return" capsulizes his view: "This cannot be understood then of the deliverance out of Babylon, but ought to be referred to the kingdom of Christ, under which this deliverance is both been, and is accomplished by the preaching of the Gospel." John Calvin, *Commentary on the Prophecie of Isaiah* (London: Felix Kingston, 1609), p. 136. To be fair to Calvin we must add that he was not a theocrat in the sense that he felt religious (church) officials should control civil offices, or even ought to occupy them, but only in the sense that God should rule the community through the Word. The minister's only authority was to be spiritual — teachers of the community. This is very clear in *The Register of the Company of Pastors of Geneva in the time of Calvin*, Edited & translated by Philip Edgcumbe Hughes (Grand Rapids: Wm. B. Erdmans Pub. Co., 1966), *passim*. There is thus complete spiritualization of "Israel" into the "Church," i.e., Israel here does not equal Israel in the sense of the Old Testament nation identified by that name. By some convenient logic chopping, Israel remains concretized as a nation in one part of the passage, then is immediately vaporized into no more than a type of spiritual entity known as the Church (Kingdom) of Jesus Christ. Typical application may be legitimate; absolute typical exegesis is not. Cf. Alva J. McClain, *The Greatness of the Kingdom* (Grand Rapids, Michigan: Zondervan Publishing House, 1959), pp. 141-143, for specific comment on the necessity of consistency in any valid system of hermeneutics and exegesis.

85 The dissolution of *religious* unity in the sixteenth century also shattered the old ligatures upon which basis *political* unity had functioned. The momentous shift from feudalism to sovereign centralized national governments signaled an epoch of conscious Machiavellian political chicanery to see which nation would prevail. Due in the main to Tudor brilliance, especially in the person of Elizabeth I, England was able to remain aloof from the entanglements and dreadful consequences of

actual war, if not entirely from the chicanery. Elizabeth's skillful political maneuvering, learned early in childhood when a clumsy move could have cost her very life, effectively preserved the peace for Britain. The recognized treatment on this theme is Garrett Mattingly's monograph *The Armada* (Boston: Houghton Mifflin, 1959).

86 Garrett Mattingly, *op. cit.* Hensley H. Henson, *Puritanism in England* (London: Hodder and Stoughton, 1912), p. 116.

87 *Ibid.*, pp. 116-117. The implications of Psalm 1:2, 3; 30; 36:5-10; Deuteronomy 5:29, 29:9; Exodus 19:5, Proverbs 28:25 and literally hundreds of other passages seemed clear enough.

88 Bishop George Carlton, *A Thankful Remembrance of God's Mercy in an Historical Collection of the Great and Merciful Deliverance of the Church and State of England, Since the Gospel Began Here to Flourish, from the Beginning of Queen Elizabeth* (London: I.D. for Robert Mylbourne and Humphrey Robinson, 1624).

89 *Ibid.*, p. 26.

90 *Ibid.*, pp. 26-27.

91 *Ibid.*, p. 89.

92 "An Admonition to Parliament (1572)" in William Haller, *Elizabeth I and the Puritans* (Ithaca, New York: Cornell University Press for the Folger Shakespeare Library, 1964), p. 1.

Chapter III

Albion and Zion: The New Jerusalem

Religious Break with Rome

The breach with Rome under Henry VIII created a spiritual vacuum[1] in England, and the Roman Church lost her place as the sole religious guide.[2] The struggles of the middle decades of the sixteenth century under Edward VI, Mary Tudor, and the first years of Elizabeth's reign further enhanced the sense of striving and of loss rather than bringing the religious unrest to equilibrium or filling the spiritual vacuum.

Elizabeth had come to the throne in 1558. Her father, Henry, can be said to have seized the church—albeit always under the guise of sedulous legality. Her brother, Edward, and her sister, Mary, had in contrary ways and with unhappy consequences tried to reform it. Elizabeth saw clearly that she must rule it, or herself be ruined. As head of the nation, she maintained control of religion, without bothering overmuch either for logic or zeal. The only religious test required of her subjects was willingness to swear fealty to herself as suzerain of the church. This posture, while tending to a broad quasi-toleration (except when someone got in her way), left things hanging, openended, unsettled, pleasing really no one, least of all the earnest reformers.[3]

To Reform the Church and Establish the Kingdom of Christ

In this connection we can be instructed best by the reflections of a succeeding and similarly engaged generation. On the eve of the revolution in November 1640, in the last margins of the period under study, we find spokesmen consciously and deliberately paralleling their own struggle and hoped for victory in language clearly meant to be reminiscent of earlier days.[4] On the first fast day[5] of the Long Parliament, e.g., two preachers Cornelius Burges and Stephen Marshall were commissioned to deliver sermons[6] from Jeremiah 50:5[7] with the specific purpose of reminding that body of its "spiritual heritage and duty to keep England's covenant with God, restore Zion and reestablish true religion and undefiled."[8] The two preachers were at pains to leave no room for doubt, therefore, as to the relevance of the familiar doctrine of covenant and return to Zion pictured in the chosen passage. These notions they applied to the Protestant struggles under Henry, Edward and Mary. Now again, the more thorough reform[9] of the nonconformist groups, in this case led by the Puritans, found themselves in the same position, vis-a-vis the *via media* of the Established Church and the manifest compromise it required. Both Burges and Marshall reviewed for Parliament in no uncertain terms that they were themselves, as the heroes of the faith of that earlier epoch, of the elect called by the Lord; they were in covenant to rebuild Zion and overthrow false gods and their priests. The preachers assured them that the Lord would successfully consumate His work in them, His elect. This covenant, moreover, was more than merely personal; it was national. Its bonds were on all Englishmen severally as well as on each true believer individually. England's destiny could be summarized, as Foxes *Actes and Monuments*,[10] the great martyrology, pictured it, in the agelong struggle of Christ and Antichrist; the pope was Antichrist, Rome was Babylon; England, believing England, the elect champion of true faith, was the appointed of God to be the special agent of Babylon's defeat and Antichrist's downfall. Henry VIII had driven him out; Edward had reformed the church; but Mary had brought back popery and its minions. Elizabeth "that glorious Deborah" had overcome "the hydra of stout popelings" at home and their supporters abroad. Thus, for all the perfidy of Antichrist, the Lord delivered England out of Babylon, protected her from the treachery of the Spaniard and his

Armada,[11] "gunpowder, treason[12] and many other perils."[13] Marshall proclaimed further:

> All the Nations in Christendome have been in grevious perplexities many years round about us; we have bin hitherto kept as another Land of Goshen, where light hath still shined when all others have been in darkness.[14]

In order to arrive at this halcyon state the Puritan mind was determined to finish reformation and establish the Kingdom of Christ. The Scriptures and the Providence of God there revealed were seized as both the force and means of its mediation by which to accomplish that end. If England were obedient it would flourish, if it were disobedient, it would perish, as the Scripture seemed to say:

> And it shall come to pass, if ye harken diligently to my commandments which I command you this day, to love the Lord your God, and to serve him with all your heart and with all your soul, that I will give you the rain of your land in his due season, the first rain and the latter rain that thou mayest gather in thy corn, and thy wine, and thine oil. And I will send grass in thy fields for thy cattle, that thou mayest eat and be full. Take heed to yourselves, that your heart be not deceived, and ye turn aside, and serve other gods, and worship them; And then the Lord's wrath be kindled against you, and he shut up the heaven, that there be no rain, and that the land yield not her fruit; and lest ye perish quickly from off the good land which the Lord giveth you (Deuteronomy 11:13-17).

The Telling Influence of the English Bible

The direct influence of the Bible, as the foregoing facts lead us to expect,

> now widely read in the Genevan Version began to tell in many directions. . . . The parallel between the English nation and the People of Israel, which was generally drawn, and seems to have established itself in the public mind almost as a postulate, confirmed that intimate association of Church and State which was the cornerstone. It would appear that the Old Testament was more widely read than the New, certainly its spirit rather than that of the Christian Scriptures coloured the religious thought of the nation. The course of events on the continent, where the Counter-Reformation seemed to be threatening a total destruction of the Reformed Churches, strengthened in English minds the notion that the English people held a special position in the providential scheme of history analogous to that held by the ancient

Israelites. This notion was eminently congrous with the prevaling
Calvinism, which suggested the idea of Divine Election as belonging to
the privileged and faithful nation.[15]

More and more as the lines of the religious settlement had
begun to become visible and were finally implemented and
accepted by the mass of Englishmen under Elizabeth, it was
apparent that another religious guide had taken the old one's
place. That new spiritual power was the Bible.[16]

John Richard Green capsulizes the situation with one sentence in his *Short History of the English People*, "England became
the people of a book and that book was the Bible."[17] By the
end of Elizabeth's reign the book of books for Englishmen was
already the Bible.[18] Shakespeare may have been the greatest
glory of the age but he was not the greatest influence:

> No greater moral change ever passed over a nation than passed over
> England during the years which parted the middle of the reign of Eliz-
> abeth from the meeting of the Long Parliament. England became the
> people of a book, and that book was the Bible. It was as yet the one
> English book which was familiar to every Englishman: it was read in
> churches and read at home and everywhere its words, as they fell on
> ears which custom had not deadened, kindled a startling enthusiasm.
> What the revival of classical learning had done on the Continent was
> done in England in a far profounder fashion by the translation of the
> Scriptures. It came at a psychological moment in the moral and politi-
> cal development of our people. It not only entered into the warp and
> woof of our literature, but seemed to give point, emphasis, and expres-
> sion to the new ethical, social, and religious impulses with which the
> country was at that time stirred.[19]

In the religious ferment of the day, coupled with the intense
contest with Spain, the faith of the people became riveted in
the Scriptures.[20] Tyndale's prophetic word, before paying
with his life at the stake for the sin (he was burned for heresy)
of translating the Scriptures into English, that the day would
come when the ploughboy would know as much of the Bible
as the learned doctors of theology came largely and rapidly
true.[21] And it tells us something about our own nature and
time to note that the Bible of Elizabethan England, the Authorized or so-called King James Version, continues in our own
day as the most beloved, quoted, read, purchased of all the
versions. The time is still far distant when it will be replaced

in the hearts of the English speaking world, much less replaced in actual use.[22] With its faith rooted in Holy Writ, the minds of pious Englishmen, saturated in the Scriptures turned with their best energy to accomplishing the goal toward which every believer is admonished to strive — to establish the kingdom of Christ.[23]

The Parallel Struggle of Old Testament Israel and Puritan England

As the sixteenth century drew to a close the England of rising Puritanism was therefore powerfully constrained by the parallel story of struggle in the journey of Old Testament Israel from slavery to freedom.[24] These whole-souled believers saw themselves as walking the same path. The Sacred Word, the promises and covenant of God recorded between God and His people, became uniquely their own. To the devout Bible-reading Protestant of the day, the "Land of Promise" was as his own Fatherland and the Hebrew patriarchs were as his own (spiritual) ancestors. He had express New Testament authority for calling Abraham his father (Matthew 3:9, 22:32; Mark 12:26; Luke 3:8, 16:22ff., John 8; Stephen's sermon in Acts 7; Romans 4; Hebrews 11:8-17, etc.) Hence he had a kind of patriotism and Zionist-like zeal stronger than that of many contemporary Jews. The Scriptures had come to contain the symbols of their own national future; the genius of The Book carried into the very heart and soul of England.[25]

The preachers were anything but slothful in telling the people that by reading and studying this Book, this one particular Book among all the products of the burgeoning book and pamphlet trade (which functioned roughly described, popularly, in demand and use, much like radio or television does for many of us today), they could discover for themselves the way to salvation, the key to the mystery of good and evil, the perfect rule by which to govern their personal lives, fashion the laws of the church and state, and judge the acts of rulers. With such expectations in mind, people made it their business to read the Bible. What they discovered there was not an abstract, systematic outline of religious precepts but the richly imaginative representation of

> the life of a people recognizably like themselves—patriarchs, prophets, judges, and kings; husbands, wives, and their families, all involved in the common predicaments of personal, family, and public life. And running through the whole, from Genesis to Revelation, was the saga of a people acutely conscious of their own identity as a people, believing themselves to have been singled out and set apart from all others for special purpose and destiny by an inscrutable almighty power who keeps them under His constant care and observation and may be expected to break in upon them at any time with his commands and judgments. . . . However habituated to reading . . . whatever English books he may have read, he never had anything to read so exciting to the imagination as the Bible.[26]

The Bible as an Imaginative Experience

The common complaint against the Puritans as stern, unimaginative, repressive biblical dogmatists in this regard, says Harold Fisch,[27] speaking specifically of the poetry of John Milton,[28] is really "too hasty a conclusion."[29] "For the reading of Scripture" he continues,

> was not a matter of accepting dogmas; it was a matter of being exposed to a direct, even blinding spiritual illumination. . . . The tremendous effect which the Bible had upon men, the awe, the terror, and ecstacy which it undoubtedly inspired, should be sufficient to convince the skeptic that the men of the Reformation were concerned with real and mighty facts of experience. . . . It was a first class imaginative experience.[30]

Interestingly, the system of Christian theology in the England of that day, Calvinism, *is* a major example of authoritatively constructed doctrine. But behind and beneath, running through and spilling out the language of his theology was Calvin's own experience of the light of God, itself too dazzling for mortal eyes, therefore, reflected in the "mirror"[31] of Scripture, as a self authenticating, intellectually constraining power, purely on its own merits:

> Scripture exhibits fully as clear evidence of its own truth as white and black things do their color, or sweet and bitter things do their taste. . . .[32]

Let this point therefore stand: that those whom the Holy Spirit has inwardly taught truly rest upon Scripture, and that Scripture indeed is self-authenticated; hence, it is not right to subject it to proof and reasoning. And the certainty it deserves with us, it attains by the testimony of the Spirit. For even if it wins reverence for itself by its own majesty, it seriously affects us only when it is sealed upon our hearts through the Spirit. Therefore, illumined by his power, we believe neither by our own nor by anyone else's judgment that Scripture is from God; but above human judgment we affirm with utter certainty (just as if we were gazing upon the majesty of God himself) that it has flowed to us from the very mouth of God by the ministry of men.[33] We seek no proof, no marks of genuineness upon which our judgment may lean; but we subject our judgment and wit to it as to a thing far beyond any guesswork! This we do, not as persons accustomed to seize upon some unknown thing, which, under closer scrutiny, displeases us, but fully conscious that we hold the unassailable truth! Nor do we do this as those miserable men who habitually bind over their minds to the thralldom of superstition; *but we feel that the undoubted power of his divine majesty lives and breathes there. By this power we are drawn and inflamed, knowingly and willingly, to obey him, yet also more vitally and more effectively than by mere human willing or knowing!* [italics mine][34]

The Certainty of Biblical Prophecy

We have seen that the *sine qua non* of Puritanism was the authority of Scripture.[35] It was used constantly in straightforward fashion.[36] The Bible said what it meant and meant what it said, and that was that. The Bible to these utter Reformation men, was *sola fidei regula* and not merely *prima fidei regula*.[37] The prophecies too, therefore, that spoke of a restored Zion, cherished as part of their own heritage, the reign of the Messiah in a kingdom of peace and justice, were an important feature of Puritan faith,[38] because the Word of God was more than true; it was TRUTH, to be trusted completely. Scripture, in sum, was all sufficient.[39] Hence it was not difficult to make a doctrine out of belief in the prophecies regarding Jewish return as explicit and unmistakable promises that would certainly be fulfilled.[40] If the Bible said so, it would be so. This kind of profound trust in the prophecies came more and more to the fore as the events of their own day pressed upon mind and heart the increasingly apocalyptic dimensions of their own time. Specific formulations on the theme of Jewish restoration in increasingly fuller detail were not long in forthcoming.[41]

The numerous passages speaking directly on the question were the bedrock on which the Puritan millennialists built and enlarged upon the doctrine of the Restoration of the Jews.[42]

The Immediate Situation

Out of this milieu, the birth and development of the idea of Jewish restoration in a land where Jews had in the flesh been formally excluded for nearly three centuries (since 1290) is no longer an anomaly, though it is doubtful that any Jews were personally known by the various restoration advocates.[43] These foundational changes in English Christianity were taking place hard on the heels of those desperate days in which the golden age of Jewish philosophy and culture was being forcibly terminated in Spain by pogrom and expulsion. Soon, numbers of Jewish neo-Christians from Iberian persecution began founding small communities in England and also the Netherlands. These Marrano families were the first wave of pioneers of Jewish resettlement in Britain.[44] A great ambivalence seems initially to have characterized the relationship of these "underground" Jews and the English people. A mixture of attitudes, admiration and hate, mistrust and esteem, is reflected in the literature of contemporary authors.[45] Marlowe's *Jew of Malta*, e.g., and Shakespeare's *Merchant of Venice* amply document the fact. At the very period when the Israel of the Old Testament had become strongly identified as the model of the English nation, the Jews on the contemporary scene were regarded with intense interest of sundry and contrary varieties.[46]

Concurrent with and partially preliminary to these events, England was undergoing an introduction to Hebrew studies. The stimulus of the Reformation generally, but initially, in the main, having its birth in the sensual interests of Henry VIII and his consequent matrimonial difficulties,[47] Hebrew learning gradually became a matter of vivid interest. So high did interest soar that by the time of the Act of Uniformity in 1549, use of Hebrew had spread so widely and penetrated to sufficient depth that private devotions were being carried on in that tongue. Formal authorization to use the Hebrew Testament was granted in the Act.

Obviously, however, if serious, sustained study and investigation were to be carried on in so remote a tongue, someone with intimate, preferably firsthand acquaintance was necessary. Accordingly, from this time onward a few Jews, usually converted ones, could be found in and around the universities. The earliest was John Immanuel Tremellius (1510-1580). Converted to Roman Catholicism and afterward persuaded to Protestantism, he came to England seeking refuge from the religious wars of the Continent during the middle years of the sixteenth century. There he found both hospitality and a position at Cambridge. On Mary's accession to the throne, however, he fled back to the Continent and ultimately became professor of Hebrew at Heidelberg, publishing a number of scholarly works. In 1565 he was back in England, Elizabeth's accession in 1558 having made return safe for the sizeable group of exiles who had had to stay beyond Mary's reach,[48] or risk the fires at Smithfield.

Of less ability and influence, Philip Ferdinandus made his way via conversion from his birthplace in Poland (1555) to an education at Oxford. He proved to be a popular paedagogue, lecturing to large groups who paid him tuition at both his Alma Mater, Oxford, and at Cambridge. His little volume of Mosaic precepts, published in 1597, was the first serious contribution to scholarship of things specifically Jewish in England.[49]

Other lesser lights, a certain Rabbi Jacob, a Jacobus Bernatus, and a Jacob Barnett,[50] et al. sparsely dotted the scene. While their record is not brilliant these played a significant role in that they familiarized the Englishman, after an absence of 300 years, with the person of the Jew and began the diffusion of Hebrew studies. Their disciples were really the ones to establish Hebraics on a permanent and important basis. By the reign of James I there had developed a competent nucleus of English Hebraists of genuine scholarly ability. Letter writing and other personal exchange in travel and business contacts further enriched this period of education. The end result of it was the Authorized Version of the Bible of 1611. Executed straight from the original languages by translators of remarkable skill and preparation for their day, the product was as accurate as the tools of the time afforded.[51] A truly magnificent rendering of poetic grandeur and genius, the Authorized Version is still the single greatest monument to the beauty and power of the English tongue, perhaps the most influential of all forces which have shaped that language, fit rival to the originals from which it was derived.[52]

The Jew, however, remained *persona non grata* in England until several years after Manesseh ben Israel's intercession before Cromwell (i.e., 1664).   Though professing Jews remained barred until that time,[53] we have seen that there is probably no people or land on earth which so habitually and deeply imbibed of the Hebraic ethos. Albion and Zion had merged virtually into one entity in the minds and hearts of Englishmen. From such a context and from among this people, now growing more and more intimate with things Jewish, the early millennarian protagonists for the restoration of the Jews to their Palestinian homeland arose.

The dimensions of the New Jerusalem were to be a great deal larger than the piety which first envisioned them, in its wildest dreams, anticipated. We are ready to turn, now *in situ*, to these men and the idea which sprang from them and their time.

Notes

1 Williston Walker, *A History of the Christian Church* (New York: Charles Scribner's Sons, 1959), pp. 358ff.

2 In January, 1531, Henry VIII, arguably a genius at despotic intrigue, charged the whole body of English clergy with violation of the old statute of Praemunire (of 1453) for recognizing the Pope's authority in the person of the Papal legate, Cardinal Wolsey. In this act he effectively intimidated the clergy into recognizing him as "single and supreme Lord and, as far as the law of Christ allows, even supreme head" of the Church of England, and at the same time extorted a large sum as the price of pardon. Formal separation from Rome took place in May of the following year when Henry forbade both payment of the annates to the Papal court and all appeals to Rome. This break in the old lines of recognized authority was for the bulk of Englishmen not satisfactorily repaired until the religious settlement outlined in the Thirty-Nine Articles composed and ratified under Elizabeth in 1563. By then, however, strong lines of dissent had formed and the *Articles* provided the back board against which the voice of the growing parties of nonconformity could be sounded. J. J. Scarisbrick, *Henry VIII* (Eyre and Spottiswood, 1968); also William Haller, *The Rise of Puritanism* (New York: Columbia University Press, 1938), pp. 6-10.

3 Williston Walker, *op. cit.*, pp. 358ff. Cf. William Haller, *op. cit.*, pp. 6, 7.

4 William Haller, *Liberty and Reformation in the Puritan Revolution* (New York: Columbia University Press, 1955), pp. 17-19.

5 The "fast days" of Parliament were regular, officially designated days whereon the whole body sat to hear a morning and afternoon sermon from the Scriptures, to pray, to concentrate upon refurnishing mind and soul with the appointments by which piety was to be nourished and spiritual duty to be informed and implemented. The influence of the pulpit was of primary importance for herein lay the overriding endeavor of the Puritan movement: to preach the Word. Hence, also, pulpit and printed sermon were the chief instruments in pressing for the desired reforms of government, worship, church discipline beyond the limits which the prelacy had established and which the Elizabethan settlement had neither required nor wished to go. William Haller, *op. cit.*, pp. xi-xv. All of this emphasis on biblical preaching was specifically to the end that reformation be complete, in their metaphor, "that the New Jerusalem be established." The result, however, was not Zion, though magnificently striven for, but something like the modern

English State. H. H. Henson, *Puritanism in England* (London: Hodder and Stoughton, 1912), pp. 267-294. For the overall picture: Hugh Redwald Trevor-Roper, *The Crisis of the Seventeenth Century* (New York: Harper and Row, 1968).

6 Cornelius Burges, *A Sermon Preached to the Honourable House of Commons Assembled in Parliament at their Publique Fast, Novem. 17, 1640,* 1641; Stephen Marshall, *A Sermon Preached before the Honourable House of Commons, now assembled in Parliament, at their publike Fast, November 17, 1640,* 1641.

7 "They shall ask the way to Zion, with their faces thitherward saying, Come, and let us join ourselves to the Lord in a perpetual covenant that shall not be forgotten."

8 So complete was the identification with the Old Testament strivings and yearnings of Israel that the logic carried over rather explicitly in the continuing debate and battle with prelacy and the Westminster divines. A particular example is in the person of one John Selden who because of his gifts with languages and wide learning in history and law was especially vexing to his prelatic opponents. They accused him, significantly, of "arrogance and glory in his Jewish learning," insisting on the *jus divinum* of his views, "always ready with proof that the Jewish State and church was all one, and that so in England it must be, that the Parliament is the church." The story is recorded of Selden that often in the course of debate he would rise and tell his clerical counterparts "Perhaps in your little Pocket Bibles with gilt leaves (which they would often pull out and read) the translation may be thus, but the Greek and Hebrew signifies thus and thus." John Aubrey, *'Brief Lives,' Chiefly of Contemporaries, Set Down by John Aubrey, Between 1669 & 1697* edited by Andrew Clarke (Oxford: Clarendon Press, 1898), II, pp. 219-225. Bulstrode Whitelocke, *Memorials of the English Affairs from the beginning of the Reign of Charles the First to the Happy Restoration of King Charles the Second* (Oxford: University Press, 1853), p. 71. Such men were frequently bitterly assailed and the labels of "antinomian, Anabaptist, churchless, lawless men, bent upon impeding the reparation of Zion" were desultorily attached to all the nonconformist parties, especially the Puritans. Arthur Sutherland Pigott Woodhouse, *Puritanism and Liberty* (Chicago: University of Chicago Press, 1951) *passim.*

9 "The real representatives of Protestantism in this country [England], both in its political and religious aspects were the Puritans." W. B. Selbie, "The Influence of the Old Testament on Puritanism," *The Legacy of Israel,* edited by Edwyn R. Bevan and Charles Singer (Oxford: Clarendon Press, 1953), p. 407.

10 Commonly known as *The Book of Martyrs*, this work was the immediate fruit of Mary's attempt to restore the old religion by prosecuting the new for heresy. The 2000 folio pages and 60 woodcuts told essentially the same story of every martyr, with numerous interest-sustaining varia-

tions of personal detail. It was the story of one who has awakened to
the light and embraced the truth revealed in the Word and who stands
by what he believes in the face of every argument, temptation and
ordeal to which he is subjected. The narrative generally included a
dramatic scene in which, relying on the Scriptures alone, the martyr
refutes all the arguments his inquisitors can bring against him and
marches off exultantly to testify at the stake before a "cloud of wit-
nesses." William Haller, *Elizabeth I and the Puritans*, pp. 25, 26. To the
above must be added that *The Book of Martyrs* was probably first in
importance after the Bible itself in sustaining the piety and impulse to
reform among the nonconforming groups. Moreover, it enlarged on
the content and method in which Puritan apologists held the New Testament to be both God's revealed word and a valid historical record, a
body of constitutional precedents as it were, by which the acts and deci-
sions of the church in later times were to be determined. The same
men were consequently bound to assert that tradition, the fathers,
councils, and church historians, rightly weighed, must agree with Scripture or be without avail. And they had finally to explain how and why
the church as seen in the New Testament so quickly fell away from its
original purity and remained so long in corruption and under afflic-
tion. For answer to that question they constructed out of the same evidence of fathers, councils, and historians, with resort also to secular and
profane authorities, their own account of what had happened in the
church from the beginning to their own day. The true church, they
said, had been betrayed when priests, prelates, and popes conspired
with rulers to persecute the saints, suppress the gospel and promote
idolatry, ignorance and superstition for the purpose of deceiving the
people and enriching themselves. This was the common Protestant
view of church history, but since the accession of Elizabeth, it had taken
popular hold and was embellished with specific English character and
application. In 1559 we find Bishop Alymer proclaiming: "God is
English. . . . out of England Wycliffe, who begate Husse, who begate
Luther, who begate the truth." He continues later to the effect that if
Christ were to be born yet again, He would do so "of England, among
Englishmen." William Haller, "John Foxe and the Puritan Revolution," in *The Seventeenth Century: Studies in the History of English Thought
and Literature from Bacon to Pope* by Richard Foster Jones *et al.* (Stanford,
California: Stanford University Press, 1951), pp. 209-224. *The Book of
Martyrs* was a documented explication of this theme. Foxe had been
one of Aylmer's fellow exiles during Mary's reign. On this notion Foxe
served both Protestant piety and English patriotism by picturing all history on a balance with England as the fulcrum, the English church as
the crucial force, and the work to be done was in claiming the souls of
men from antichrist for Christ and His Kingdom. The climax, according to Foxe, was soon to come in the imminent approach of Christ's
final triumph in England. William Haller, *Foxe's Book of Martyrs and the
Elect Nation* (London: J. Cape, 1963) gives a fully orbed study on Foxe
and his book.

11 The rivalry between England and Spain in the last two decades of the sixteenth century was a Gordian knot of religious intrigue, Machiavellian politics and royal deceit. Felix Raab, *The English Face of Machiavelli* (London: Routledge and Kegan Paul, 1965), *passim*. Though Philip II of Spain had in 1559 actually offered his hand in marriage to Protestant Elizabeth of England in order to thwart French designs through the person of Mary Stuart, Queen of Scots, events had altered the picture by 1587 to the point where Philip sent a great Armada against England. In a series of savage naval engagements in the English Channel in 1588 the smaller but fast ships of Sir Francis Drake and John Hawkins outmaneuvered, disorganized and largely destroyed, with the help of severe weather, the larger, more powerful but bulky and awkward galleons of Spain. The few Spanish vessels that escaped were able to do so only by fleeing up through the North Sea and around the northern coast of Scotland. The defeat of the Armada meant that England was to remain Protestant, meant the birth of modern English sea power and also meant the beginning of decline of Spanish power.

12 Jame I, (son of Mary Stuart, Queen of Scots and great grandson of Margaret, daughter of Henry VII) though reared a Presbyterian, favored episcopacy on the principle of "no bishop; no king" seemed, at the outset of his reign to be veering towards the Roman Catholics. However, his attitude soon changed. In February, 1609, he ordered priests banished, and soon Parliament confirmed the Elizabethan laws against them. This led to what was to become known as the Gunpowder Plot associated with the name of Guy Fawkes. Its purpose was to store a cellar under Parliament buildings with barrels of gunpowder and to blow up both houses, along with James and his eldest son. The plot was discovered and the chief conspirators were shot or executed. This aroused much anti-Roman Catholic feeling and led Parliament to enact even more stringent acts against those of the persuasion. Kenneth Scot Latourette, *op. cit.*, p. 816.

13 William Haller, "John Foxe and the Puritan Revolution," *loc. cit.*, *passim*.

14 Stephen Marshall, *Sermon*, p. 19.

15 H. Hensley Henson, *Puritanism in England* (London: Hodder and Stoughton, 1912), pp. 115-116.

16 Persuasion in Parliament, most of the debates, the speeches, in short, the real source of power and authority brought to bear increasingly and well nigh exclusively on every situation, contest and problem, was to argue from or cite the Scripture. The sermons in Parliament tell us more of what was really going on than the published catalogued debates in the vast compilations and collections still carefully preserved. (Cobett's *Parliamentary History* and Hansard's *Parliamentary History of England* now exceed 750 volumes.)   Hundreds of sermons were preached on themes as Thomas Wilson's *David's Zeale for Zion, Psalm 69:9, "the zeale of thy house hath eaten me up"* wherein Parliament's duty

was declared as being eaten up by zeal for God's house; the business of God's house was the preaching of the word; Parliament, therefore, must bend every effort to raise up preachers (*contra* the practise of the Established Church clergy in neglecting preaching). Thomas Wilson, *David's Zeale for Zion: A sermon preached before Sundry of the Hon. House of Commons at St. Margarets at Westminster, April 4, 1641* (London: n.p., 1641), *passim*. Two years later Wilson was commissioned for another, similar sermon, this time on Hebrews 11:30, entitled *Jerichoes Downfall.*

Another important representative sermon is Samuel Fairclough's *The Troublers Troubled, or Acan Condemned, and Executed, Joshua 7:25* wherein Parliament is forcefully reminded how Achan had brought the anger of the Lord upon Israel by disobeying Joshua and how Israel heeding Joshua, took Achan and all his people and stoned them in the vale of Achor. Fairclough told his hearers that they too were in covenant with God to destroy from their midst every troubler of the Lord's people: "Up for the matter, belongs to you, wee also will be with you; wee, even all the godly Ministers of the Country as *Aaron* and *Hur* with *Moses* and *Joshua* [emphasis his]."

Samuel Fairclough, *The Troublers Troubled, or Achan Condemned and Executed. A sermon Preached before sundry of the Hon. House of Commons, Apr. 4, 1641* (London: Henry Brome, 1641), p. 29. William Haller, *op. cit.,* pp. 1-31, comments at length on the influence of the Bible through the Puritan preachers.

17 John Richard Green, *Short History of the English People* (New York: Harper and Brothers, 1893), II, pp. 933ff.

18 William Haller, *Rise of Puritanism*, p. 14.

19 W. B. Selbie, "The Influence of the Old Testament on Puritanism," *op. cit.*, p. 407f.

20 The Bible was to the pious Englishman of the day the very word of God "given by inspiration of God, profitable for doctrine, for reproof, for correction, for instruction in righteousness: That the man of God may be perfect, thoroughly furnished unto all good works" (II Timothy 3:16, 17). Moreover, the Scriptures "came not in old time by the will of man: But holy men of God spoke as they were moved by the Holy Ghost" (II Peter 1:21).

The threat of Spanish invasion struck terror in the breast of every nation in that day for Spain was still the first power of Europe and her reputation for ruthless suppression was both legendary and earned. When the Armada appeared in the Channel, therefore, Queen Elizabeth herself appeared bareheaded before her troops, riding through the ranks declaring: "I am come among you at this time being resolved . . . to lay down for my God, and for my Kingdom, and for my people, my honour and my blood, even in the dust. I know that I have but the body of a feeble woman, but I have the heart of a King, and a King of

England too." Quoted in Arthur L. Cross, *A Shorter History of England and Greater Britain* (New York: The Macmillan Company, 1920), p. 260.

21 Christopher Wordworth, *Ecclesiastical Biography; or, Lives of Eminent Men, Connected with the History of Religion in England; From the Commencement of the Reformation to the Revolution* (London: Francis and John Rivington, 1853), Vol. II, p. 193.

22 Statistics from the American Bible Society show sales of the Authorized King James Version are still three to one over all other versions combined. American Bible society, "A Distribution Comparison of English Versions by The American Bible Society," *National Distribution Minutes* (New York: American Bible Society, February 25, 1969), pp. 4-5.

23 Observe the words of the Lord's Prayer, Matthew 6:9ff., and the rest of that chapter, especially verses 24ff. through verse 33, "Seek ye first the Kingdom of God. . . ." For further amplification cf. H. H. Henson, *op. cit.*, p. 116ff. William Haller enlarges on this fact: "The converse of the duty of believing the Bible was the duty of doubting everything else" (*The Rise of Puritanism*, p. 238). Moreover, "no church and no opinion could be wholly reprobate unless it denied the fundamental truths of Scripture of man's ability to apprehend them." *Ibid.*, p. 239.

24 H. G. Wood, "Puritanism," *Hastings Encyclopaedia of Religion and Ethics* (New York: Chas. Scribner's Sons, 1919), Volume X, p. 513. Cf. especially the comments relating to Puritan realization of "Jewish ideals."

25 *Ibid.*, p. 512.

26 William Haller, *Elizabeth I and the Puritans* (Ithaca, New York: Cornell University Press, 1964), pp. 30-31.

27 Dr. Fisch, now of Bar-Ilan University, Ramat-Gan, Israel, describes his life (educated in England) as a journey from Albion to Jerusalem. He wrote in 1964 that "Albion is never wholly divorced from his spiritual partner and shows traces of Jerusalem even when he most vigorously repudiates all that Jerusalem stands for. . . . Jerusalem has as much need of Albion as Albion has of Jerusalem." Harold Fisch, *Albion and Jerusalem* (New York: Schocken Books, 1964), p. ix.

28 E.g. Kathleen Nott in *The Emperors Clothes* (Bloomington: University of Illinois Press, 1958), pp. 169, 194, complains that religious dogma is the enemy of poetry, that Milton's poetry was "monumental and static," and that he was "the portentous and comet-like cause which accounted for much of the devastation in poetic language." Beside the more than adequate rebuttal by Dr. Fisch, Milton's own iconoclastic temperament, his very Puritan encounter with the Bible as an imagination-firing experience rather than a source of dogma seems to be the chief offense and stumbling-block to those who thus criticize him. Milton was himself often at pains to heap ridicule on the old scholasticism which thus

pontificated and dogmatized, often over trivia. Observe Milton's reaction to the scholastic curriculum at Cambridge:

> They reek of the monkish cells in which they were written . . .
> they produce nothing but boredom and disgust. . . . Their subject
> matter is trivial, feeble and dull, their style is dry and lifeless. The
> questions with which they occupy themselves are never decided,
> are not worth deciding and are only the more confused the longer
> they are disputed. The net result of all the labor spent upon them
> is to make you a more finished fool and cleverer contriver of con-
> ceits, and to endow you with a more expert ignorance. . . . No
> wonder, since all these problems at which they have been working
> in such torment and anxiety have no existence in reality at all, but
> like unreal ghosts and phantoms without substance obsess minds
> already disordered and empty of all true wisdom.

Eustace Mandeville Wettenhall Tillyard, *Studies in Milton: Private Corre-*
spondence (London: Challo and Winders, 1951), pp. 67-73.

29 Harold Fisch, *op. cit.*, p. 3.

30 *Ibid.*, p. 4.

31 John Calvin, *Institutes of the Christian Religion*, translated by Ford Lewis
Battles, edited by John T. McNeill, Volume XX, *The Library of Christian*
Classics (Philadelphia: Westminster Press, 1960), Book III, Chapter 2,
section vi, p. 76.

32 *Ibid.*, Book I, chapter 7, section ii.

33 Cf. II Peter 1:21.

34 John Calvin, *op. cit.*, Book I, chapter 7, section 5, p. 80.

35 William Haller, *Elizabeth I and the Puritans*, p. 24.

36 This should not be construed to require a woodenly brittle literalism,
but rather to refer to the kind of interpretation which is true to the natural or normal implication, i.e., what the author of a given passage
meant to convey. We arrive at this on the basis of the principles of *usus*
loquendi, grammatical-syntactical hermeneutics and exegesis with full
appreciation for metaphor, simile, personification and other literary
devices. This would, allow us, e.g., to find in the language of Hosea 7:8
"Ephraim is a cake not turned," not a caricature of literalism which
insists that the author wished to convey the notion that Ephraim must
exist here as a batch of dough cooked only on one side like a pancake
that did not get flipped, but rather a figure of speech which means to
call the northern kingdom, Ephraim, here in synecdoche for all the
tribes in the north, "half-baked," and to mean pretty much the same
thing that we do still in the twentieth century when we use this term.
Only if thus approached does the Bible make sense in the first place or

is the representative literary flowering of the epoch under study, a Milton, Bunyan or Defoe, possible of comprehension — not *in spite of* their Puritanism but *because* of it.

37 Cf. Bernard Ramm, *Protestant Biblical Interpretation* (Boston: W. A. Wilde Company, 1956), *passim*.

38 The idea of theocracy was not new. Calvin had worked at it in Geneva. Many utopian schemes had been tried. Norman Cohn's *Pursuit of the Millenium* (New York: Harper Torchbooks, 1961) documents several movements and a variety of local experiments. The most explicit in England of this period was a radical group among the nonconformists and Puritans who were known as Fifth Monarchy Men. They had in common the idea of the return of Christ to earth to reign and establish a "Fifth Monarchy" to succeed Assyria, Persia, Greece and Rome. Their practical program varied greatly, leading ultimately to an abortive attempt to bring in the millennium by force of arms. Thomas Venner, a cooper by trade, and other leaders, among whom were some highly placed officers in the Parliamentary army were at first tolerated but finally had to be dealt with severely.

Venner himself was hanged and quartered; other prominent leaders, General Thomas Harrison and General Robert Overton were beheaded. Louise F. Brown, *The Political Activities of the Baptists and Fifth Monarchy Men in England During the Interregnum* (Washington: American History Association, 1911). *Oxford Dictionary of the Christian Church*, pp. 503-504. Henry M. Clark, *History of English Non-Conformity* (London: Chapman and Hale, 1911), Vol. II, pp. 352, 353. On pp. 129ff., Clark adds the interesting comment that The Fifth Monarchy Men of this period were the "spiritual successors to the Anabaptists of Edward VI and Mary's time in that they mixed religious and revolutionary propaganda." For the interrelation of all the nonconformist groups with good explication of each, Clark's *Non-Conformity* is currently the most complete. John Archer, *The Personall Reigne of Christ* (London: Benjamin Allen, 1642) is a typical example of the Fifth Monarchist position.

39 William Haller, *The Rise of Puritanism*, p. 14. A pervasive Calvinism was the key to this outlook.

40 W. B. Selbie, "The Influence of the Old Testament on Puritanism," in *The Legacy of Israel*, edited by Edwyn R. Bevan and Charles Singer (Oxford: Clarendon Press, 1943), pp. 407-408. Cecil Roth, *A History of the Marranos* (New York: Harper Torchbooks, 1966), pp. 252ff.

41 *Vide* the bibliographical section on source materials for a partial listing. Cf. also footnote 32, Chapter One for comment on the prolific production of materials centered in this theme during the succeeding decade.

42 Cecil Roth, *History of the Jews in England* (Oxford: Clarendon Press, 1941), pp. 145-158.

43 *Ibid.*, p. 149.

44 *Ibid.*, pp. 136-137.

45 Cecil Roth, *History of the Marranos*, p. 257f.

46 The waning years of the sixteenth century in England witnessed a miniature anti-Semitic storm. The most popular play in London in 1594 was Marlowe's *Jew of Malta*. The extravagances of it seemed to parallel and anticipate the character and fate of a certain Dr. Lopez who openly declared himself to be a Jew, was accused of a plot against the Queen, and after a lengthy, partisan trial was executed in June of that year. Shakespeare's *Merchant of Venice* portrayed the cruder aspects of the popular view of the Jew as a kind of new Judas. Cecil Roth, *History of the Jews in England*, pp. 143-144.

47 Henry's desire to annul his marriage to Catherine is one of the better known marital episodes of history. The interest here is in the fact it was to bibilical authority that all parties to the contest appeal, and further, that the Bible was cited on both sides of the question. Leviticus 18:16 seems strictly to forbid cohabitation between a man and his brother's wife, while Deuteronomy 25:5 specifically prescribes marriage if the brother died childless in order that his name should be perpetuated. The situation was exegetically very uncertain. That very uncertainty presented all kinds of possibilities to those inclined to intrigue. Thus it suddenly became advantageous to have specifically Jewish authority and tradition to which to turn and use. Richard Crooke, sent by Henry to seek the opinion of learned canon lawyers, also sought the assistance of a certain Marco Raphael, an apostate Jew, who was very obliging. Crooke reports from Venice early in 1530 that he had daily sought the advice of several Jews and he mentions six by name. Henry required that the Rabbinical statements be brought to him personally for consideration. The upshot of the matter was that most of Henry's informants were not much more than unctious confomers and a levirate marriage in Bologna between a Jew and his brother's widow in that very year completely discredited all the arguments which Henry's agents had mustered together. Nonetheless the episode, together with the contemporary Reuchlin-Pfefferkorn controversy in Germany, started to rebuild the aura of respectability long lost to Hebrew learning since the earliest period of the Christian era. Scarisbrick's *Henry VIII* is the best authority on the biblical and legal aspects of the divorce but also see Garrett Mattingly, *Catharine of Aragon* (London: J. Cape, 1950), pp. 173-311.

48 Irving Carlyle, "Tremellius, John Immanuel," *Dictionary of National Biography*, LVII, pp. 186-187. Interestingly, Tremellius became an outspoken Calvinist, which position sent him to prison on several occasions even while enjoying the relative safety of his Lutheran hosts in Germany.

49 Cecil Roth, *History of the Jews in England*, p. 147.

50 *Ibid.* Roth speculates further that Rabbi Jacob, Jacobus Bernatus and Jacob Barnett, likely, were one and the same man.

51 In this respect the Authorized Version was a great advance on that of Coverdale, who knew no Hebrew. His precursor, William Tyndale, was, on the other hand a competent scholar. The translators of both the Geneva or Breeches Bible (1560) and the Bishops Bible (1568) were also familiar with Hebrew. The earliest English Hebraist of any great skill was Hugh Broughton (1549-1612). The first Hebrew grammar for English use was John Udall's *Key to the Hebrew Tongue* (Utrecht, 1593), composed while he was in prison for his part in the Marmelate Tracts. For complete history of bibliography in this regard consult Cecil Roth's, *Magna Bibliotheca Anglo-Judaica* (London: The Jewish Historical Society of England, 1937). The Authorized Version was the culmination of efforts of a long line of pious Englishmen to put the Word of God into the vernacular. The translators knew their task well enough to avoid the pitfall of laboring on the level of academic, Latinized English and learned tongues. But neither did they vulgarize it into the everyday banalities. Their skill has for its monument the intelligible, plain, and beautiful idiom of common speech yet suitable both to lofty subject matter and at the same time able to communicate forcefully to the mind and heart of the unlearned. The chapter entitled "Rhetoric of the Spirit," pp. 128-172 in William Haller's *Rise of Puritanism* is a brilliant essay on this aspect of Nonconformist-Puritan aspiration and accomplishment.

52 Cecil Roth, *History of the Jews in England*, pp. 147-148.

53 For a full treatment of the story of Manasseh's requests and Cromwell's desire to comply, any of the standard Jewish histories has the facts. The most readable, though brief, is Cecil Roth's.

Chapter IV

Revelation, Resurrection and Restoration

Francis Kett (d. 1589), a descendant of the famous Norman family of that name, is the hero of this first segment of our narrative. The most distinguished member of the Kett family, Robert Kett of Norwalk, was the leader of the first agrarian revolt, also during the reign of Elizabeth, and paid for his temerity on the scaffold.[1] Francis took B.A. and M.A. degrees at Cambridge in 1569 and 1573 respectively. We find him, though a clergyman, described as a "doctor of physick" and listed as author and publisher in 1585 of *The Glorious and Beautiful Garland of Mans Glorification Containing the Godly Misterie of Heavenly Jerusalem.* The book is distinguished by a lengthy dedication to Queen Elizabeth and florid prose. Relatively little of Kett is known except in relation to this one product of his pen and the ensuing difficulty in which it engaged him, ending finally in martyrdom.

By 1588 *The Glorious and Beautiful Garland* had reached highly stationed if not appreciative readers. In the autumn of that year, Edmund Scambler, bishop at Norwich summoned Kett to his court and preferred Articles of Heretical Pravity against him. The verdict of condemnation to death was handed down with undisguised passion. It was exceeded only by the dispatch with which the machinery to execute sentence was set in motion. In a letter dated October 7, 1588, Scambler urges the civil head, Lord Burghley, to a "speedy execution" of Kett as a "dangerous person of blasphemous opinions."[2]

The next information about Kett comes from an eye witness to his execution on January 14, 1589. A certain William Burton, minister in Norwich was on hand to view and record the proceedings.   Interestingly enough, Burton was willing to vouch for Kett's godliness and piety:

> ... how holy he would seem to bee ... the sacred Bible almost never out of his handes, himselfe alwayes in prayer ...[3]

but classed him as an "Arrian heretique," glories in his fate and is quite certain of his eternal damnation as "a devill incarnate."[4]

Whatever the details, Kett was burned alive in the castle ditch at Norwich:

> When he went to the fire he was clothed in sackcloth, he went leaping and dauncing: being in the fire, above twenty times together, clapping his hands, he cried nothing but blessed bee God ... and so continued untill the fire had consumed all his neather partes, and untill he was stifled with the smoke.[5]

Even after his death Kett's enemies continued variously to caricature his views with odium, as universalism, anti-trinitarianism and gave especially short shrift to his millenarianism, the worst, apparently, of all his sins, as "enthusiastic." They declared him to hold that

> Christ wyth his Apostles are nowe personally in Iudea gathering of his church and that the faithful must goe to Ierusalem there to be fed with Angelles foode.[6]

Even cursory reading of *The Glorious and Beautiful Garland*, however, discloses all the cardinal points of biblical orthodoxy, with copious proof texts.[7] The methodical piety of Kett's careful hermeneutic is quite plain, straightforward and inevitably brought him to conclusions unacceptable to the Anglican churchmen of his day. Kett foolishly (or courageously, the line between the two—if there is one—is exceedingly fine) declared openly what many others covertly held:

> The first golden stayre of Christianitie, is to believe the holy Scriptures and Gospell of God, simply syncerely, and truely: The second staire is, to reverence the worde of God, with a pure hart in all obedience and diligence to taste how sweete the Lord is: and this is the grice [price] of true Religion: The third staire is, to goe forward by the word of God, unto the meditation of heavenly life, having your conversation in heaven, from whence you look for a saviour to deck and beautiffe

you with glorie: And this is true holiness and godliness: The fourth
goodly stayre is to continue and persevere in ye word of God and
treuth. . . .⁸

In this brief statement, we have the matter, in sum, already:
The Word of God believed, reverenced, meditated upon, and
persevered by, without reference to prelate or other outside
authority is the way to

> . . . all steadfastness of faith, love, hope and patience immoveable . . .
> perfect constancie to obtain ye victory, and . . . to enter into the
> Christall sea of glory, (to stand in the number of the elect that hath got
> ye victorie of the beast, of his image, of his mark and of the number of
> his name) . . . singing the song of Moyses the servant of God.

From these statements, if they represent a suggestive pattern
and if the logic thus outlined is followed to a final port of call,
it should be of little surprise to us that in an age when the
divine right of kings still prevailed, that such a bold proclamation of what amounted to total loyalty to another authority
would inevitably run afoul of the powers that be. For a millennium and more this idea had stood, a monolith without fis-
sure, master both in things temporal, and spiritual. It was now
beginning to erode away in a good many minds, and edgy
monarchs were the more scrupulously sensitive about their
prerogatives. Such jealousy, as Kett was soon to learn, is a
very dangerous and potent force. The things he was saying, in
that time, smacked of sedition — whatever their theological
implications.⁹ A substantial share of the surprise and some of
the joy of discovery is blunted by apprehending that such
total, overwhelming absorption in Scripture, given the place
and moment in history, would conceive and bring to birth as
an irresistably logical, integral, necessary and organic part of
its system, the notion of Jewish national return to Palestine.
And Mr. Kett cannot disappoint us; he jumps with both feet
into the matter by telling his readers that they must

> desire onely to be fed with the wisdome that proceede from this our
> heavenly heardman; *imbracing no other word of doctrine but that which he
> gave us from Jerusalem* [italics mine].¹⁰

The use of Old Testament metaphors and other figures is
nearly complete, introducing us to what is to follow: Salvation

equals belonging to the house of Jacob;[11] Esau's house equals the place of carnal desire;[12] heaven equals to dwell in New Jerusalem;[13] true Christianity equals to accept and follow the Holy One of Israel;[14] God's throne equals the stoole of David, whose seat is Jerusalem,[15] and so on.

Though we should not expect Kett to hand us a full blown exposition of our idea, he did come through clearly enough to exhume in the minds of all who read his book the long buried *Opiniones Judaicae* and in thus exposing them to the air, to attract criticism from distinguished sources, specifically censuring his "stubborn heresy" of "belief in the return of the Israelites."[16] There are some few explicit statements, however, occurring as components of the doctrine of God (His attributes):

> the Lord, mindful of his promise to Jacob, said: I will root Jacob *againe* [italics mine], and Israel shall be greene and beare flowers, and fill the whole world with her fruit, then shall the desert and wilderness rejoyce, and the wasted groundes florish like a lillies: And I will power waters vpon the drie ground, and rivers vpon the thirstie, and shall give waters in the wildernes and streames in the desert.[17]

Again:

> who [i.e. God] shall bring redemption to the captive, and restore Israel, and set vp his honour in Iuda, and in Davids stoole, that all nations shall honour him: yea kings and princes shall arise and worship this holy one of Israel.[18]

And in a Messianic flavored passage:

> In the latter daies the hill of the Lords house, shall be set vp higher than anye mountaines, and the people shall prease vnto it, and the multitude of gentils host to it, for the law shal come out of Syon and the word of God from Ierusalem.[19]

The most significant feature of Kett's role in our story is not strictly in the millenarian element of his views tending to the restoration of the Jews, nor in the fact he considered Judea and Jerusalem as the scene of coming redemption and looked to a gathering of God's people in the Holy Land, nor even in his understanding of Israel as Israel and not merely a prefigurement of the Church, all of which we have observed. But singular importance must be attached to the catalytic action his declarations on the idea, though admittedly shadowy, generated in the world of scholarship.   Also, without Kett's appearance the continuing development of the new idea thus spawned would have been delayed for want of someone courageous enough to speak.

Hard on the heels of Kett's execution in 1590, a Latin work was published by the most distinguished textual critic of the day and Calvinist theologian, Andrew Willett (d. 1621),[20] entitled *De Universali et Novissima Judaeorum Vocatione*.   In it, one must judge, apparently, suggested by the martyr's fate, Kett is declared culpable expressly for his outrageous belief in Israel's return.[21]   Although he quarrels with Kett and addresses his arguments against such an expectation, in this work Willett must be regarded as the first Englishman systematically to treat in any kind of discursive fashion the notion of Jewish national restoration.   These several facts may be deduced from the import attached to the topic—official assignment of a whole treatise to the idea—and the suggestive juxtaposition of the book's public issue in concert with Kett's trial and execution.   Willett foretold and advocated the general conversion of the Jews to faith in Christ, as outlined in Romans, chapter eleven.   He disputed, however, that the biblical passages involved presented any evidence that the Jews should regain a sovereign state of their own.   This people, he pointed out, were not successful in re-establishing their commonwealth under the more auspicious circumstances of antiquity, or with Emperor Julian's help.   Nor did 1500 years of Messianic dreaming, hoping against hope, bring them a single step nearer realization.   Do they now spin yet more fantasies of restoration when they are a more dispersed, confused, many tongued people, so that discrimination among them by tribe is quite impossible.[22]

From a very interesting passage early in *De Universali etc.* we learn that the reputation of Solomon Molko and David Reubeni had reached England and Willett was informed thereon.   Willett parallels Francis Kett with Molko.   In doing so we have the clearest evidence that Kett's views had impressed at least Willett as a preaching of Jewish restoration:

> In this heresy of the belief in the return of the Israelites that most infamous man has indulged too much who proclaimed himself King Solomon, but for such a great blasphemy suffered due punishment [at the stake] under the Emperor, Charles V, at Mantau Italy [in 1532]: and Kett, our Englishman, who, having been caught in a similar heresy and stubbornly maintained it, was by a most just sentence recently condemned to death by fire and flames, and burnt at Norwich.[23]

Of the others who followed Kett, were influenced by him and throughout this initial period of beginnings and development were criticized, censured, thrown in gaol, none paid the supreme price he did. The idea he espoused, far from revolutionary, however, was as hoary with age as the Bible. Neither Kett's execution nor Willett's learned arguments were able to suppress this belief, once born. It had already influenced others and began soon to be developed more fully, continuing within the organic context of Biblical exposition and theology.

Inasmuch as the title of Thomas Draxe's first work is partly identical, and the content thereof parallel with Andrew Willett's work, it seems possible that he, the next writer to treat the topic of Jewish restoration, was influenced by Willett's work and had knowledge of Francis Kett. Draxe (d. 1618) was a distinguished theologian of a "worshipfull family," Cambridge education and respected reputation as a man of letters and quiet life.[24] In 1608 he published *The VVorldes Resvrrection, Or the gnerall calling of the Jewes, A familiary Commentary vpon the eleventh Chapter of Saint Paul to the Romaines, according to the sense of Scripture* . . .[25] The key to Draxe's views is his Calvinism, the principles of which are apparent and operative from the first line of the table of contents,

> Can God's covenant with his Elect bee made frustrate through mans unbeliefe. Neg.,[26]

to the last sentence of the book,

> We must in all our words and works, consultations and actions, acknowledge, praise and honour God as the chiefe good and the most excellent cause of all things, and constantly maintaine and advance his glory: otherwise if we honour not him he will never honor vs here, much lesse glorifie vs in the life to come.[27]

From this basic thrust from the ground of God's everlasting covenant, His sovereign decrees in the handling of the universe and everything therein, the essence of Draxe's outlook in the matter at hand is predictable:

> Jewes are beloved for their Father's sake (as Solomon was never wholly deprived of God's spirit and favor for David's sake) it proceedeth not from their works or persons, but only from God's gracious and everlasting covenant, the fountain and roote of it. The summe of the covenant is, *that God will be their God and the God of their Seede*, and therefore there must be some to whom the covenant must be made good and fulfilled, and there are loved for the covenant's sake.[28]

In Draxe's view, earthly restoration of the Jews *must* happen, God's majesty and glory are at stake. This event is required to vindicate before all men, from first to last, the glory and honor of God so long sullied by sin. It was on this basis that God originally chose Israel—to be a demonstration people of Himself revealed, to the nations of earth. It was for this reason that he brought them out of Egypt—so that

> the Egyptian shall know that I am the Lord when I stretch forth mine hand upon Egypt and bring out the children of Israel from among them.[29]

On this basis Moses reasoned with God to spare Israel from his consuming wrath for their idolatry at Mount Sinai—what will the nations say of Thee if thou destroy this people?"[30] For this reason the very realm of nature groans in travail waiting "to be released from decay."[31] And for this reason we, too, argues Draxe, await His coming because we shall be "like him;" we shall be glorified before men as joint heirs with him in the Kingdom—when every knee shall bow and every tongue confess him Lord.[32]

That the Jew owed his preservation to the inscrutable designs of Divine providence ("for who knoweth the minde of the Lorde?")[33] is outlined by Draxe with a candor and warmth uncharacteristic of his time:

> It is a marvelous work of God, and not without mystery, that the Jewes, wandering and dispersed in all countries almost, should still continue such a distinct and unconfounded nation, . . . and so constant keeping and observing of (as much as they possibly may) their ancient

laws, rites, and ceremonies. . . . They have been in the time of greatest persecution, when the tyrants of the world sought to extinguish and root out the Scriptures (and still are) the faithful keepers of the Old Testament: and all this may put us in some good hope of their future calling and conversion.[34]

The "Calling of the Jewes" was, we see, conversion. The astonishing thing is that Draxe takes Christians severely to task for their gross misbehavior toward the Jews. Draxe was a protagonist for toleration and readmission to England, as well as restoration, well before the former notions are historically generally traced and treated. He writes courageously:

> We must not roughly either contemne much less condemne the Jewes, nor espelle them out of our coasts and countries but hope well of them, pray for them, and labour to win them by our Holy zeale and Christian example.[35]

The frankness of his feelings is fused together with a general statement of his conclusions in the matter:

> Then shall the miserable and reduced Jewes be brought home, the hearts of God's people replenished with inmenkable [immeasurable, incalculable] joye, all nations shall glorify God and we shall in short time be fully and finely perfected and glorified.[36]

In a work[37] published later in the same year (1608) Draxe elaborates on the necessity of the Jews' conversion as a preliminary antecedent to their restoration.

> The second signe yet to be fulfilled is the generall calling and conversion of the nation of the Jewes (in the places and countries where they shalbe and are residing) and this shalbe the reviving and reioycing of the world both in respect of Jewes and Gentiles, and this is most plaine as by Lv. 21. ver. 24 . . .[38]

It appears that no matter what subject to come from his pen in any kind of systematic discourse, restoration of the Jews had somewhere to be mentioned. A third work published in 1608,[39] a fourth in 1613[40] and a fifth in 1615[41] refer to his view that

> *Iewes* shall towards the end of the world, be temporally restored into their owne Country rebuild *Ierusalem*, and have a most reformed, and flourishing Church and Commonwealth . . .[42]

None of the later works of Draxe treat the idea at length but do distinctly allude to the idea. From the titles above it is clear that the notion of Jewish restoration was to Draxe an integral component of Christian eschatology, and the content is precisely that.

Systematic treatment *par excellence* of the idea of Jewish restoration came in 1615 via English translation in Amsterdam of the learned Thomas Brightman's (1552-1607) plodding Latin work *Apocalypsis Apocalyseos*,[43] first published two years posthumously in 1609. It appeared in England under the title *Revelation of the Revelation, that is, The Revelation of St. John Opened Clearly with a Logicall Resolution and Exposition Wherein the Sense is cleared, out of Scripture, the Events also of Thinges Foretold are Discussed of the Church Historyes.* In Brightman's work we come to what, probably, at this early juncture, was the single strongest impulse in Great Britain in support of the doctrine of Jewish national restoration. This may be seen in that he was a man of winsome, evangelical persuasion and life, approached the central issue of the doctrine with a bold frankness and in the uniquely enduring nature of the contribution and inspiration he supplied to similarly minded authors for most of two generations.[44] Originally written, apparently, about 1600, before Queen Elizabeth's death—the exact date is unknown—and first printed at Frankfurt (1609), it was published again in Latin at Heidelberg (1612), with English editions at Amsterdam (1615) and Leyden (1616). Of particular note in this connection is the collection of his works and their reissue at London in a single massive volume as late as 1644.[45] As a Puritan scholar, one of the fathers of English Presbyterianism, with education through M.A. and B.D. degrees at Cambridge, Brightman was a constant student. He carried his Greek Testament with him always, reading completely through it every two weeks—even while riding horseback so as to lose no time.[46] His commentary on the Revelation was probably printed on the Continent in its earlier editions because of his disaffection with the Established Church of England, which he thought was the Laodicean Church of Revelation 3:14-21. The Laodicean Church was the lukewarm church which Christ said he would spew out of his mouth. The sign of this lukewarmness on the part of the Church of England, as Brightman saw it, was the retention of popish practices. In his own words:

> The most mighty King Henry . . . had cast out the Pope, be [i.e., but] he retayned the Popish superstition.[47]

While conceived, apparently, as an *Opus Mysticum*, its main subject to declare the certainty of the overthrow of Antichrist (Papal Rome), Brightman plods verse by verse through Revelation expounding the trumpets, seals, visions, vials and so on with few of the flourishes of color and style that characterized both the earlier and later authors on that book. We arrive at his fundamental argument for Jewish restoration where he comments on Revelation 16:12,[48] The vision of the sixth Angel who pours out his vial at the command of the great voice and the Euphrates River is dried up is seen as a component in the preparation for passage across of the kings of the East spoken of in the verse. Brightman then equates the Jews with the "Kings of the East," finding providential analogy between their crossing the Euphrates and the parting of the waters of the Red Sea in the Exodus from the land of Egypt:

> *And the sixth Angell povvred out his viall upon the great River Euphrates.* This River is not either Tyber, or any other block house of Rome, the destruction whereof was taught vs in the former Viall that went next before; for why should one and the same thing being once done, be done againe and afresh? But it is that which slideth through Mesopotamia at the Eeast side of Iudea, as wee have seene above Chapter 9.14. Yet this River is put here metaphorically for any impediment, by which the passage into the Cuntry may bee stopped. The former event of this Vial is the drying vp of the waters thereof, as the red Sea was dried vp of old by meanes of the East winds that blewe, and as it was done when the Iewes passed over Iordan into the land of Canaan, Exod. 14. Josh. 3. The ende why the waters are dried vp, is that the waye of the Kings that come from the rising of the Sunne might bee prepared. But who are these Kings? Are they the foure Angells of whom we reade, Chapter 9:15. The consideration of the time will not suffer this interpretation to stand. That Trompet sounded many yeares before this; this Viall began not to bee poured out as yet; it followeth after the sacking and razing of Rome, which flourisheth yet, and which that Trompett sawe flourishing a longe time, what then, are they those Kings of the earth and of the whole world of whome mention is made

in the 14. verse of this Chapter. But these Kings to whome Euphrates giveth place, are Kings of the East onely, and not of the whole world.

It would bee tedious to rehearse much more to confute the interpretations of other men; It seemeth to me that that people is here signified by these Kings, for whose sake Done the Scriptures declare that the waters were dried vp of old, namely the Iewes, to whome the redd Sea gave passage, and Iordan staid his course till they all passed over, making a way thorough the deppes with their feete. This miracle is proper to this people alone.[49]

He amplifies this aspect yet further:

the whole East shall be in obedience and subjection unto them, so that this people are not called kings unworthily, in regard to their large and wide jurisdiction and empire.[50]

This state of affairs is to follow the destruction of the Turks, Calling of the Jews, i.e., their turning to Christ and becoming a Christian nation.[51]

The essential nature and purpose of this newly established Jewish commonwealth was a peaceful one:

to make the goodness of God shine forth to all the world when they shall see Him to give to that nation (which is now and hath been for many ages scattered throughout the whole world and inhabited nowhere but by leave and entreaty) their owne habitations where their fathers dwelt. . . .[52]

Brightman's view can be distilled into one passage:

What, shall they [the Jews] returne to Ierusalem againe? There is nothing more certain, the Prophets doe every where directly confirme it and beate vppon it.[53]

That these opinions and views had a most telling effect can be judged from the exultation, some thirty seven years after Brightman's death, of the anonymous editor of his commentary on the Song of Solomon:

Led God so shine upon us with the light of his Countenance, that there may always be a *Brightman* in Britain, to the setting forth of the glory of God. . . .[54]

In a special work on the book of Daniel[55] Brightman calculates the time these events will take place. He intentionally designed it for the Jews and states in the preface that for this reason he is basing his argument exclusively on parts of the Old Testament (Daniel and Song of Songs).[56]   Though his speculations in this work are of little interest to us now, except as curiosities,[57] the publication of an English version in 1635, in excess of twenty years after the Latin original (1614), shows how deadly seriously the matter was taken at the time.

With succeeding writers we turn a corner into literature which, with a few exceptions, is extension and development of the spade work done to date, especially by Thomas Brightman.

Notes

1 Alfred Goodwin, "Kett or Ket, Francis," The *Dictionary of National Biography*, edited by Sir Leslie Stephen and Sir Sydney Lee (Oxford: Oxford University Press, 1960), pp. 74-5. Hereafter *The Dictionary of National Biography* will be abbreviated *DNB*.

2 *Ibid.*, p. 74.

3 *Ibid.*

4 Alexander Gordon, *DNB*, II, p. 18.

5 Alfred Goodwin, "Ket or Kett, Francis, *DNB*, XI, p. 74.

6 *Ibid.*

7 Francis Kett, *The Glorious and Beautiful Garland of Man's Glorification Containing the Godly Misterie of Heavenly Jerusalem* (London: Roger Ward, 1585), *passim*. The entire work is couched in language which rehearses in detail each of the forces and circumstances discussed in the previous chapters. Chapters II, III and IV of Kett's work contain a general statement of orthodoxy over the whole of systematic theology.

8 *Ibid.*, p. D4.

9 Kett's outspoken Puritanism did not help him survive:

> It is a repugnance to the ordance of God to hold back the frute and sweete taste of the Gospell from the people by concealing it under a cloke of an unknown language and strange tongue . . . it is apparent, that it is the duty and part of princes and governors to follow herein the example of Jehosophat, causing the worde of God plainly to be taught among their subjects in the mother language (as Moyses law was to the children of Israel) . . . so that it standeth you upon [it] to have care of your souls, that no man make you to shoote at a wrong marke.

Ibid., pp. 17-8. Little wonder he succeeded soon in raising the hackles on the back of so many persons in a position to do him no small amount of harm.

10 *Ibid.*, p. C3.

11 *Ibid.*, p. V1.

12   *Ibid.*, p. V8.

13   *Ibid.*, p. IV5.

14   *Ibid.*, p. V2.

15   *Ibid.*, p. I6.

16   Andrew Willett, *De Universali et Novissima Judaeorum Vocatione* (Cambridge: Ex officina Johannis Legati Contabrigiensis Typographi, 1590), p. B4.

17   Francis Kett, *The Glorious and Beautiful Garland, etc.*, p. C2. Cf. Isaiah 27, 35, 44.

18   *Ibid.*, p. I6.

19   *Ibid.*, p. I8.

20   John Frome Wilinson, "Willett, Andrew," *DNB*, XXI, pp. 288-292.

21   Andrew Willett, *op. cit.*, p. B4.

22   *Ibid., passim.*

23   Ibid., p. B4. "In ista heresi de Israelitarum reversione nimium sibi placnit homo ille impurissimus qui se Solomonem regem praedicabat, at dignas tanta impietate poenas Mantuae in Italia sub Carolo quinto Caesare subiit and sustinuit: and Kettus ille nostrus Anglus instissima sententia nuper ignis and flammae adjudicatus est, Norvicci crematus, in consimili, heresi, deprehensus, obstinate persistens."

24   Gordon Goodwin, "Draxe, Thomas," *DNB*, VII, pp. 7-8.

25   Thomas Draxe, *The VVorldes Resvrrection Or the generall calling of the Jewes, A familiar Commentary vpon the eleventh Chapter of Saint Paul to the Romaines, according to the sense of Scripture and the consent of the most indicious interpreters, wherein above fiftie notable questions are soundly answered, and the particular doctrines, reasons and uses of every verse are profitably and plainly delivered* (London: Printed by G. Eld for John Wright, 1608).

26   *Ibid.*, p. A1.

27   *Ibid.*, p. 124.

28   *Ibid.*, pp. 102-103.

29   Exodus 7:5.

30   Exodus 32, 33.

31   Romans 8:16-25; cf. Isaiah 11:6-9.

32 Phillipians 2. Thomas Draxe, *op. cit., passim.*

33 *Ibid.,* p. 115. "How vnserchable are his waies and his iudgements past finding out." p. 120—Constantly Draxe uses Biblical statement for a springboard into his discussion and the greater share of his argument as well.

34 *Ibid.,* p. 105f.

35 *Ibid.,* p. 57

36 *Ibid.,* p. 93.

37 Thomas Draxe, *The Chvrches Securitie, Together with the Antidote or preservative of ever waking Faith. A treatise conteyning many fruitefull instructions, moralities and consolations fit for the time and age wherein we live. Hereunto is annexed a sound and profitable treatise of the generall signes and forerunners of the last judgement* (London: Imprinted by George Eld, and to be sold by John Wright, 1608).

38 *Ibid.,* sheet 95.

39 Thomas Draxe, The Lambes Spouse (London: n.p. 1608).

40 Thomas Draxe, *The Earnest of OVR Inheritance: Together With A Description of the New Heaven and of the New Earth and a demonstration of the Glorious Resurrection of the bodie in the same substance. Preached at Paul's Crosse the second day of August, 1612* (London: F. K. for George Norton, 1613).

41 Thomas Draxe, *An Alarvm to the Last Ivdgement or An exact discourse of the second coming of Christ, and of the generall and remarkeable Signes and Forerunners of it past, present, and to come; soundly and soberly handled, and wholesomely applyed, wherein divers deep Mysteries are plainly expounded, and sundry curiosities are duely examined, answered and confuted* (London: Printed by Nicholas Okes for Matthew Law, 1615).

42 *Ibid.,* p. 22. Cf. pp. 74-81, Chapter XIIII, "A third generall and memorable Signe of the approach of the last judgement; namely the conversion of the Jewes."

43 *Apocalypsis Apocalyseos idest Apocalypsis D. Joannis analysi et scholiis illustrata; ubi ex Scriptura sensus, rerumque praedictarum ex historiis eventuXXs discutinuntuXXr. Huic Synopsis praefigitur universalis, et Refutatio Rob. Bellarmini de antichristo libro tertio de Romano Pontifice ad finem capitis decimi septimi inseritur* (Franc.: n.p., 1609).

44 Brightman's works and he himself are specifically referred to in the majority of theological works treating the millennium, and especially the idea of Jewish restoration, both to attack and to approve it, from his own day to the present. His contemporary, Thomas Draxe refers in *Alarum to the Last Judgement etc.,* to "master Brightman," *(passim)* and

quotes him copiously, specifically where he outlines Jewish return to "theire Countrey" as one of the signs to the Last Judgement. Draxe asks, like Brightman, "Shall the Jewes be restored to their Countrey?" And he answers with more caution than Brightman but with his characteristic language:

> It is very probable, First, all Prophets seeme to speak of this returne. Secondly, they shall no longer bee in bondage. Thirdly, God having for so many ages forsaken his people shall the more notably shew them mercy (*Ibid.*, p. 76ff.).

And as recently as the Autumn of 1968, Brightman, and his like-minded younger contemporary Joseph Mede (1586-1638), are subjects of an article by Robert Clouse, entitled, "The Apocalyptic Interpretation of Thomas Brightman and Joseph Mede," *Bulletin of the Evangelical Theological Society*, Volume 11, No. 4, Fall 1968, pp. 181-194. The exalted esteem of the immediately succeeding generation may be seen in the title of an anonymous pamphlet published in 1641. *Brightman's Predictions and Prophecies: Written 46. yeares since; concerning the three Churches of Germanie, England and Scotland, Foretelling the miserie of Germanie, the fall of the pride of Bishops in England by the assistance of the Scottish Kirk. All which should happen (as he foretold) between the years of 36. and 41.* (n.p., 1641), wherein Brightman is compared to "Sybills (so often and frequently alleged by the Fathers) who many yeares before predicted the Incarnation of Our Blessed Savior" (p. 7).

45 Leroy Edwin Froom, *Prophetic Faith of Our Fathers* II, p. 512.

46 James Mew, "Brightman, Thomas," *DNB*, II, p. 1247.

47 Thomas Brightman, *The Revelation of St. John With an Analysis and Scholion in The Workes of that Famous, Reverend, and Learned Divine, Mr. Tho. Brightman* (London: Cartwright, 1644), p. 125.

48 "And the sixth angel poured out his vial upon the great river Euphrates; and the water thereof was dried up, that the way of the kings of the east might be prepared."

49 Thomas Brightman, *op. cit.*, pp. 547-548.

50 *Ibid.*, p. 548.

51 *Ibid.*, p. 549, 860ff.

52 *Ibid.*, p. 549.

53 *Ibid.*

54 Thomas Brightman, *A Commentary on the Canticles or the Song of Solomon wherein the Text is Analised, the Native signification of the Words Declared, the Allegories Explained, the Order of Times whereunto they relate Observed*

(London: Printed by Iohn Field for Henry Overton in Popes-head-Alley, 1644), p. 976.

55 Thomas Brightman, *A Most Comfortable Exposition of the Last and Difficult Part of the Prophecies of Daniel — Wherein the restoring of the Jews and their calling to the faith of Christ, after the overthrow of their last enemies is Set Forth in Lively Colours* (London: n.p., 1635).

56 *Ibid.*, sheet Aaaaaa2.

57 E.g., he gives the dates for the beginning of the Apocalyptic period as 1650 and expected it to last until 1695.

Chapter V

Turks, Tartars and the Ten Tribes

No less an eminent person than Queen Elizabeth's ambassador to Russia, Giles Fletcher (1549-1611), and, significantly, a disciple of Thomas Brightman, begins the next episode of our story. Fletcher was a poet, historian and prolific writer on various subjects. Two of his sons, Phineas and Giles Fletcher the younger, came by poetic gifts honestly, exceeding in this discipline their father's fame. Fletcher's chief recorded merit is his diplomatic genius, by which he proved "a faithful agent for Queen Elizabeth at the Pallace of the Great Czar of Muschovy."[1]

In the years 1588-1589, Fletcher, though he came to court with impeccable credentials as "master extraordinary of the court of requests" was treated with "greatest indignities." Queen Elizabeth sent formal complaint to the Czar, remonstrating on the manner in which Fletcher had been treated. In spite of these difficulties, he succeeded in securing for English merchants valuable advantages and concessions. After his return from Russia he published a book about this then still very remote country: *Of the Russe CommonWealth; or, Manner of Government by the Russe Emperour (commonly called the Emperour of Moskovia), with the Manners and Fashions of the People of the Country* (1591) which was, apparently, authoritative enough to be reprinted under various titles until as recently as 1856.[2]

Another fruit of Fletcher's Russian sojourn, the one with which we are concerned, is a precise, scientific outline and essay devoted to the question of the Lost Ten Tribes of Israel. It was not put into print until some sixty years after his death. This took place in the following manner. A book entitled *Israel Redux: or the Restauration of Israel; or the Restauration of*

Israel exhibited in two short treatises. The first contains an essay on some probable grounds that the present Tartars, near the Caspian Sea are the posterity of the ten Tribes of Israel, By G. F. LL.D. The second, a dissertation concerning their ancient and successive state, with some Scripture evidences of their future conversion and establishment in their own land,[3] was edited and published by a certain Samuel Lee (1625-1691) a widely learned scholar and Puritan divine.[4] In Lee's "Preface or Epistle to the Reader" it is said that he

> obtained this Manuscript of Dr. Fletcher's Grandson, Mr. Phineas Fletcher, a Worthy Citizen of London, together with his kind leave to pass it into Publick Light; give me I pray, the liberty of a line or two to acquaint thee, that this Author was a faithful Agent for Q. Elizabeth of famous memory, . . . and hath given us some fruits of his inquisitive travels . . . also collected some observations about the Tartars, Confining upon the Territories near the Caspian Sea . . . endeavoring by some probabilities to evince that the 10 Tribes of Israel, antiently carried Captives by Salmanasser into the Northern Mountainous Crags of Assyria . . . are at this day mixed among those Barbarous Nations.[5]

That such prominent mention of Fletcher and his essay is made by so widely read and distinguished a man as Dr. Lee, after so long a period had lapsed since the date of its composition, speaks plainly of the weight attached to the work. Just when the essay was actually written is not known. Fletcher died in 1611 and in the tract he refers to the work of Thomas Brightman,[6] whose work did not appear before 1609. We may deduce from this that the essay on the Ten Tribes was possibly the last piece of work to come from Fletcher's pen.

More important to our topic than the rather speculative hypothesis, the involved logic and evidences thereto which Fletcher produces, are the allusions he makes to the notion of Jewish restoration, using this position as a biblical certainty, by which to support and lend credence to his main thesis that the Tartars equal the Lost Ten Tribes. For example, he cites Romans 11:22,[7] states that God's Justice and Mercy requires the "calling again" of the Jews,[8] then argues:

> [Therefore] the 10 tribes are preserved by God unconfused with other nations . . . [they] were not destroyed by Assyria, only transplanted.[9]

A most revealing illustration of the employ of this principle is in the instance of Fletcher's appeal to Thomas Brightman's interpretation of Revelation 16:12, as proving the necessity of God's preservation of the Ten Tribes in order that a people, i.e., the "Kings of the East" there described (identified as Israel),[10] indeed do exist to cross back over the Euphrates when God dries it up in the latter days:

> The pouring of the 6th vial to dry up the river Euphrates for the Kings of the east means for Israel, the 10 tribes, to return. For the tribes of Judah and Benjamin are not dispersed in the north and not in the east but in the west and southern parts of Asia, Africa and Europe. What is more, the people mentioned to pass over are kings and not just ordinary people.[11]

And for the same purpose, yet fuller explication in the last paragraph of the treatise:

> As for the manner of their passing over the said River, whether it shall be actual drying of the River, or a removing of all impediments, which may stop or hinder their speedy passage in this their expedition towards their Country, I will not argue at this time. That it shall be an actual exiccation of the River, with no less miracle, than the drying up of the Red Sea, of River *Jordan*, when they passed towards the Land of *Canaan*, that so this work of God, which shall be famous in all the World, even the restoring of this people, may be observed by other Nations, with great reason and probability is affirmed by *Th. Brightman*, the last interpreter of that Book [Revelation], whom God endued with special gifts, and great brightness after his name, for the full clearing and exposition of that Prophecy, above all that hitherto have written of it. FINIS.[12]

In his shorter compositions, the second part of the book, Dr. Lee writes "concerning the Place and State of the dispersed Tribes of Israel."[13] He uses Fletcher's essay as a spring board from which to launch into the question "whether the Ten Tribes shall return out of their disperson."[14] And then to affirm:

> I am fully perswaded that the reduction of the ten tribes from their great and ancient dispersion to their own Land is a Scripture truth, though not yet accomplished, in evidence whereto I shall give in several arguments from the sacred records.[15]

From this point Dr. Lee leads the reader through a veritable catalogue of Bible proof texts, citations of the classics of geography and history, Strabo, Ptolemy, Pliny, Olearius, etc., Jewish authors, Josephus, Benjamin of Tudela, various of the Patristic writers, Origen, Jerome, Justin Martyr and so on, in great variety and length. Everywhere buttressing his argument are two key passages:

> The Lord shall set his hand again, the second time, to recover the remnant of his People . . . and shall assemble the outcasts of Israel, and gather together the dispersed of Judah from the four corners of the Earth.[16]

and:

> I will cause the Captivity of Judah, and the Captivity of Israel to return, and I will build them as at the first.[17]

Though the scholarly Dr. Lee registers his readiness at the end of his first composition to leave

> full determination to farthur and future inquiries of Merchants and travellers, to be discuss'd and argu'd among the Learned.[18]

he adds another 30 folio sheets under the title, ἐπεισάγμα (i.e., "Additions"), containing a

> Discourse of the grand Charter of the Donation of the Land of *Canaan* to *Israel* . . . Together with a short Natural History of the Animals, Vegetables, and minerals found in that country, and of its present Fertility,[19]

which "additions" will be to the reader, the author is certain, "No less useful, than delightful."[20]

Of interest to us is the thematic weaving of Jewish restoration through the entire fabric of even this "Natural History." The author, it appears, is simply unable any other way to begin his "additions" than by quoting the Prophets:

> And ye (the 12 Tribes of Israel v. 13) shall inherit the Land: Concerning which I lifted up my Hand to give it to your Fathers. Ezek. 47:14.[21]

then by introducing his second topic in similar fashion

> Having discoursed on the return of *Israel* into their own Land . . . I hope it may not be counted inexpedient to delineate the ample and stately Charter whereby they held title to it, and the circumference of its Bounds and the extension of its Limits from the great River *Euphrates* to the *Egyptian* Sea, which the Lord hath declared, yea sworn that all the 12 Tribes of Israel shall possess in the latter days.[22]

Before putting the matter to rest, his passion not quite spent, the author waxes lyrical, in language reminiscent of and richly flavored by various portions of the Bible:

> till the Righteousness of Zion shine forth as brightness, and the salvation thereof as a Lamp that burneth, Not doubting but when the Israelites have finish'd their appointed time of dispersion that other Lands of their further and remoter wanderings, and intermixtures, that they shall as certainly return to, as ever they went out of their Ancient Land. For the mouth of the Lord hath spoken it.
>
> To which purpose I have connexed a Dissertation about their first Exile State, and their continuance in those and some of the Adjacent Regions in succeeding Ages. The certainty of their return in God's due time after the destruction of Anti-christ to a very glorious estate both Scriptural and Temporal, to adore our blessed Lord the Crucified Messiah, the King of Kings. and Lord of Lords, when the Tribes of that Land shall look upon him whom they have pierced, and mourn as for an onely Son, and be in bitterness as for a First-born; when the Lord shall make them an eternal excellency, the joy of many Generations when that people shall all be righteous, and shall inherit their Land for ever.[23]

And to his fellow Christians, his Puritan piety evangelically aglow, the mantle of his broad learning resting lightly on his shoulder, tempering, if not entirely setting aside the otherwise characteristic religious parochialism of his day, Dr. Lee implores:

> Let us pray for Israel, as once that Church did for us; We have a Sister and she hath no breasts; For alas they were cut off by the barbarous Heathen, that she may prove an Amazon, or like the Schythian Queen Tomyris successful against all her enemies. If Zion be a wall rebuilt again, let us build upon her a Place of Silver. If a Door, let's enclose her with Boards of Cedar. Make haste Oh Beloved Saviour, unto both the Flocks of thy Companions, of Israel and the Nations, and be like a Roe or a young Hart upon the Mountains of Spices. So prays a humble and hearty well-wisher to the brightness of Israel's Rising,
>
> Samuel Lee.[24]

That belief in the continued existence of the Israelite tribes—as distinguished from Judah and Benjamin, who, apparently, were properly to be identified as constituting "the Jews" in a narrow sense—was a facet both of Christian and Jewish Millennial Messianic views, as we already have seen.[25] This opinion we have explored above in the treatise of Giles Fletcher, conveyed to us and confirmed by Samuel Lee.

Fresh impulse was given to this interest in the Tribes by the appearance in English of an Italian tract bearing on identically the same theme. The title is very striking:

> *Newes from Rome. Of two mightie Armies, as well footemen as horsmen: The first of the great Sophy, the other of an Hebrew people, till this time not discovered, comming from the Mountaines of Caspij, who pretend their warre is to recouer the Land of the Land of Promise, and expell the Turks out of Christendome. With their multitude of Soldiers, and new invention of weapons.*
>
> *Also certain prophecies of a Iew serving to that Armie, called Caleb Shilocke, prognosticating many strange accidents, which shall happen the following yeere, 1607.*
>
> *Translated out of Italian into English by W. W.*[26]

The opening sheets of the tract contain a letter dated June 1, 1606, from a Signior Valesco to "The Renowned Lord, Don Mathias de Rensie of Venice,"[27] whereby information is conveyed intended to

> advertise your Lordship of certain great, horrible and fearefull things that hapned in this quarter . . . to provide for the perill and danger that at this time hangeth over theyr heads.[28]

The pamphlet is of considerable literary interest, as the Shakespearean scholar, James Orchard Halliwell-Phillips (1820-1889) uses it as the cardinal piece of evidence in his theory that the name of Shylock in Shakespeare's *Merchant of Venice*, first staged in 1596, was suggested by this tract.[29] If the theory is right, it seems a fair "educated guess" that Shakespeare himself was not unaware of the Millennial-Messianic currents among contemporary Christians and Jews. To some degree this knowledge may have had some influence in shaping the play of the humiliated Jew's derisive rebellion. The author of the tract outlines in apocalyptic colors the approach of a great conflagration and warns of its awesome dimensions and terrors.

We are informed that war is soon to be waged by "Hungarie, Bohemia and Moscovia" with the purpose of driving the "terrible Turke" from Europe,[30] and of a "Hebrew people so far unknown, mighty and marvellously swift," about to recover the Land of Promise.[31] The Hebrew tribes, the narrator continues were driven by Alexander the Great beyond the Caspian Mountains (i.e., "mts. of Caspij") where they remained secluded for many centuries until "Dutch Captaines arrived in their region and taught them modern warfare and introduced modern weaponry. A mighty army, mustered together, trained, equipped, zealous, is described in detail as to its harness, size, horses, astonishing swiftness of movement, etc., and said to be presently on the very borders of Palestine.[32]

At the very end of his narrative, in a spirit of solemnity, the author of this rare pamphlet exhorts all Christians to pray to God to withhold the impending cataclysm of calamities and to convert their hearts:

> there will be great remoovings of the earth in divers places, so that for feare thereof, many people will be in a strange amazement and terror.
> These punishments are prognosticated by this learned Jew, to fall uppon the whole world by reason of sinne, wherefore it behooveth all Christian[s] to amend their evill lives, and to pray earnestly unto God to with-hold these calamities from us, and to convart our harts wholy to him, whereby we may find favour in our time of neede, through Jesus Christ our Lord. Amen.[33]

Summary of Data

We have, now with our survey of content of the above literature, isolated the distinctive principles of that doctrine of Jewish restoration which emerged and marched on through succeeding generations. In sum they are as follows: The Jews are to be "called" (i.e., converted as a nation), and together with the posterity of the Ten Tribes of Israel, will be restored to the land assured them by Divine eternal, immutable decree.

From this point onward we will be dealing more with development of the idea than with origins. Birth had come, charac-
teristically in travail, in the martyrdom of Francis Kett;
Andrew Willett, by his opposition, succeeded in overcoming
the long-standing inertia in prompting greater movement and
breadth to the idea and, quite unintentionally, in coaxing
coherence from its protagonists; Thomas Draxe was certain of
the Jews' conversion, cautious about their restoration; Thomas
Brightman was absolutely sure of their calling and restoration,
confiding further his calculations for the same; Giles Fletcher,
via Samuel Lee, assumes the truth of Brightman's expositions
and explores the involvement of the Ten Lost Tribes; the
anonymous writer of *Newes from Rome, etc.* certifies the Ten
Tribes participation in concrete, particular terms.

Notes

1 Samuel Lee (editor and author of parts), *Israel Redux: or the Resauration of Israel; or the Restauration of Israel exhibited in two short treatises. The first contains an essay on some probable grounds that the present Tartars, near the Caspian Sea are the posterity of the ten Tribes of Israel. By G. F., LL.D. The second a dissertation concerning their ancient and successive state, with some Scripture evidences of their future conversion and establishment in their own land* (London: S. Streater for John Hancock, 1677), sheet A2.

2 Thompson Cooper, "Fletcher, Giles," *DNB*, XIX, pp. 299-300. The 1856 edition of this work of Fletcher's is published under its original title in *Russia at the Close of the Sixteenth Century* by Edward Bond (London: McHalykut Society, 1856).

3 Fletcher's part of the work is that segment of the title which is an *Essay on Some Probable Grounds that the Present Tartars, near the Caspian Sea are the Posterity of the Ten Tribes of Israel*. His initials are juxtaposed immediately thereafter.

4 Miss B. Porter, "Lee, Samuel," *DNB*, XXXII, pp. 378-379.

5 Samuel Lee, *op. cit.*, sheet A2.

6 Giles Fletcher, *Essay on some Probable Grounds, etc.*, p. 27.

7 "Behold therefore the goodness and severity of God: on them which fell severity; but toward thee, goodness, if thou continue in his goodness: otherwise, thou also shall be cut off." The context of the passage tells us who "thee" is here. It may be succinctly summarized in verses one and two: "Hath God cast away his people. For I also am an Israelite, of the seed of Abraham, of the tribe of Benjamin. God hath not cast away his people which he foreknew."

8 Giles Fletcher, *op. cit.*, p. 3.

9 *Ibid.*, pp. 3, 7.

10 Thomas Brightman, *A Revelation of the Revelation*, p. 548. Cf. chapter IV, *supra*.

11 Giles Fletcher, *op. cit.*, p. 14ff.

12 *Ibid.*, p. 27.

13   Samuel Lee, *op. cit.*, p. 29.

14   *Ibid.*, p. 30.

15   *Ibid.*, p. 78.

16   Isaiah 11:11, 12.

17   Jeremiah 33:7.

18   Samuel Lee, *op. cit.*, ἐπεισάγμα, sheet A3f.

19   *Ibid.*, p. 78.

20   *Ibid.*

21   *Ibid.*, frontispiece.

22   *Ibid.*, sheet A.

23   *Ibid.*, sheets A3-A4; cf. Isaiah 62:1; 60:5, 22; Zechariah 12:10; Matthew 24:30; Revelation 1:7.

24   *Ibid.*, sheets A3v, A5r; cf. Song of Solomon 8:8, 9, 14.

25   The appearance of David Reubeni in Europe (1624) and the stir caused by the tale he brought with him about a kingdom of the tribe of Reuben existing somewhere in Tartary, mixed together with the actualities of the facts behind Judah Halevi's (c. 1085-1140) *Kuzari*, are representative of the continued interest within Jewish circles on this question.

26   The tract is anonymous, and the rest of the bibliographical data is only partial: "Printed by I.R. for Henry Gosson, and are to be sold in Pater [noster Rowe at the signe of the Sunne]. The bracketed data is a projection of the British Museum listing, made on the basis of partial visibility of the remainder of the line, which was damaged by someone overly zealous to have an even bottom edge hence cropped off most of the lower portion of the letters on the last line of the sheet. There is no indication of the date of publication.

27   *Newes from Rome, etc.*, Sheets A2 and A3.

28   *Ibid.*

29   James Orchard Halliwell-Phillips, *Halliwell's Shakespeare* (London: The Halkyut Society, 1853), Volume V, p. 277.

30   *Ibid.*, sheet A3ff.

31   *Ibid.*, sheet A5.

32   *Ibid.*, sheet Bff.

33   *Newes from Rome etc.*, sheet B5.

Chapter VI

A Manifesto for Jewish Restoration

By the end of the first decade of the seventeenth century, Brightman, Draxe and Fletcher had died. But of their belief in Jewish national restoration anything but atrophy for lack of advocates set in. Far from it.

A brilliant lawyer, not a divine like Brightman and Draxe, but like Fletcher a layman, by name Henry Finch (1558-1625), picked up the strands of the doctrine from the isolated miscellaneous allusions and adumbrate development thus far extant, which we have in course noted. He turned again to the Scriptures and produced in 1621, *The World's Resurrection or The Calling of the Jewes. A Present to Judah and the Children of Israel that Ioyned with Him, and to Ioseph (that valiant tribe of Ephraim) and all the House of Israel that Ioyned with Him.*[1] The book was published anonymously, which veil, while soon pierced, reflects favorably on Finch's judgment of the distempers of his times and on his instincts, if not overly clever, for self preservation. The book had been published for a matter only of weeks when the roof caved in on the author's head. In the persecution which ensued, Finch lost his reputation, his possessions, his health[2] — all precipitated by his belief in Jewish national restoration. This much alone would justify a place in the history of the idea. But beyond this, Finch's public standing and his labors as a man of letters in promoting the doctrine have confirmed for him a focalizing role in its history. Extended treatment is required.

The Contribution of Sir Henry Finch: Prospectus

Henry Finch was a man of extraordinary personality and accomplishments. His recognized abilities, professional esteem

and achievement lifted him to high station.[3]   Against this
backdrop, the consequent scholarly and ecclesiastic criticism
on his views, royal acrimony against his person and sequestra-
tion of his property—leaving him in his late sixties deprived of
any substance in goods or name to sustain life—stand starkly
in relief. This dramatic discrediting attracted a great deal of
attention and cast a tragi-color mantle over the idea of Jewish
restoration. No doubt, as human nature still responds, the
darkly sinister rumblings and rumors accompanying Finch's
fall from favor attracted the lion's share of the public curiosity.[4] But in the process a floodlamp was caused to shine on
rising Christian belief in the certainty of the biblical pronouncements about a coming restoration of the Jews to their
ancient national homeland in Palestine.[5]

The novel feature of Finch's treatment of the issue was the
quasi-political character it here and there assumed. This was,
in the main, the element that caused him to run afoul the
authorities, in this case none other than King James I
himself.[6] The implications, politically, were readily made by
thoroughly   conditioned   readers[7]—even   though   Finch
practised the art of understatement in this regard. Moreover,
King James was precisely the kind of man, it seems, at pains
for occasion to be piqued and despotically to react.[8]

Finch's legal training and background, and probably more
importantly, his attempt to be truly complete in examining the
subject in a limited treatise, explain the inclusion of political
content. Finch, as most expositors before and since of similar
hermeneutic, found it impossible to treat the topic, at least
from a biblical perspective, without becoming enmeshed in
things political.[9]   In that day, not long in advance of the
docking of the ideological ship *Divinum Ius Regum* (Divine
Right of King) at its final port-of-call—if indeed it did not run
aground or break up in heavy seas, heaving not at all into any
harbor—European monarchs were especially defensive for
what they considered their special prerogatives.[10] This royal
testiness can be understood, if not appreciated by those of us
who have never enjoyed it, not only as a jealous guarding of
supposed royal rights to unchecked arbitrariness, unlimited
dissipation of the public treasury, license in one's sensual

interests, etc., associated popularly with kingly behavior. But also, kings of the time resisted any encroachment on their powers as an affront of office, which office existed in their eyes, as a kind of theocratic vicarage at very God's behest, to personify the nation, to safeguard it, to oversee it, in every regard touching its works, ways and welfare, as a Divinely appointed patron, steward and benefactor, to enhance it.[11] The theory is noble but its application in practice, unhappily, man being what he is, is tyrannous, more often than otherwise.

King James, intelligent and cunning as undeniably he was, well earned the description given him by King Henry IV of France as "the wisest fool in Christendom."[12] Vain in his theological learning and self-styled expertise as a biblical exegete, James' reaction to Finch's book was nearly as vitriolic as it was foolish. James deduced ill-begotten, evil-intentioned political overtones in the notion of Jewish national restoration. This he saturated with characteristic spleen and suspicion. The vivid blend of revolutionary colors in which millennial context Finch's treatment necessarily, because biblically derived, was ensconced, probably was more the source of James' reaction than any frank evaluation of the content. And James cordially despised the pious Puritan spirit which in Finch was genuine and prominent.[13]

At this juncture we will do well to trace in some detail the unfolding of these events and especially the inmixing, partly as cause, partly as result, of Finch's person and of his development of our idea.

Sir Henry Finch: Man, Lawyer, Biblical Student, Literateur, Advocate of Jewish National Restoration

Born in 1558, son of Sir Thomas Finch, Knight Marshall of the Army, Henry was educated at Oxford's Oriel College and admitted to the Bar at Grey's Inn in 1585. He entered Parliament in 1593 for Canterbury and was returned by election in 1597.[14]

As a lawyer he achieved a lasting recognition through the considerable merit of his lengthy four volume legal treatise Νομοτεχνία, published in 1613, and dedicated to King James I.

As an exposition of the common law, *Finch's Law*, as it was called, was superceded only by Blackstone's *Commentaries*.[15] In any case, Finch's skill and learning in this work was of sufficient distinction to earn him a respected reputation in the rarified altitudes of the legal elite among his contemporaries. No less than Francis Bacon invited him to assist in the monumental task of "reducing the concurrent statutes heaped one upon another to one clear uniform law;" and the King about the same time, personally sought his opinion on the "conveniency of monoply patents intended to be granted to inns and alehouses."[16]

Jurisprudence and the arid, tediously lexical labors of codifying dusty statutes were by no means, however, his only interests. Finch's genuine urbanity and erudition mark him as representative of the renaissance characteristics of Elizabethan England. Like his contemporaries, Finch was a man of wide horizons, well read in classical literature, the writers of which he was wont often to quote, and of facile pen. Above all, of chief interest to us, Finch was an eager and deep student of the Bible and theology. His legal training made his logic tight. The same exemplary lucidity displayed in *Finch's Law* was similarly engaged in the biblical exposition to which he put his hand. His dominantly legal mind fastened in the breast of a fervent, religious devotion, drew Finch, like a magnet, to meditations on the mysteries of Divine government.[17]

Predictably, given the nature of that epoch, and Finch's propensities, Calvin's supremely logical, consistent theology, arguing from the sovereignty of God and the self-authenticating nature of the Bible,[18] appealed both to Finch's honed intellect and the warmth of his piety. Anchored to these moorings, matters religious and legal were in Finch's mind handled by the same mental machinery. What he says himself grandly and succinctly, in the prefactory note to his *Sacred Doctrine of Divinitie, Gathered out of the Word of God* (1599), will eloquently state the case:

> And for my parte, I am of that iudgement, that it is so far from being unmeet for a Gentleman of the Innes of the Court, to deale in these Holy Studies, that I could wish of the Lorde, that the Noble Men of the Court itselfe, and all others whose wits are either by nature or

education more pregnant, would fine and file them upon such endeav-
ours as these are. So should they fitt themselves not only to pass from
the Princes Court into the Lordes owne Court, their to reigne for ever
more; but should able themselves ten thousands times better to all
honourable services of the Prince and countrie in a wiser and more
polique government of the Commonwealth than Macchiauel that
cursed hell hound can furnish thereof. For besides many draughts of
policy, here and there scattered throughout the whole Scripture, especially the stories: that one book of Proverbs as it were the Lord's owne
Politickes, is able to yielde more sound precepts of sure and safe government, than, I will not say Macchiauel but than all Macchiauels in the
world when they shall have met and shall beaten out their brains about
that consultation.[19]

We see here that kind of Puritan personality and outlook
which we have earlier sketched in terms of the general ethos
of the time, fully active—well nigh personified—in Henry
Finch. Reinforcing this disposition was the similar bent of his
personal friend and publisher, William Gouge (1578-1653),
teacher of Hebrew at King's College, Cambridge, and Rector
of St. Anne's, Blackfriars. Of unique interest to us is not
merely the fact Gouge was a Hebraist, but, especially, a disciple of Philip Ferdinandus, the baptized Jewish scholar whom
we have already met.[20]

Gouge, some twenty years younger than Finch, was known
as an "Arch-Puritan" on account of his abstemious life and
strict piety. The famous lawyer gained in Gouge a zealous
admirer, particularly of his theological studies and inquiries
into "The Lord's owne Politickes."[21] Persuaded by Gouge's
enthusiasm,[22] Finch permitted him to publish *An Exposition of
the Song of Solomon called Canticles, togither with Profitable Observations Collected out of the Same* in April of 1615. In his "Preface to
the Christian Reader," Gouge declares:

> Heerin therefore (good Reader) thou art much beholding to the
> learned Author of this booke, who hath taken so good pains in
> expounding this rare Song. Such is the Author, such is the worke, that
> neither father nor child need to bee ashamed of one another. The
> author is a man of great place and note in the Commonwealth; his
> humility will not suffer him to have his name made known. Though by
> profession he be not a Divine; yet in knowledge of those learned
> tongues wherein the Scriptures were written, and in understanding of
> the mysteries contained in them, he is a very deep & profound Divine.
> The many learned treatises which he hath made, some in Hebrew,

other in English; some heretofore published, other still lying by him, are evidences of more than I have sayd. . . . Thus I have shewed thee (Christian Reader) that this *Song of Songs* is worthie to bee expounded; yea that necessarie it is, it should bee expounded: that the Author of this worke is well able to performe so weightie a worke; and that he hath taken good paines in performing it. Do thou his paines for thine owne good. If thou aske me why I meddle so farre in it, as to publish it, I answere, *For thy good*; had it not been for me, thou haddest not seene it.[23]

Apparently, Finch was of a type which one either deeply admired or just as cordially disliked. He had few acquaintances, otherwise only intimates and enemies.

An Exposition of the Song of Solomon etc. shows Finch following the long accepted approaches to the Song of Songs in using it as a metaphorical picture of Christ and the Church.[24] His hermeneutic can best be seen in a passage directly pertinent:

The manner of writing (in Song of Songs) is that which we call active, or representative, that is wherein Persons onely are brought speaking, the author himselfe, saying nothing: and the persons here are Christ, the Church and sometimes, but very surely, the friends of them both: In all which the Church, burning with a desire of Christ longeth, and is important till shee be joined vnto him. For hether tend all her passions, exclamation, testifications of her love, commendations of her spouse, Christ again by kinde gentle and loving speeches comforteth and cheereth vp the Church with certaine hope of that happie and blessed time: for hether tend all his commendations of her present, and promise of future graces, the accepting of her unfeigned repentence.[25]

Finch's transformation of the outspoken sensuousness of Song of Songs to pious devotional literature reflects the intense crises of the Church of that day, whereby the frankly passionate expressions of yearning in this love-song, more than ever, are regarded as a key to the mystery of the impending marriage of the Bride (the Glorified Church) and the Lamb (the risen, glorified Christ), in other words, the spiritual union of the Church and her Lord:

The Bookes of *Solomon* the Iewes compare not vnfitly to the Temple which he built. Whereof this song of songs, or most excellent song resembleth the holy of holies or the most holy place: Being a declaration of the blessed and sweet coniunction betweene Christ and his Church, and of the contract, and eipousels (espousals] made betweene

them, whilest the Church is now militant vpon earth. All which time is
as it were a bidding of the banes vntil by his second coming from
heaven our spirituall marriage with him shall be solemnized and made
vp.[26]

The clue to our theme is Finch's allusion to "his [Christ's]
second comming." In following the traditional allegorical
equation for the book's interpretation, Finch applies it to what
he calls "the Church of the Iewes"[27] which

> . . . it is not possible to containe . . . within the narrow boundes of
> Ierusalem . . .

but rather

> shall be made the Catholicke Church of all the world; a new manner
> of Citie must bee built: wherefore plucking downe the mid-wall of par-
> tition, a new wall, and new gates shall bee made to engage the Citie: a
> new government and discipline, new officers, pastors, teachers, etc. to
> administer it. New, not in substance, which hath alwaies been the same,
> even among the Iewes, but newly established, bewtified, and translated
> to the Gentiles.   Neither shall this be any disgrace to the now
> Ierusalem, everything shall bee then so farre more glorious and more
> excellent. A house of saints shall bee erected by the preaching of the
> Gospell, to bee the Pallace of the great King: a stately and magnificent
> pallace, all of silver. . . .[28]

The author takes leave of his reader by declaring:

> In expounding the Text, the author hath held himself close to the
> Hebrewe.[29]

This statement prepares us with that final note on which to
turn to Finch's next later work, his *magnum opus* expressly
treating Jewish restoration. It begins with a dedication in
archaic Hebrew characters, used again, translated into
English, as part of the title.[30]
The vision of a revivified, and gloriously rebuilt New
Jerusalem which we have seen in Finch's *Canticles*, bears
already traits of the early Christian eschatological views discussed in chapter two of the present work. Lactantius,[31] e.g.,
et al., are alluded to throughout. Finch revives these old views
but with an effect that was epoch-making in terms of its gener-
ous size (247 pages) and the attention posterity soon visited

both on book and author. The title tells us a good bit itself: *The World's Resurrection or the Calling of the Jewes and (with them) of all Nations and Kingdoms of the earth, to the faith of Christ. A Present to Judah and the Children of Israel that Ioyned with Him, and to Joseph (that valiant tribe of Ephraim) and all the House of Israel the Ioyned with Him.* The latter half of the title Finch lifts straight out from the English rendering of the first part of the Hebrew dedication. The rest of the dedicatory inscription may be appropriately added here as spring board to his doctrine.

> The Lord give them [i.e., the Jews] grace, that they may return and seeke Jehovah their God, and David their King, in these latter days.[32]

Like his other theological work, this book was published anonymously, again by William Gouge, Finch's friend and disciple. And once again Gouge praises the author in the prefactory epistle as a scholar "who hath dived deeper into the mysteries that I can doe," giving special emphasis to Finch's "great understanding of the Hebrew tongue." Beside this preface there is a "letter to the Christian Reader," and "Epistle Dedicatory," the latter addressed to "all the Seed of Jacob, farre and wide dispersed" and yet another dedication to "the children of Israel, written for their sake in Hebrew."[33]

Finch goes on to explain the nature of this, his present to the Jews:

> Daughter of Tsion by fleshly generations: Jerusalem which sticcest close to carnall rites and ordinances, and to the legall worship:[34] To you I bring this present, wherever you dispersed. A spark out of a Diamond; one drop out of that Sea, which the whole Ocean cannot holde. Flowing from the infinitens of wisdome revealed in the Scriptures. Concerning thy repayre, and thee home againe, and to marry thee to himself by faith for everymore. . . .[35]

While Finch makes the offense allegedly committed by the Jews corporately the reason behind the calamities which have befallen them in the *Galut*, he declares his anticipation of a radical change in their heart and fortune immediately pending at the hand of the Lord:

> Out of all the places of thy dispersion, East, West North, and South, his purpose is to bring thee home again, and to marry thee to himselfe by faith for evermore. In stead that thou wast desolate and forsaken,

and sattest as a widow, thou shalt flourish as in thy youth. Nay, above and beyond thy youth. . . . Out of thee shall come gems and precious stones, richer than of the Saphire; ruddier than the Carbuncle, shining above the Topaze. Ezraes, Nehemies, Mordecaes, builders of a better Temple than that which thou hast doated upon so long. . . . Thy gates shall be made of pearles, and thy street of pure gold. All the Gentiles shall bring their glory into thy empire, and fall downe before thee. . . .[36]

The body of the text is a very catalogue of biblical evidence with complete description and explication by the author. He bases the development of his argument on grammatico-historical exegesis. He uses the prophecies in a manner which clearly reflects acquaintance with the early Christian Fathers, and the immediately preceding millennial writers (as Thomas Brightman). At the same time he betrays the precision of an highly trained legal mind:

> Where *Israel, Iudah, Tsion, Ierusalem*, etc. are named in this argument, the Holy Ghost meaneth not the spirituall Israel, or Church of God collected of the Gentiles, no nor of the Iewes and Gentiles both (for each of these have their promises severally and apart) but Israel properly descended out of Iacobs loynes.[37]

The theme is expanded along the same lines of logic and evidence:

> The same iudement is to be made of their returning to their land and ancient seates, the conquest of their foes, the fruitfulness of their soile, the glorious Church they shall erect in the land it selfe of Iudah, their bearing rule farre and neere. These and such like are not Allegories [of the kind we saw in Finch's treatment of Song of Solomon], setting forth in terrene similitudes or deliverance through Christ (whereof those were types and figures) but meant really and literally of the Iewes. It was not possible to devise more express or evident tearmes, then [i.e., than] the Spirit of purpose vseth to cut off all such construction. Neither were *Iosias* or Cyrus more plainely named hundred of yeares before they were borne, then [i.e., than] these things are plainely delivered for the confirming of that peoples faith. Wherefore wee need not be afraid to averre and mainteyne, that one day they shall come to Ierusalem againe, be Kings and chiefe Monarches of the earth, swaye and governe all, for the glory of Christ that shall shine among them. And that is it *Lactantius* faith, Lib. 7. Cap. 15. *The Romane name (I will speake it, because it must one day be) shall bee taken from the earth, and the Empire shall returne to Asia, and again shall the East beare dominion, and the West be in subiection.*[38]

The approach of this position, distinctively Christian, is yet remarkable close to the central ideas of Jewish Messianism. It cuts cleanly through the old practice of ascribing the curses of the prophecies to the Jews while reserving the blessings to the Church and Christians. It means that there is again a Jewish history, a history with continuity from biblical times through intervening ages to the present and, most importantly, into the future. Jews in Galu*t* are construed as a nation, in some way intact and distinct, the destiny of which is solidly declared in the Scripture and determined by Divine providence, just as in the Biblical period. Their ultimate, sure deliverance, in Finch's mind, consists of their spiritual redemption and restoration to their ancient land.

Methodically, Finch outlines his expectations "of these most high and ample promises. Such and so great as are altogether incredible, but that the mouth of the Lord had spoken them" in a series of "aphorisms or positions"[39] bearing directly on our theme. They are given here in full because of their comprehensive scope and overall usefulness in demonstrating the broad dimensions of his exposition:

1. The first head concerneth the Iewes refusall of Christ, Whereupon shall follow
2. Both their reiection to be no more his Church and people.
3. (Notwithstanding which, a small remnant, a hole seed, shall be left. *Rom.* 11.5.)
4. And also their long desolation.
   The second head is of the calling of the Iewes.
5. Of this remnant God will be pleased to gather a Church vnto himselfe,
6. In the last dayes. Ezech. 38.8. Hoshea 3:5.
7. Not of a few, singled out here and there, but of the Nation in generall. Rom. 11.25, 26, 27. Cantic. 8.10.
8. And that of the ten Tribes as well as of the rest of the Iewes. Ezech. 37.16, 19. Hosh. 1.11. Ier. 3.12, 13. etc. Esay 11.12, 13. Obadia vers. 20. Zach. 10.6. Rom. 11.26.
9. But this extendeth not to euery one. Some there shall be, refractarie Spirits, that will not euen then stoope to

Christ. Against whom the wrath of God shall be euident. Rev. 21.8. Dan. 12.2. Esay 65.11, 12, 13, 14, 15, 16, 17.

The third head respecteth the beginnings of their conversion; of whom it shall be, and when, and the things that shall follow thereupon,

10. The first conuerted shall be out of the Northland and the East quarters. Dan. 11.44. Esay 41.26, 27.
11. And that about the time when the Turkish tyrannie shall haue lasted 350 yeares. Dan 7.25. 12.7.11. Ren. 9.15.
12. They shall repaire towards their owne country. Esay 11.15, 16 & 51.10, 11. Ier. 3.18. Hosh. 1.11.
    Things following vpon it are
13. In the way, Euphrates shall be laid dry for them to passe, as once the Red Sea was. Rev. 16.12. See Esay 11.15. & 51.10, 11.
14. The tidings of this shall shake and affright the Turkish power. Dan. 11.44.
15. A marueilous conflict shall they have with God and Magog, that is to say, the Ture. Ezech. 38. & 39. Rev. 20.8.
16. And shall be in sore distresse. Dan. 12.1.
17. This conflict shall be in their owne country, the land of Iudea. Rev. 20.8, 9. Esay 25.10. Ioel 3.2. Ezech. 29.2, 4. Zach. 14.2.4. 3, 4, 5. Dan 11.44, 45.
18. A noble victorie they shall obtaine.
19. God from heauen miraculously fighting for them. Rev. 20.8, 9, 10. Esay 27.1 & 31.8,9. Ezech. 38.18, 19, 20, 21, 22, 23. Zach. 14.3, 4, 5.
20. It seemeth the maine blow where the Grand Signior himselfe must fall, shall be at, or neere Ierusalem. Rev. 10.16. & 20.9. Ioel. 3.2. Ezech. 39.16.
21. The vtter ouerthrow of the whole Armie, perhaps shall be beside the Sea of Gennezaret, otherwise called, the Lake of Tiberias. Ezech. 39.11.
22. This conquest of Gog and Magog commeth 45 yeares after their first conuersion, which is the 395. yeare and last period of the Ottoman Empire. Reu. 9.15. Dan. 12.12.

The fourth head is their flourishing state of Church and Common-wealth, after this victory once obtained. For,

23. They shall dwell in their owne Countrey. Ier 3.18, and 23.8. Ezech. 37.21, 22. Amos 9.14, 15.
24. They shall inhabite all the parts of the land, as before. Obad. 15. 19, 20. Ier. 21. 38, 39, 40. Esay 27, 12. and 65. 10.
25. They shall liue in safety. Esay 60.18. Hosh. 2.18.
26. They shall continue in it for euer. Ezech. 37. 25. Amos 9.15.
27. The land shall be more fertile then [i.e., than] euer it was. Ezech. 36.35. Hosh. 2. 21, 22. Ioel 3.18. Amos 9.13. Zach. 14.10.
28. The Countrey more populous then [than] before. Esay 49. 19, 20, 21. Ezech. 34, 31. and 36. 37, 38.
29. There shall bee no separation of the ten tribes from the other two: but all make one entire Kingdome. Ezech. 37.22, 24. Hoshea 1.11.
30. And a most flourishing Common-wealth. Dan. 7.27.
31. Touching their Church, it shall bee most glorious. Esay 4. and 24.23. and 60.1, 2. Reu. 21. and 22. Dan. 12.3. Ier. 3.16, 17. Ioel 3.19, 20.
32. Which glory shall appeare in outward beauty. Esa. 24.23. and 30.26 and 6.20 and 62.1, 2, 3, 4. Reu. 21.23. and 21.5. Zach. 14.6, 7.
33. Sanctity. (all prophane purged out) Ioel 3.17. Zach. 14.20, 21. Reu. 22.3.
34. Purity of doctrine. Ezech. 37.23. Hosh. 2.16, 17. and 14.8. Zach. 13.2, 3.
35. Excellency of the new covenant. Esay 61.8. Ezech. 37.26.
36. Abundance of spirituall graces. Faith, Knowledge, Zeale, Piety, etc. Esay 25.6.
37. Cheerefull obedience. Esay 66.7, 8.
38. Multitude of beleeuers. Hosh. 1.10, 11. Zach. 10.10.
39. Happinesse and prosperity. Esay 25.8. and 51, 13. and 60.19, 20. Reu. 21.4.
40. Ioy. Esay 30.29. and 35.10. Hosh. 2.15. Zach. 10.7.
41. Safety. Zach. 10.12. and 14.11. Jer. 23.6 and 33.16.

42. Stability. Esay 26.1. and 33.16. Ier. 30.20.
43. Perpetuity. Esay 60.21. Hosh. 2.19. Ioel 3.20.
44. The fift and last head is, that after their call, Ashur and Aegypt, all those large and vast Countries, the whole Tract of the East and of the South shall be conuerted vnto Christ. Esay 19.23, 24, 25. and 27.12, 13. Micha. 7.11, 12. Zach. 10.10, 11, 12. and 14.8,9. Psal. 69.31. and 72.9, 10, 11. Rev. 11.14. The chiefe sway and soueraignty remaining full with the Iewes. So as,
45. All nations shall honour them. Rev. 21.24. Esay 49. 23. and 60.3, 5 etc. and 61.9 and 66.10, 11, 12. Zephan 3.19, 20. Rev. 16.12.
46. And the enemies of the Church by them subdued, Numb. 24.17, 18, 19. Esay 11.14. Ioel 3.19. Obad, vers. 18. Zach. 10.11, and possessed, Esay 14.2 and 61.5. Ioel 3,8. Amos 9.12. Obad. vers. 17.19. shall willingly or perforce come vnder Christs obedience.[40]

Though he rejects "Jewish fables"[41] (Rabbinical concepts and abrogated ceremonies, etc.), we have above a comprehensive statement of what Finch examines exhaustively before his readers. Every germane element of the idea of Jewish restoration developed to date out of the Scripture is covered. "The truth of e[a]ch position," he tells us,

> . . . I will not here stand to discusse. This Treatise following (where they are noted in the margent) doth aboundantly proue them all.
>
> The time drawing neere, wherein these things foretold so long before, come now to be accomplished, how sweet a thing it is, to looke into the prophesies that giue assurance of it.
>
> May it therefore please the iudicious and learned Reader, to weigh the Scriptures following: which professedly, and of purpose, speake of these things.[42]

To be sure, no deeply metaphysical meditations are before us here. Finch's work, although principally titled *The Worldes Great Restauration* is occupied all but incidently with the subject of its secondary title *The Calling of the Jews*. In accordance with the view of earlier espositors, Finch sees both conversion and restoration of Jews *and* the Ten Tribes, i.e., a whole nation of Israel, "not a few, singled out here and then."[43] The initial mustering together will be from the north and east. In the process of the journey to their own country, the Euphrates will dry up for them to pass over (from Brightman,). Once in their land they will be set upon by the Turk, the "little horn" of Daniel's fourth beast. The other three monarchies in Daniel's vision are those of Persia, Macedonia and Rome. The catastrophes attendant upon these events culminate in establishment of the Jewish Kingdom and, according to Finch's timetable (again, borrowed from Brightman) will take place between 1650 and 1695. Finch exceeds Brightman not in basic exposition but in exhaustive survey and in the mixture of religious and political aspects into one, and in the projection of an ideal, perfect theocracy in a redeemed Holy Land.[44]

From these statements we are able to see that the Kingdom, of spiritual destiny and function in the divine plan, has nonetheless very tangible and concrete expression. They (i.e., the Jews) are going to dwell in every corner of the land; they will live in safety; they will continue there in perpetuity; the land will be more fertile and populous than before; there shall no longer be a separation between the northern kingdom (ten tribes) and the southern (two tribes). It shall be, in sum:

> . . . a body politic where unto all other corporations in the world are but counterfaits . . . knowledge, wisdom, pietie, justice, temperance, honour and magnanimity will be found.[45]

Finch leaves no margin for doubt that his vision is to be understood concretely.

> Then shall be established that most glorious kingdom of Ierusalem, under which all the tribes shall be united. So ample shall be their dominion that not only the Egyptians, Assyrians, and the most extensive countries of the East, converted by their example, but even the rest, the Christians, shall of their own accord, *submit* themselves and acknowledge their primacy.[46]

This sublime vision is the note on which the book closes. A bolder, more vivid coloring to the doctrine is difficult to imagine, especially set off against the dark prospects of contemporary realities. The most helpless and persecuted of all peoples are to be exalted to boundless power and glory, which events signal and mediate at the same time the redemption of all mankind. It was for Finch's day a revolutionary doctrine indeed.

In a period consciously practicing absolutism in Church and State it is hardly surprising that *The World's Great Restauration* provoked hot opposition. James I was then King of England. His belligerence toward Puritanism in general and his resentment against Parliament in particular presaged an approaching storm. A brief sketch of him and the character of his reign and time will help us at this point. He was conscientious where his interests were at stake, industrious, genuinely concerned for religion, and possessed a good portion of the astuteness of his Scottish upbringing. But the personal anomalies which publically were exposed by the undisciplined living of his most visible associates failed to enlist the confidence, or even to command respect, of his best subjects:

> It was not only by living in an intellectual world of his own that JAMES failed to gain a hold on the hearts of Englishmen. The riotous profusion of his Court gave wide offence. In July, 1606, when his brother-in-law, CHRISTIAN IV. of Denmark, visited him, ladies who were to act in a dramatic performance before the two kings were too drunk to play their parts and the offence was left uncorrected. His own life was a double one. He liked the company of the learned, who could discuss with him questions of theology and of ecclesiastical politics, but he also liked the boon companionships of the hunting field; and though his own life was pure, and his own head, according to his physician's report, to hard to be affected by wine, he himself indulged in coarse language, and took no pains to avoid the society of evil livers.[47]

After the Hampton Court Conference of 1604 where the nonconforming parties presented their requests to him, James had done his level best to live up to his promise to make the Puritans conform themselves or "harry them [i.e., the Puritans] out of the Land."[48] The vitriol of his distaste for the Puritans is reflected in the instruction he gives to his son on the art of king-craft in his *Basilicon Doron*: "Cherish no man more than a good pastor; *hate not any man more than a proud Puritan*."[49] It seemed that by a strange fatality every conspicuous act and public utterance ran cross grain to the sentiments of the time. Puritanism by its opposition to Romanism had come to be almost synonymous with patriotism; therefore

James' dalliance with England's mortal enemy Spain in an extended but unsuccessful attempt to negotiate a marriage treaty, shocked, enraged and alienated the major portion of his subjects.[50] From James' heavy hand many fled to the Continent. The year 1620 witnessed the voyage of the Mayflower to America. Interestingly, in the years 1618-1620 a certain John Traske and various of his followers were imprisoned for "Judaizing" for advocacy and observance of a strict Sabbath.

Beside these internal circumstances within England, sweeping historic changes were taking place elsewhere which coincided with the publication of *The World's Great Restauration* (1621) and doubtless added to its impact.

The Thirty Years' War was just in its beginning stages. A Catholic Empire was advancing with Spain in its vanguard. James' son-in-law, Frederick, then king of Bohemia and head of the Protestant Union, had just been defeated in the Battle of White Hill, near Prague.[51] The Ottoman Empire was in decline. In 1571 the battle of Lepanto signalled an irreversible break in Ottoman sea power.[52] The Treaty of Torok (1606) was the high water mark of Turkish conquest and momentum.[53] With these things in the foreground, we are able to understand why the political implications of Finch's book were quickly realized and pounced upon by those in a position to lose advantage thereby. In particular, the book did not escape the notice of the witty, widely read theology buff who occupied the throne, who wrote,[54] disputed and harangued. A collision between the exegetical lawyer and "the wisest fool in Christendom" was both imminent and inevitable.

The King construed the book of his Serjeant-at-law (Finch's anonymity was short-lived) as a personal libel. Not only were the author's overall religious views in direct opposition to the Episcopal opinions of James, but even more so to the King's theory that his reign had been a perfect theocracy. There is little doubt that James, too, was included among the group of monarchs who would bow before the ruler of the Jewish Kingdom proposed by Finch. Both Finch and his publisher were soon arrested and examined before the High Commission. The High Commissioner was a creation of King James to serve as an implement for having done with overly ardent

Protestants. It took a number of weeks before either Finch or Gouge could obtain release, and then only upon disclaiming in writing "the opinion which His Majesty thinks is asserted in his book" and after abject apology "for having written so unadvisedly."[55]

The affair was not ended, however, with the mere release from jail of author and publisher. In each body where public opinion in that day could be sounded, there was reaction to this manifesto of Jewish restoration. Parliament, Pulpit and University each mounted an assault on the idea.

Notes

1 [Henry Finch], *The World's Resurrection or The Calling of the Jewes. A Present to Judah etc.* (London: Edward Griffin for William Bladen, 1621).

2 James McMullen Rigg, "Finch, Sir Henry," *DNB*, VI, p. 13.

3 *Ibid.*

4 Beside King James' personal outrage, no less than three other celebrated notables, Archbishop William Laud and John Prideaux, Regius Professor of Theology at Oxford, each a contemporary of Finch, and the eminent historian Thomas Fuller, all censure, ridicule and heap contumely on Finch as worse than "a dreamer, a madman who thinks with the misbegotten brains of a Jewish zealot." John Prideaux, "De Judaeorum Vocatione," *Orationes Novem Inavqurales, De Totidem Theologiae Apicibos, scitu non indignis, pront promotione Doctorum, Oxoniae publica prophonebantus in Comitijs* (Oxioniae: Iohannes Lichfield, and Guilielmus Turner, 1626), p. 110. Each of these men is discussed in the text to follow.

5 Finch's critics wrote as though they were composing an epilogue. It was not, however, to be that way. The more his antagonists harangued, the more attentive, sympathetic, tentatively persuaded, and sizeable Finch's own listening and reading publics became. In this regard, while certainly of small personal comfort to him, Finch was the critical influence, by virtue of his very humiliation, which finally overcame the generally negative predisposition against the idea.

6 James is recorded to have been all but apoplectic in rage at the notion in Finch's book that the sovereigns of the world would one day bow to a Jewish king, an idea implicit in millennial doctrines of Jewish restoration. Franz Kobler, "Sir Henry Finch 1558-1625," *Transactions of the Jewish Historical Society 1945-1951)*, XVI, p. 116.

7 See chapter three.

8 H. H. Henson, *Puritanism in England*, pp. 51-55, 58-62.

9 After quoting *ad seriatim* from Leviticus 26, Deuteronomy 7, 28 and 30, Nahum Sokolow's indignant cry of outrage against Jewish unbelief in national (hence political) restoration is illustrative:

Here we have in plain words, simple and clear, the fundamental idea of Moses: the Jewish national future and the possession of the land forever. This cannot be explained away by sophistry. In vain, some Jews declare: We are not nationalist Jews, we are religious Jews! What is the Jewish religion if the Bible is not accepted as an Inspired Revelation? It is strange and sadly amusing that some Jews, adherents of the monotheistic principle, describe themselves as Germans, Magyars, and so on, "of the persuasion of Moses." If this is not blasphemy, it is irony. The real Moses, the Moses of the Pentateuch, brands Dispersion as a curse, and his whole religious conception, with all the laws, ceremonies, feasts, etc., is built up on the basis of the covenant with the ancestors, a covenant immovable and unalterable. No matter whether Jews call themselves religious or nationalistic, the Jewish religion cannot be separated from nationalism, unless another Bible be invented.

Judaism, or the Jewish religion, is based first upon the teaching of Moses, and next upon that of the prophets, and it is a favorite claim of the modern school of Jewish reform that their Judaism is "Prophetic Judaism," in opposition to the Judaism of orthodox Jews, who lay particular stress on the Talmud. But what do the Prophets teach?

History of Zionism, II, p. 162-163. For an astonishingly similar Christian statement *vide* Wilbur M. Smith, *Israeli/Arab Conflict and the Bible*, pp. 9-41.

10 Franz Kobler, *op. cit.*, p. 115.

11 *Vide* the remarks on the origins of absolutism in the legacy of Alexander the Great's political thought in Wallbank and Taylor, *op. cit.*, I, pp. 149-150. Cf. John of Salisbury (ca. 1115-1180), "The Nature of a True Prince," *The Portable Medieval Reader*, edited by James Bruce Ross and Mary Martin McLaughlin (New York: Viking Press, 1964), pp. 251-259. This essay was written in the twelfth century. Also valuable is the shorter and more pointed essay by Frederick Barbarossa (ca. 1122-1190), "The Independence of the Temporal Authority," *ibid.*, pp. 259-261.

12 W. M. Southgate, "James I of England," *World Book Encyclopedia* (Chicago: Field Enterprises, 1964), II, p. 21.

13 H. H. Henson, *op. cit.*, pp. 51-55, 58-62.

14 James McMullen Rigg, *op. cit.*, p. 12.

15 Written in legal French, the dedicatory epistle in Latin, it consists of four volumes. The first surveys jurisprudence with many citations of Plato and Cicero. The second treats common law, customs, statute law; the third, procedure; and the fourth, special jurisdictions (as of bishops,

admirals, etc.). The English version, *Law, or Discoures thereof in Four Books, written in French by Sir Henry Finch, Knight, His Majesty's Serjeant at-law, done into English by the same author* was issued in 1627. James McMullen Rigg, *op. cit.*, p. 13.

16 James Spedding, *Life and Letters of Bacon* (London: Longman, Green, and Longman and Roberts, 1873), VI, pp. 71, 84, 99.

17 Franz Kobler, *op. cit.*, p. 111

18 Johann Jakob Herzog, "Calvin (Latinized form of *Cauvin* or *Caulvin*), John," *The Schaff-Herzog Encyclopaedia of Religious Knowledge* (New York: Funk and Wagnalls Company, 1891), p. 369. It is worth citing the distinguished Professor Herzog in this connection:

> Leaving out of view his correspondence, the writings of Calvin divide themselves into the theological and the exegetical. In regard to the latter, it suffices now to say that they have never been excelled, if, on the whole, they have been equalled. He possessed all the requisite qualifications for an exegete—knowledge of the original tongues, good common sense, and abundant piety. His expositions are brief, pithy, and clear. His theological writings are remarkable for their early maturity and their unvarying consistency. Beside his minor writings, we possess that masterpiece of Protestantism, the *Institutes of the Christian Religion*, which came fully grown into the world, like Minerva from the brain of Jupiter. He really produced at twenty-six a book in which he had nothing to change at fifty-five.

19 [Henry Finch], *The Sacred Doctrine of Divinitie, Gathered out of the Worde of God, Together with an Explication of the Lordes Prayer* (London: [Published by William Gouge], 1599), sheets A6-A8.

20 Reverend Alexander Gordon, "Gouge, William," *DNB*, XXII, pp. 273-275.

21 [Henry Finch], *The Sacred Doctrine, etc.*, sheet A7.

22 Gouge's admiration is unbounded. He writes in a brief dedicatory epistle in *An Exposition of the Song of Solomon* (sheet A):

> To the Author of this Work the Publisher thereof wisheth Grace in this world and Glory in the world to come.

> Right Worshipfull: It pleased you as a testimonie of your love to bestow these your labours on me written with your owne hand: they being mine by a free donation on your part, I think I have power to doe with them what I will. Wherefore I have been bold to publish them; knowing that they are welworth the publishing, and that thorough [i.e., through] God's blessing they may bring much spirituall comfort, and profit to God's Church. Long con-

tinued custome requireth that they should have a Patron. What better Patron can they have then the true proper parent? Who for eminencie of place can adde great countenance vnto them, and for excellencie in learning can maintain them. For mine own part I acknowledge myselfe many waies much indebted vnto your worship. . . .

23 William Gouge, "Preface to the Christian Reader," in [Henry Finch] *An Exposition etc.*, sheets A2, A4.

24 [Henry Finch], *op. cit., passim.* The allegorical language is sensitive, beautiful and extreme. One illustration will suffice. The outspoken sensuality of chapter 4:2-5 he first reproduces then comments (sheets E3-E4):

> *Thy teeth are like a flock of even shorn sheep, that come up from the washing, which all of them doe bring forth twinnes, and there is not a miscarrying one among them.*
>
> *Thy lips are like a thread of scarlet and thy talke is comely: they temples within thy locks are as a piece of pomegranet.*
>
> *Thy neck is as the towre of David, built for armories: a thousand targets hang therein, all shields of mighty men.*
>
> *Thy two brests are as two young hindes; the twins of a roe which feeds among lillies.*

Goe vnto her teeth, they are equall, shining, double rewed, whereby she cheweth the meate of heavenly doctrine, both for her selfe and others. The Law of Grace is in her skarlet lippes, speaking things comely and for edification. Temples like a rose to see to, & of the hew of a Pomegranet, bending beyond the haire. So naturall is her bewty, and her face her owne: for what needth shee the dyings or colourings of worldly glory to set forth her spirituall bewty? or of humane wisdome to adorne the simplicity of the Gospell? Is her face onely and the parts thereof worthy to be commended? doe not the rest as well excell? her neck of holy discipline, and the goverments to assist the ministry of the Worde, and that compleat armour of proofe which every Christian sighteth with, holdesth her vp and keepeth her steddy more strong than all the weapons of any tower of armourrie can doe. Lastly her pappes, plumpe, round, faire, and full of all good nourishment of the sincere milk of the word of God (I Peter 2:2), that flowes from a streame out of both her brests of that olde and new Testament.

25 *Ibid.*, p. 3.

26 *Ibid.*, sheet B.

27   *Ibid.*, pp. 63, 72.

28   *Ibid.*, p. 63.

29   *Ibid.*, p. 124.

30   [Henry Finch], *The World's Resurrection or the Calling of the Jewes etc.* (London: Wm. Gouge, 1621), Frontispiece. A later edition (same year) shows Edward Griffin and William Bladen as publishers.

31   *Ibid.*, sheet 34.

32   *Ibid.*, frontispiece.

33   *Ibid.*, sheets A-A9.

34   The epistle continues in this vein, with praise and blame for the Jews juxtaposed side by side in quick contrast.

35   *Ibid.*

36   *Ibid.*, pp. 24ff.

37   *Ibid.*, p. 6.

38   *Ibid.*, pp. 6-7.

39   *Ibid.*, p. 2.

40   *Ibid.*, pp. 2-6.

41   *Ibid.*, p. 2.

42   *Ibid.*

43   *Ibid.*, p. 60.

44   *Ibid.*, *passim.*

45   *Ibid.*, Heading four.

46   *Ibid.*, p. 194f.

47   Samuel R. Gardiner, "Jame I," *DNB*, XXIX, p. 170.

48   H. H. Henson, *Puritanism in England*, p. 54.

49   *Ibid.*

50   William Haller, The Rise of Puritanism, pp. 51ff. *Vide* also "James I," *The Oxford Dictionary of the Christian Church*, edited by F. S. Cross (London: University Press, 1966), pp. 712-713.

51 Wallbank and Taylor, *op. cit.*, I, p. 560.

52 *Ibid.*, p. 553.

53 *Ibid.*, p. 541.

54 James was himself a biblical expositor on things prophetic. He had a special interest in the book of Revelation and wrote a commentary on it when only twenty years of age (1586) entitled *A Paraphrase Upon the Revelation of the Apostel S. John*. In the "Preface to the Reader," James bishop of Winton remarks:

> I may safely say; That *Kings* have a kinde of interest in that Booke [The Revelation] beyond any other: for as the execution of the most part of the *Prophecies* of that Book is committed unto them; So, it may be, that the Interpretation of it, may more happily be made by them: And since they are the principall Instruments, that GOD hath described in that Booke to destroy the *Kingdome of Antichrist*, to consume his State and Citie; I see not, but it may stand with the Wisedome of GOD, to inspire their hearts to expound it.

In James I, *Workes of the Most High and Mightie Prince, James, King of Great Britaine*. Edited by Iames [Montague] Bishop of Winton (London: Robert Barker and Iohn Bill, 1616), sig. D4r. Interestingly, King James declares:

> The faithfull praiseth God for the Popes destruction . . . and for the plagues which are to light on him and his followers. . . . The Pope by his Pardons makes merchandise of the soules of men. Heaven and the Saints reioyce at his destruction, albeit the earth and the worldlings lament for the same.

Everywhere James calls Rome by the term Babylon. James I, *Workes, etc.*, pp. 47, 57.

55 James McMullen Rigg, *DNB*, VI, pp. 12-13.

Chapter VII

Eminent Attempts to Write an Epilogue to the Doctrine

Until his death in October 1625, Finch remained in embarrassed circumstances. The genealogists note that his son John, from time to time in this short span of less than four years, had to be surety for him in preventing arrest for debt.[1] But neither the fall from favor of the famous author and his publisher, nor their deaths a few years thereafter meant the end of the affair. Records from Parliament reveal a most interesting reaction. In May 1621,[2] among other matters, a bill concerning the Sabbath was introduced. In flowing rhetoric, the term "Lord's Day" is therein advocated as a better alternative to "Sabbath," because as Sir Edward Coke, Chief Justice of the King's Bench and pre-eminent law-writer, put it:

> . . . many were inclined to Judaism and dream that the Jews shall have regiment and kings must lay down their crowns to their feet.[3]

John Pymme, later one of the chief and great leaders in the Great Rebellion, refers directly to the strict observance of the Sabbath by the Traskites and speaks of:

> . . . other opinionists concerning the terrene Kingdome of the Jewes.[4]

Yet more explicitly, Sir Thomas Barrington mentions:

> a book or two . . . lately set forth of the Jews ruling over the world.[5]

A certain Mr. Sheppard, a Puritan member of the House of Commons, on hearing the bill[6] read a second time, and after following the argument for the change it proposed, is recorded to have risen and said:

> This bill is idle and indiscreet, first for the title of it. Everyone knoweth that *Dies Sabbati* is Latin for the Sabbath-day, and *Dies Sabbati* is Saturday, as it is taken in all writs, returns, and amongst lawyers. So as it is no otherwise than if it should be titled, "An Act for the Observing of Saturday, Otherwise called Sunday."[7]

Because of Mr. Sheppard's extreme Puritan sympathies as an advocate of seventh day worship, the bite of his sarcasm was not left unchallenged. Before the session was over Sheppard's defense of the despised *Opiniones Judicae*, here epitomized by his outburst in favor of retaining the term "Sabbath," was punished by forcible physical expulsion from the Chamber. He was returned to it on his knees in humiliation at session's end to hear sentence pronounced on his misdeed by Sir Jeremy Horsey:

> In 35 Eliz. there was preferred a bill into this house, that such as came not to Church on the Sundays should pay, for every Sunday he was absent, 12d. Mr. Sheppard was then called in to the bar, and there on his knees heard his sentence, viz., That the house doth remove him from the service of this house, as being unworthy to be a member thereof.[8]

That feelings over this issue ran at somewhat higher temperature than those normally associated with phlegmatic Englishmen is to say a good deal less than the truth. But again, the temper and circumstances of the time being what they were, such reactions against any and everything smacking of affront to the works and ways of the Establishment were suspect, if not of sedition outright, at least of dangerous insult to Crown and Church. In this way, nonetheless, an essentially irrational and unnecessary challenge to the ideas, not of a Jew but of a distinguished Englishman, denied the word "Sabbath" an official place in England.

Further reaction to Finch's work and his ideas is recorded in two other contemporary documents. Each is noteworthy both for what it says and for its author. The most vehement of the two is the attack made by Archbishop William Laud. Under King Charles I he became the Crown's first minister, chaplain to His Majesty and holder of the dubious distinction as the most cruel, ruthless oppressor of Puritanism and freedom of worship in England.[9]   He chose for his phillipic against

Finch's book (mentioning the author and specific page numbers of the work throughout) the occasion of the King's birthday, preaching before His Majesty on June 21, 1621, at the King's hunting lodge in the forest at Waltham. He chose for his text Psalm 122:6, "Pray for the Peace of Jerusalem."[10] Laud's ill-tempered heaping up of sarcasm and contumely reflects the genius of his personality at its biting best. Upon reading his derision of Finch and the invective he piles line on line, one wonders why Finch did not suffer the same fate of Francis Kett. Ironically, however, that fate awaited Laud himself. Out of the very ideas he that day paraded for to scoff, arose the piety which brought him under the ax on January 10, 1645. But let us hear Laud at length. In content and tone the following passage is representative:

> I had now done with *Rogate pacem*, pray for peace, but that *Jerusalem* is come again in my way. . . .[11] But it is a strange *Jerusalem*. Not the old one, which is literall in my Text, for which *David* would have prayers; not that which succeeded it. *Jerusalem* of *Jew* and *Gentile* converted, for which we must pray: But a *Ierusalem of gold and precious stones* (as is is described. *Apoc.* 21.) *which shall be built for them againe upon earth in greater glo[r]y than ever it was. And this Ierusalem upon earth, is that which is called the Heavenly Ierusalem, Heb. 12:122. And the new Ierusalem, Apoc. 21.2*, [Latter underlined passage italicized by Laud is taken from Finch, pp. 44 and 66.]
>
> So it is not now sufficient that the Jewes shall be (in God's good time) converted to the faith of Christ, as the Apostle delivers it, Rom. 11. *But these converted Jewes must meet out of all Nations: the ten Tribes, as well as the rest, and become a distinct, and a most flourishing Nation againe in Jerusalem And all the Kings of the Gentiles shall do homage to their King* [Finch, p. 79].[12]

After thus reciting Finch's position, Archbishop Laud explodes:

> Good God! What a fine people have we here? *Men in the Moone!* [emphasis his].[13]

His scorn continues:

> I will not trouble you with any long discourse, wherein this error meets with or parts from the Chiliasts; nor is it worth any settled confutation; Onely I cannot desire you *Rogare pacem*, to pray for any peace to this Jerusalem. It was an old error of the *Jewes*, (which denyed Christ come) that when their *Messias* did come, they should have a most glori-

ous temporall Kingdome, and who but they? I cannot say the Author of this vanitie denies Christ come, God forbid; But this must say, that many places of that old Testament, which concerne the *Resurrection* from the dead, and which looke upon *Christ* in his first or second comming, are impiously applyed to this returne of the Jewes, which (saith he) [i.e., Finch] is to them as a Resurrection from the dead.[14]

Whereupon Laud pronounces Finch

. . . an exquisite Arithmetician[15]

because he is able

. . . beside the first coming of Christ in the flesh, and his second to Judgement, (which are all the personall commings of Christ that ever Scripture revealed, or the Church knew) hath found a *Third*, betweene *One* and *Two*, namely, his comming to this conversion of the Jewes.[16]

And his argument continues, citing in order from pages 48, 105, 56 and 75 of Finch's work:

But see a little: I will not be long passing.
Shall *Jerusalem* be built againe after this eversion by the Romans? The Prophet Esay saith *no*, *Esa.* 25. But this (saith our author) is not meant of *Ierusalem, but of her enemies.* Yes, it is meant of *Ierusalem*, as well as other Cities, as appeares *ver.* 6, 7. and is confirmed by Saint Hierome, . . . And suppose the place to be doubtfull, wether meant of Ierusalem or not, yet that other is unavoydable, *Ier 19.11. I will breake this City and this people, as one breakes a potters vessel, that cannot be made whole again.*[17]

The remaining elements of the notion of Jewish restoration are not spared:

For the Ten Tribes comming in to the rest. The Good Man [Finch] should doe well to tell us first; where those ten Tribes have been ever since before the Baylonish Captivity, or poynt out the Story that sayes they remained a distinct people. No: they degenerated, and lived mixed with other nations that captived them, till not onely their Tribes were confounded, but their name also utterly lost, for almost *two thousand years since; And yet now forsooth we shall see them abroad againe.* It is strange we should not know our friends all this while. For within these seventy foure yeares they shall have quite rooted out both the *Pope* and *Turke*, our two great Enemies; And shall begin within less than these thirty years. *I cannot tell here whether it be Balaam that prophesieth, or the Beast he rod on.*[18]

In the concluding portion of his sermon, Laud borrows further from Finch's book, pages 46, 102 and 163, as yet one more jumping off place for his scoff.

> . . . As for the Kings of the *Gentiles* that they shall serve this King of Ierusalem, you neede not beleeve that till you see it. If Christ be King there, I make no question, but the Kings of the *Gentiles* will easily submit to him: But if it be any other, they have reason to hold their own. And it seems it is not well resolved yet, who shall be King; For *pag.* 46 and 102 The *Author* tells us, Christ shall be King there, And *pag.* 163, *One shall be King whom the Jewes shall set up among themselves.*[19]

Finally, Laud links Finch to England's arch enemies, the aggressive Jesuit teachers and missionaries:

> I will follow this vanity no further. Onely doe you not think the Papists will triumphe, that such monstrous opinions are hatched among us? Sure they will; yet they have little reason here: For two of their learned *Iesuits* are of opinion, (they are *Salmer:* and *Lori:*) that the Apostles did not sin, when lead with the errour of the *Iewes*, they thought Christs Kindome should be temporall, Act. 1.6. which is the ground of all this vanity. And *Tullius Crispoldus*, one of theirs, left notes behind him (which are yet in manuscript in the Library at Milan) which agree in all things almost with this present folly. So whatsoever is amisse in this *Iewish* dreame, the *Primogenitus*, the first borne of it, after the *Iew*, is theirs. Onely herein their care out goes ours; They keepe the Frensie locked up, and we publish it *in Print*.
> I will leave these men to their dreame of the *Jewes*.[20]

That the greater share of Laud's tirade is, generously described, argument *ad hominem* is clearly evident. But the ridicule on the part of the learned was not yet over. If in a less spectacular fashion, because his remarks were delivered in Latin in the hearing of only a small coterie of scholars, Regius Professor of Theology at Oxford, John Prideaux[21] took the occasion of his inaugural address to deliver an oration entitled "De Iudaeorum Vocatione," i.e., "The Calling of the Jews." Prideaux thus used the same title for his remarks as Andrew Willett had done some thirty years previous in exorcizing what he thought to be the malevolent notion of Jewish restoration then newly resurrected by Francis Kett. And Prideaux's view of the matter, singling Finch out for special attention and odium, closely resembled that of the Elizabethan scholar. He opens his discourse:

It is known to nearly all, how, amidst our other calamities, Judaism has lately prevailed, to the disgrace of divines and the scandal of the weak. Three opinions are flying about on this subject: that of the madmen, who think that the legal ceremonies to be recalled, that of the dreamers, in whose brains a Jewish monarchie-throne and the frame of a temple are floating; that of the zealots, who are looking shortly for I know not what sublimated doctrine, and doctors more than angelical and seraphic from them [the Jews] were converted. . . .[22]

We need not survey in detail the rest of Prideaux's diatribe. It follows hard on the heels of the contemptuous pattern we have seen practiced by Archbishop Laud. Prideaux goes the same route in scornful rehearsal of Finch's predictions,[23] alluding specifically to Thomas Brightman, "that Chiliast,"[24] and lists Jewish Messianic efforts from the time of Bar Kochba[25] to Solomon Molko.[26] "Such Hebrew roots" says the learned Professor Prideaux, "have been swollowed by some without a grain of salt," adding with regret that some among this group are "otherwise learned and orthodox."[27]

All along the way there is rebuttal consisting in the main of running quotations from Jerome, Augustine, Thomas Acquinas, Duns Scotus, Melancthon, Oecolompadius, Calvin, Luther, Belarmine, and so on,[28] exhausting virtually every theological source up to the day which constitutes, for Prideaux, an "evangelical consensus"[29] against these "devils,"[30] "fanatics,"[31] and "ignorant obdurate apostates."[32] "Such evidence," he states in the last paragraph is "evidence irrefutable."[33]

Finch was silenced. But his "heresy" would not die with him. True, his lamentable experience, with that of his pub- lisher William Gouge, taught other advocates of the idea dis- cretion. And the general repression suffered under the despotic, arbitrary hand of Charles I, and Archbishop Laud, his hatchet man, in the succeeding critical decades until out- break of the Puritan Revolution, taught the lesson of caution. More than one witness, however, rises in this period to give voice to the doctrine. Succeeding history was to show quite mistaken what one might normally assume. Neither Laud or Prideaux, for all the coercive power of their positions, and the mighty blows they indeed did administer, could kill the idea.

To the final episode in our narrative we now turn. We shall discover that the doctrine of Jewish national restoration comes into its own, is held by some of the most illustrious of England's sons, and is reflected in passages of literature from the pen of a genius.

Notes

1 James McMullen Rigg, *DNB*, VI, p. 13.

2 There is a frustrating conflict of dates in the records. Cobett's edition of *Parliamentary History* for the period gives this debate under the date of 1620; Hansard's *Parliamentary History* records it under the date of 1621. The latter seems more likely because Finch's book was itself not published until 1621.

3 Great Britain, *The Parliamentary History of England from the Earliest Period to the Year 1803 (36 volumes), From which Last Mentioned Epoch it is Continued Downard in the Work Entitled "The Parliamentary Debates" (775 volumes to 20th Dec. 1968)* (London: T. C. Hansard *et al.*, 1806 onward), volume I, p. 1190.

4 *Ibid.*, p. 1191.

5 *Ibid.*, p. 1190.

6 Its full title was "An Act for the Keeping of the Sabbath, Otherwise Called Sunday."

7 *Parliamentary History of England, etc.*, I, p. 1190.

8 *Ibid.*, p. 1191.

9 H. Kolde, "Laud, William," *The New Schaff-Herzog Religious Encyclopedia*, VI, p. 421.

10 Archbishop William Laud, "Sermon Preached before His Majesty, on Tuesday the 19. of June at Wanstead, Anno 1621. Psalm 122:6, 7: 'Pray for the Peace of Jerusalem; let them prosper within thy walls, and prosperity within thy palaces,'" *Seven Sermons Preached Upon Severall Occasions* (London: Printed for R. Lowndes, at the White Lion in S. Pauls Church-yard, 1651).

11 *Ibid.*, p. 23.

12 *Ibid.*, p. 24.

13 *Ibid.*, p. 25.

14 *Ibid.*, p. 26.

15 *Ibid.*

16 *Ibid.*

17 *Ibid.*

18 *Ibid.*, p. 27.

19 *Ibid.*, p. 28.

20 *Ibid.*, p. 29.

21 E. G. Hawke, "Prideaux, John," *DNB*, LXVI, pp. 354-355.

22 Notum est fere omnibus, quomodo inter caeteras *fundi nostri calamitates,* invaluit nuper Iudaismus, in *Doctorum* opprobrium, & *Infirmorum* scandalum. Tres circumvolitant hac de resententiae. *Insanientium*; qui *revocanda* censent esse *legalia.* Somniantium, quibus *Iudical thronus monarchiae & templifabrica* natant semper in cerebro. *Zelotarum,* qui nescio quam *sublimatarn Doctrinan & Doctores* plus quam *Angelicos & Seraphicos,* a *convertendis* propediem expectant. John Prideaux, "De Iudaeorum Vocatione," *Orationes Novem Inavgvrales, De Totidem Theologiae Apicibvs, scuitu non indignis, pront promotione Doctorum, Oxoniae publica proponebantus in Comitijs* (Oxioniae: Iohannes Lichfield, and Guilielmus Turner, 1626), p. 110.

23 *Ibid., passim.*

24 *Ibid.*, p. 117.

25 *Ibid.*, pp. 114, 115, 116.

26 *Ibid.*, p. 127.

27 Hujusmodi excitarunt afflatus *radices Hebraica,* sine *grano salis* a nonnullus ingestae . . . quam doleo *viros* alioqui satis *doctos, & orthodoxos* tanti sacere, vt commendatam cuperent. *Ibid.*, pp. 116-117.

28 *Ibid.*, pp. 112ff.; pp. 120ff.

29 *Ibid.*, pp. 111-112, 119.

30 *Ibid.*, p. 125.

31 *Ibid.*, p. 126.

32 *Ibid.*, pp. 119-120.

33 *Ibid.*, p. 128.

Chapter VIII

Acceptance as Respected Doctrine

Continuity of the doctrine of Jewish restoration up to, with and beyond Finch is established by more than the attacks made upon him. In the same year of his book's publication and his imprisonment, in the person and writings of Joseph Mede, or Mead, (1586-1638), the distinguished biblical scholar, after Brightman's death the most celebrated and often quoted protagonist for the idea, we find vigorous advocacy of the idea. Mede, professor of Greek at Cambridge, was a man of widely recognized learning and genuine accomplishment. His many works in philosophy, history, mathematics, physics and the disciplines of antiquities were conspicuous. The British Museum *Catalogue* requires four full folio pages of fine print to list his publications. He twice refused the provostship of Trinity College, Dublin, as well as numerous official positions, preferring to remain a teacher.[1] To his extensive correspondence we owe considerable debt for direct information on our topic. He writes to Sir Henry Stuteville:

> Christ's College Camb. March 31, 1621.
> Sr.
> . . . Sr Henry Finch was last week examined before the High Commission about the book he wrote *(The World's Great Restauration)*, but wonderful privately. He gave up his answer in writing, which was sent to the King, & expected from him what should be his censure. . . .[2]

A week later another letter follows:

> Christ's College Apr. 7 [1621].
> Sr.
> . . . I have seen Sr Henry Finch's *The World's Great restauration, or Calling of the Jews, & with them of all the Nations of the Earth, to the Faith* of Xt. I cannot see but for the main of the discourse I might assent unto him. God forgive me, if it be a sin; but I have thought so many a day.

But the thing, which troubles His Majesty, is this point, which I will write out for you *verbatim*; "The Jews & all Israel shall return to their land & antient Seats, conquer their *foes*, have their Soil more fruitfull than ever. They shall erect a glorious Church in the Land of Judah it self & bear rule far and neare." . . . We need not be afraid to aver and maintain, that one day they shall come to Jerusalem again; be Kings & chief Monarchs of the Earth; sway & govern all, for the glory of Xt; that shall shine amongst them. And that is it Lactantius saith Lib. 7. Cap. 15. *The Romans name I will speak it, because it must one day be, shall be taken from the Earth, & the Empire shall return to Asia. And again, shall the East bear dominion & the West be in subjection.* In another place Ashur & Egypt, all these large & vast Countries, the whole tract of the East & South, shall be converted to Christ; the chief Sway & sovereignty remaining with the Jews. All nations shall honour them.

Some say the King says he shall be a pure King, & he is so auld that he cannot tell how to do his homage at Jerusalem.

This with my best respect,
Yours ever,
Joseph Mead.[3]

Mede's fame as an expositor rests chiefly on his *Clavis Apocalyptica*,[4] bearing thematically on the doctrine here in view.[5] Beside the direct remarks on the point in the two excerpts from his letters which we have already seen, in *The Key to the Revelation*, Mede alludes to our idea in outlining his scheme of "Synchronisms" for the events pictured in that book. The "scattering of that holy people [i.e., the Jews] at length finished . . . that last of wonders"[6] will be consumated and the "New Jerusalem, that beloved city," shall serve as "the seat of the Imperial Kingdom of the Lord God Omnipotent."[7]

The striking thing about Mede is the residual power of his influence in the views of subsequent writers and times, manifest by continuing scholarly interest in him to the present day. The following remarks were written so shortly ago as 1968, commenting on Mede in this particular connection:

> Mede's work became very popular in England and he can be credited with the revival of premillennial studies in the English speaking world. Other expositors were to alter his approach but he re-established and popularized the study of the literal kingdom of God in modern thought.[8]

The same year that Mede's *Clavis Apocalyptica* was first published (1627), there appeared in England another work in Latin, *Diatribe de mille annis Apocalyptica*, which had been published in Frankfort, Germany, written by the celebrated reform theologian and professor at Wittenburg and Herborne, Johann Heinrich Alsted, (1588-1638).[9] In it Alsted takes cognizance of and cites "Master Mede's work"[10] with high praise. The author consumes 276 pages cataloguing biblical evidence and "antient authority" from "the earliest expositors downward" on the point that the content of millennial doctrine, including conversion of the Jews and their national restoration,

> . . . is no novell conceit, new broached fancy, or an opinion started up yesterday, *De millenaria felicitate doctrinam non esse novam hesternam.*[11]

Interest here is in the fact there was exchange of knowledge and study of the works in this field between the continent and Great Britain. This reciprocity seems to have been accomplished rather quickly for Alsted's work and Mede's (i.e., the Latin originals), as we have seen, come on the scene but a few months apart. And Alsted's *Diatribe de mille annis etc.* aroused more interest in England than it did in his native Germany. Antagonistic English writers are found tarring him with the same brush that they used on their own millennarian scholars. Note the following title of a work written in 1645, from the pen of Thomas Hayne:

> *Christs Kingdome on Earth, Opend according to the Scriptures. Herein is examined what Mr. Th. Brightman, Dr. J. Alstede, Mr. I. Mede, Mr. H. Archer, The Glympse of Sions Glory, and such as concurre in Opinion with Them, hold Concerning the Thousand Years of Saints Reign with Christ, And of Satan's Binding: Herein also Their Arguments Are Answered.*[12]

The most significant contribution of Alsted's, however, is not the circulation among and the virtual identification of his work with that of British writers on our topic but in the unique destiny he ascribes to the doctrine. In Alsted's mind, millennial teaching is a Christian philosophy of history. In a ruminating kind of way he approaches the matter in summing up his material:

> The Questions arising in this . . . can be reduced to one quest.: whether there shall be any happiness of the Church here upon earth before the last day; and of what kinde it shall be.?[13]

The answer to the question thus posed, is for Alsted an unqualified Yes! History has no meaning unless it is going somewhere and unless it has an end (goal) and that end be in this world. Reason requires that history ought not be finally adjudicated and terminated until all its known possibilities have been fulfilled within the admitted limits imposed by that which is finite and sinful. Should there not be an age in which the unrealized and worthwhile dreams of mankind will at last come, *in* and *through* time on earth? If there is a God in heaven, if life which He created on earth is not something evil per se, then human history must come to some worthy consumation. Otherwise human life is irrational, very much like the proverb of the man building a great staircase. Step by step he sets it up, laboring wearily, often suffering painful reverses because of tragic hazards and poor materials. Now at last it is finished. But lo and behold, it is a stairway that goes no place! It is just a staircase and nothing more. But, says Alsted, the clear statements of Scripture and the reason of man in his finest moments and aspirations will not support this. Our minds and hearts can not and will not accept it. Belief in the biblical millennium as a part of history, lays a basis for a truly feasible, satisfying and coherent view of life here and now. It says that in spite of the tragedy of sin, life is something worthwhile; all efforts to make it better are worthwhile. The reason? Because all the true values of human life will be preserved and carried over into the coming Kingdom; nothing worthwhile will be lost. In the midst of opposition, corruption and reverses, man has assurance that help is on the way, help from heaven, when righteousness, justice, love shall reign supreme — "Give the King thy judgements, Oh God . . . In his days shall the righteous flourish . . . All nations shall call him blessed" (Psalm 72:1, 7, 17).[14]

That such a sublime vision reached deeply into the public imagination in every direction, penetrating well into and through intellectual circles too, is evident from the striking trace of them to be found in one of the greatest literary documents of the epoch. None other than Francis Bacon alludes to the millennial ideas of Henry Finch in his *New Atlantis* (originally written in Latin sometime between 1614-1617).[15]

While like his predecessor Roger Bacon, Sir Francis aimed chiefly at divorcing science from sheer authority and Scholasticism, and at the same time wrote brilliant essays about everyday matters, he sallies forth in highly imaginative, speculative description of a Utopian form of society.[16] In *New Atlantis* Bacon concentrates on technological advances and shows the importance of science in society, outlining his own new cultural plan based on the expected benefits. His narrative introduces us to a Jew who takes him to the "father of Solomon's House" and the latter then address him (hence also the reader) concerning the goals, preparation, function, ordinaces and rites of that ideal civilization which Bacon is forwarding. Of note to us here are the goals:

> The end of our foundation is the knowledge of causes, and secret motions of things and the enlarging of the bounds of human empire, to the effecting of all things possible.[17]

He anticipates flying machines, submarines and many other improvements in medicine, surgery, meteorology, mechanical contrivances etc.[18] The touchstone of interest to us is the frame of reference within which Bacon couches his tale. His ideal society is centered around "Solomon's House" or, as it is elsewhere identified, "The College of Six Days Works".[19] Moreover, he makes a certain Jew, named Joabin, a merchant of Bensalem, the name for the civilization, tell the story of the Jews living in that country, where they are true to their religion but also acknowledge the Divine mission of Jesus, calling him the "Milken Way" or the "Elijah of the Messiah."[20]

> By that time six or seven days were spent, I was fallen into straitacquaintance with a merchant of that city, whose name was Joabin: he was a Jew, and circumcised, for they have some few stirps of Jews yet remaining among them, whom they leave to their own religion, which they may the better do, because they are of a far differing disposition from the Jews in other parts. For whereas they hate the name of Christ, and have a secret inbred rancour against the people among whom they live; these contrariwise give unto our Saviour many high attributes, and love the nation of Bensalem extremely. Surely this man of whom I speak, would ever acknowledge that Christ was born of a virgin, and that he was more than a man; and he would tell how God made him ruler of the seraphims which guard his throne: and they call him also the Milken Way, and the Eliah of the Messiah, and many other

high names; which though they be inferior to his Divine Majesty, yet they are far from the language of other Jews. And for the country of Bensalem, this man would make no end of commending it, being desirous by tradition among the Jews there, to have it believed, that the people thereof were of the generations of Abraham by another son, whom they call Nachoran; and that Moses by a secret cabala ordained the laws of Bensalem, which they now use; and that when the Messiah should come and sit in his throne at Jerusalem, the king of Bensalem should sit at his feet, whereas other kings should keep at a great distance. But yet, setting aside these Jewish dreams, the man was a wise man and learned, and of great policy, and excellently seen in the laws and customs of that nation.[21]

It seems justified to say of this passage that we have before us from the mind of an acknowledged genius, at least a reflex of the ideas of and surrounding Jewish restoration which we found in Henry Finch and others before him—and this in the millennial-utopian context of the whole book. The author does not poormouth the Jews on any account, rather he puts words on their tongues which place them in as good a light as possible. Moreover the fancied milieu and the vocabulary, out of which the tale is spun, is rich with terms and allusions to things Jewish and Old Testament in origin. Bacon, who also suffered imprisonment in 1621 (the same year as Finch's downfall) in consequence of charges made against him, may perhaps be reflecting notions gained from his colleague at law and former collaborator. Whatever the details of the influences on Bacon or his sources in this connection—which cannot certainly be known—we are able to use this unusually candid statement as a good indication of just how thoroughly these ideas had become incorporated into the spiritual life of England in that day. We have come a long way from the despite in which Francis Kett was held for the timerity of his suggestion that the Jews were to be restored to their ancient national home.

As a certain biblical teaching and future reality seen of the prophets, the doctrine had had few friends and many enemies. What we have seen from Sir Francis Bacon's pen signals a far more lively conclusion than that which the early protagonists for the idea, by the merits of their arguments and their tenacity, could have hoped to accomplish, viz., the task of unearthing the idea and bringing it to acceptance as respected doctrine. The work was done by men who had been born and lived in the Elizabethan age, although much of the pertinent literature was not published until the reign of James I, and in some cases not translated into English from Latin until even later.

The hour for further development struck with the riotous events of 1640/41 and the approaching Civil War. Thomas Brightman's works were reprinted. An anonymous tract detailing "Mr. *Brightman's* stupendious Revelations"[22] appeared in early 1641. Hanserd Knollys in the same year in his *Glimpse of Syons Glory etc.* refers with approval to most of the Jewish restoration advocates we have met in the course of our study.[23] The Fifth Monarchy Men sound a provocative expression of the idea in their expression of an imminently approaching New World Monarchy.[24] Robert Maton issues his blunt manifesto, *Israel's Redemption*[25] and answers the challenge to it shortly thereafter with a fuller explication in *Israel's Redemption Redeemed.*[26] The learned Divines Nathaniel Holmes and Henry Jessey collect funds for needy Jews in England and Jerusalem and praise the Jewish people in numerous references to Jewish restoration in their writings on Christian Eschatology.[27]

But most instructive is that the great historian of the epoch, Thomas Fuller, in his remarkable *Pisgah-Sight of Palestine and the Confines Thereof etc.*,[28] published in 1650, in the final section of the book treating "The Jews fancy of a temporall kingdome"[29] refers to the doctrine as:

> . . . a conceit of the modern *Jews,* that one day they shall return under the conduct of their *Messias* to the Countrey of *Canaan,* and city of *Jerusalem,* and be re-estated in the full possession thereof.[30]

And here yet once more, nearly thirty years after the tragic events, Fuller traces the English version of this "conceit" back to:

> One Author [who] so enlargeth the future amplitude of the Jewish State, that thereby he occasioned a confining to himself. His expressions (indiscreetly uttered, or uncharitably construed) importing, that

all Christian Princes should surrender their power as homagers to the temporall supreme Empire of the Jewish nation.[31]

In a marginal note he identifies the "Author" to whom he has just referred as:

> M. *Finch* in his Book of the Calling of the Jews (published by *Will. Gouge D. D. Anno* 1621) for which he was imprisoned.[32]

But Fuller's criticisms, like those of Willett, Laud, Prideaux *et al.* before him, were too late, destined to be mere chronicle. The planted seed had sprouted, grown, and was beginning to bear fruit. One response to the doctrine among Englishmen was the intercession in 1648 of the pious Baptists Johann Cartwright and her son Ebenezer in their *Petition of the Jewes: For Repealing of the Act of Parliament for their Banishment out of England*. This spirit was given momentum by the Jewish community in the person of Manasseh ben Israel through his book *Hope of Israel* and his negotiations with Cromwell for the readmission of his coreligionists. The list of distinguished advocates grew apace at an amazing rate: Johann Amos Comenius, Isaac Newton, John Milton, James Harrington, Lord Protector Oliver Cromwell himself and so on and on and on.

As observed at the beginning of the investigation, we have now confirmed. There is much reason, indeed, to be

> . . . amazed at the number, the continuity and the authority of the works in question, stretching back in unbroken sequence as far as the seventeenth century [and as we have seen even beyond]. There can be no doubt that these publications played a considerable part in the evo-lution of the Zionist idea.[33]

Further than this we are not to go in the present study. It is another story.

Manasseh Ben Israel and the Readmission of Jews into England

While we have completed our study of the aborning of Jewish restoration as a biblical motif—in some cases taking quasi-political forms—in nonconformist thought and theology, there is a singularly interesting sequel which deserves mention in the present context: Jewish readmission into England. It is quite true that in characteristic English pattern this event was anything but a clearly executed *de jure* decision but was rather a *de facto* connivance. The forces and persons which brought it about are something as follows:

1. The exodus of Sephardic Jewry from Spain and Portugal subsequent to the decrees of 1492 and 1496 respectively was further intensified by the introduction of the Tribunal for Inquisition in these two countries in 1531. Maranos who had remained behind found existence in the Iberian peninsula unbearable. They fled: To the east — Naples and Venice, Saloniki and Constantinople, Fez, Tlemcen, Algiers and Tunis, Cairo and Alexandria, Jerusalem and Safed, Damascus and Smyrna; to the north — Amsterdam and Hamburg; almost every shore washed by the Mediterranean Sea, as well as the new continent of America and its isles, the Portuguese-Galician, Castilian and Catalan dialects could be heard on the lips of Jewish exiles. We turn our attention to the North Sea area, the Netherlands specifically.

2. When Charles V of Spain attempted to introduce the Inquisition into the Spanish possessions in the Netherlands, he did not anticipate the tenacity with which his high handed ruthlessness would be resisted. The northern provinces of the Low Countries declared their independence (Utrecht 1579) and won it after a bitter, bloody struggle. The defeat of the Spanish Armada a decade later (1588) further weakened Spain and precipitated another freshet of Marano immigration to this new republic in the Netherlands. Toleration was available there to the extent that we find a thriving, though relatively small, Jewish community "possessed of ample means, and engaged in commercial enterprises which redounded to the welfare of Amsterdam," their principal place of residence by the opening years of the seventeenth century.[34]

3. Within that community there had been two synagogues. A third synagogue was established (1618) when a dissident group withdrew after being offended by the stern lecturing of one Rabbi Isaac Uzziel at certain of his congretation's moral lapses. To the office of Rabbi and prominence in this latter

synagogue in 1622 arose one Manasseh Ben Israel. On this man of fertile imagination, and fecund, if also shallow, pen, the hinge of this Jewish episode of history swings.[35]

Manasseh Ben Israel (1604-1657) surpassed his colleagues in the Amsterdam Rabbinical college by his wide, albeit superficial, erudition, his versatility, and his interests which were attracted beyond the pinched limits of his immediate surroundings and community. He established a Hebrew press to supplement his meager income as a spiritual leader and earned something of a reputation as an homiletician. In an extended attempt to broaden into business ventures that would bring a more comfortable living he associated himself in a growing circle of relations with men of affairs, Jewish and Christian, at home and abroad, among them none less than the learned queen Christina of Sweden.[36]

With a certain mystical bent, and with the better part of his mature years already spent on a work called the *Conciliator* (*El Conciliador*, written in Spanish) in which supposed contradictions in the Scriptures were reconciled, Manasseh evidenced a strong attachment to the Bible and a similar kind of piety which we have before noted among various nonconformist spokesmen in Christian England.[37]

In particular, the millennarian doctrines of the Fifth Monarchy men, among others, struck a sympathetic chord in the heart of Manasseh—just as somewhat later, Puritan chiliasts quoted him in support of their thesis regarding the soon to be instituted Kingdom of God. A lively correspondence between Manasseh and the English Puritans was carried on concerning their common interest, with the double consequence of friendly concern each for the other's cause: Puritans for the Jewish presence in England, and in Manasseh's mind a growing hope in a near approaching day of Jewish deliverance.

In a small book entitled *The Hope of Israel*, Manasseh outlines the themes which he had come to hold in common with his Puritan sympathizers: The scattering of the Jewish people was complete—Manasseh accepted quite uncritically the theory that the indians of the New World were not aboriginal but the last Israelitish Tribes (migrated, according to this hypothesis, across Asia and into the Americas); moreover, that Scripture tended to show the incomplete nature of the restoration under Cyrus; and that signs of the final, future deliverance had been multiplying (mass expulsion, torture etc.).[38]

In the meanwhile England had become republican (1649). Lord Protector Cromwell had an eye to things immediately useful as well as to things divine. The commercial value of the Jews was a lesson from history Cromwell had, apparently, learned well. Overtures were made, therefore, by the British government to the Jewish community in Amsterdam and Manasseh was invited to come to England (1652). Matters were temporarily stalled, necessarily, by the anti-Dutch sentiment of merchant classes in England who feared enterprising Dutch competition, also by Royalist sympathies among the Jews of Amsterdam who had no love for regicide, and by the Dutch war. But finally in May 1655 a second invitation was extended and in October of that year Manesseh arrived in England as the guest of the Protector of the Commonwealth.[39]

From his lodgings in the Strand, Manesseh submitted his *Humble Address* to Cromwell in which he appealed for Jewish readmission into England. The Messianic thesis was strong in his plea. But stronger still, predictably, were the more concrete considerations of the tangible benefits to England's welfare that would accrue from Jewish presence.[40]

Cromwell was favorably disposed and saw personally to the convening of a great conference of statesmen, lawyers and theologicans at Whitehall in December 1644, to discuss the matter in all its aspects. The deliberations were inconclusive. There was opposition from London merchants who were understandably wary of Jewish competition in trade, and from the narrow perspectives of many of the clergy. Nonetheless, Cromwell was able to elicit from the lawyers present that nothing in English law prevented Jewish resettlement. The question of desirability had hung too heavily in the atmosphere. Hateful innuendo and other demurrers of this sort seemed to subject action to indefinite postponement. Official governmental sympathy had not been sufficient for clear-cut resolution of the issue.[41]

From the advantage of historical perspective, however, this very lack of an outright *de jure* motion worked to Jewish advantage. War with Spain in 1656 brought the question of Marano loyalty to a climax. When in 1656 a court test was settled in favor of one Antonio Rodrigues Robles, to wit, that he was, in fact, fleeing the Inquisition, and, hence, not a subject to the Spanish crown any longer, the Jewish community threw off her mask and declared her colors, both religiously and politically. Former Jewish allegiances were no longer suspect.[42]

This was back-door admission, it is true. Manasseh had failed to win open readmission for his co-religionists. He had returned to Amsterdam disappointed and broken in spirit. Worse still, he died before events vindicated his labors. Yet that very failure in his mission brought better results, probably, than had he been officially successful. An official act would, almost certainly, have been accompanied by special legislation placing some kind of onerous disabilities on the Jew compared to other citizens. Thus the Jews had been spared by typical English compromise, illogical, left handed, inconsistent, but unexpectedly satisfactory.[43]

Notes

1 "Of his character, scholarship and eminence there is no doubt." Froom, *The Prophetic Faith of Our Fathers*, II, p. 522. William Chappel, Bishop of Cork and Ross writes, "*Mr. Meade* is as judicious a man in Ecclesiastical antiquities and as accurately skilled in the first fathers of the Church both Greek and Latin, as any man living." E. N. H., "The Life of Joseph Mede," *Clavis Apocalyptica* (Dublin: Robert Moore Tims, 1831), p. xvii.

2 Robert Folkestone Williams, *The Court and Times of James the First* (London: H. Colburn, 1848), II, p. 250.

3 *Ibid.*, p. 251.

4 I.e., *The Key to the Revelation*, written in Latin, published first in 1627, then again in that tongue in 1632 and 1642 respectively, before translation into English by Richard Moore in 1643. The edition used here is a reissue of Moore's translation, published in Dublin by M. Goodwin in 1831. It is also contained in his collected *Works* published in 1648, 1669 and 1672 respectively.

5 In addition, Mede's *The Apostacy of the Latter Times* (London: Samuel Man, 1644), and his *Daniel's Weeks* (London: M. F. for John Clark, 1643) are laterally related as well.

6 Joseph Mede, *The Key to the Revelation*, p. 56.

7 *Ibid.*, p. 57.

8 Robert Clouse, "The Apocalyptic Interpretation of Thomas Brightman and Joseph Meade, *Bulletin of the Evangelical Theological Society*, volume eleven, No. 4, Fall, 1968, p. 190.

9 A. Heppe, "Alsted: Johann Heinrich," *A'llgemeine Deutsche Biographie* (Berlin: Duncker and Humblot, 1967), pp. 254-255. Alsted published extensive works in theology, paedagogy, physics, philosophy, rhetoric. British Museum *Catalogue*, volume I, pp. 165-168. As recently as 1910, Alsted's life and work was the subject of a book by Percival R. Cole in the field of education: *Johann Heinrich Alsted: A Forgotten Educator* (Sydney, Australia: Teacher's College Press, 1910).

10 Johann Heinrich Alsted, *The Beloved City or, The Saints Reign on Earth a Thousand Yeares; Asserted and Illustrated from LXV. places of Holy Scripture; Besides the judgement of Holy Learned Men, both at home and abroad. and also*

Reason it selfe. Written in Latine by Ioan. Henr. Alsedius, Professor of the University of Herborne. Faithfully Englished; With some occasionall notes. And the Judgement herein (not only of Tycho Brahe, and Carolus Gallus; but also) of some of our owne famous Divines (London: n.p., Printed in the yeare of the last expectation of the Saints., MDCXLIII), p. 80.

11 *Ibid.*, p. 247.

12 Published in London by Richard Cotes for Stephen Bowtell.

13 Johann Heinrich Alsted, *The Beloved City etc.*, p. 33.

14 *Ibid.*, pp. 33ff. For a remarkably parallel statement from our own time *vide* Alva J. McClain, "A Premillennial Philosophy of History," *Bibliotheca Sacra*, vol. 133 (April 1956), pp. 111-116; also *The Greatness of the Kingdom* (Chicago: Moody Press 1959, 1968) pp. 527-531.

15 Reverend Professor Fowler, "Bacon, Sir Francis," *DNB*, II, pp. 344, 350.

16 The present writer's copy of Bacon's *New Atlantis*, interestingly, is bound in one volume with Sir Thomas More's *Utopia*. Bacon's work parallels in content by way of scientific-technological description what More's work does in terms of sociological description.

17 Sir Frances Bacon, *The New Atlantis* (London: Joseph Rickerby, 1838), p. 252.

18 *Ibid.*, pp. 253ff.

19 *Ibid.*, pp. 234ff.

20 *Ibid.*, pp. 243ff.

21 *Ibid.*, pp. 243-244.

22 *Brightman's Predictions and Prophecies* (London: n.p., 1641), p. 2. The present writer has a xerox copy of this tract in his library. It consists of a long poem (supposedly written in 1595) predicting the calamity and misery soon to befall German, Scottish and English Christianity for their sloth at reform. The Thirty-years War was in progress on the Continent at the time of the tract's publication and the Puritan call to arms was soon to be sounded in England.

23 Thomas Goodwin [Hanserd Knollys], *A Glympse of Syons Glory: or, The Churches Beautie Specified* (London: William Sarner, and are to be sold at his Shoppe at the Signe of the Golden Anchor neere *Pauls*-Chaine, 1641), *passim*.

24 The most representative is John Archer's *The Personall Reigne of Christ upon the Earth* (London: Benjamin Allen, 1642).

25 Robert Maton, *Israel's Redemption, Or, the Jewes generall and Miraculous conversion to the faith of the Gospel: and returne into their owne Land: And our Saviours personall Reign on Earth, cleerly proved out of many plaine Prophecies of the Old and New Testaments* (London: Matthew Simons, 1642).

26 Robert Maton, *Israel's Redemption Redeemed, Or the Jewes generall and Miraculous conversion to the faith of the Gospel: and returne into their owne Land: And our Saviours personall Reigne on Earth, cleerly proved out of many plaine Prophecies of the Old and New Testaments. And the Chiefe Arguments that can be alleged against the Truths, fully answered: Of Purpose to satisfie all gainsayers: and in particular Mr. Alexander Petrie, Minister of the Scottish Church of Roterdam. By Robert Maton, the Author of Israel's Redemption. Divided into two Parts, whereof the first concernes the Jewes Restauration into a visible Kingdome in Judea; And the second our Saviours visible Reigne over them, and all other nations at his next appearing. Whereunto are annexed the Authors Reasons, for the literall and proper sense of the plagues contain'd under the Trumpets and Vialls* (London: Printed by Matthew Simons, and are to be sold by George Wittington at the blew Anchor neere the Royall Exchange, 1646).

27 A. C. Bickley, "Holmes, Nathaniel," *DNB*, XXVII, pp. 193-194. Alexander Gordon, "Jessey or Jacie, Henry," *DNB*, XXIX, pp. 370-372.

28 Thomas Fuller, *A Pisgah-Sight of Palestine and The Confines Thereof With the History of the Old and New Testament Acted Thereon* (London: Printed by J. F. for John Williams at signe of the Crown in Paul's Church-yard, 1650).

29 *Ibid.*, p. 194.

30 *Ibid.*

31 *Ibid.*

32 *Ibid.*

33 Cecil Roth, "The Challenge to Jewish History," *op. cit.*, p. 20.

34 Max L. Margolis and Alexander Marx, *A History of the Jewish People* (New York: Harper and Row, 1927), p. 488.

35 E. N. Adler, "Manasseh Ben Israel," *Jewish Quarterly Review* (April, 1904).

36 Margolis and Marx, *op. cit.*, p. 490.

37 Cecil Roth, "The Mystery of the Resettlement," *Essays and Portraits in Anglo Jewish History* (Philadelphia: Jewish Publication Society of America, 1962), pp. 86-107. A most intriguing essay.

38 Margolis and Marx, *op. cit.*, p. 492.

39 Margolis and Marx, *op. cit.*, p. 493.

40 Joseph Jacobs, "Manesseh Ben Israel," *Jewish Encyclopaedia*, Volume VIII, p. 284.

41 Cecil Roth, *History of the Jews*, p. 302.

42 Margolis and Marx, *op. cit.*, p. 443.

43 For numerous, brief pieces of material on Manasseh and Cromwell, the details of the negotiations between them and other related information, consult the volumes and indices of the *Transactions of the Jewish Historical Society of England*.

Chapter IX

Concluding Statement and Summary of Data

At this juncture in our study, we would do well briefly to survey in broad spectrum fashion some of the more likely causative forces at work behind the events, men and ideas outlined in the preceding chapters. An effort of this kind will give us a margin of understanding of the literature in the context of the times. We have been looking mainly at specimens of individual trees, now let us get a look at the forest.

Hebraic Influence on Doctrine and "Judaizing" in Christian Reform Movements

While in intent it is something of an old canard, there is partial truth in the often expressed hermeneutic sentiment that exegetic literalism leads to the "realm of Judaism." In almost every Christian epoch, therefore, hyperbolic use of the term "Judaizing" has caricatured close study of the Old Testament literary sources of Christian faith—albeit usually in a derogatory sense because the product of such study frequently came up antithetic to religions' vested interests. Both Old and New Testaments, hence, have been "rediscovered" from time to time by Christian reformers and in the conspicuous strainings of numerous sectarian movements after legitimacy.

Of primary interest to us here are the motives which resulted in the shift of gravity from the New Testament and from Pauline doctrine to the Hebrew Scriptures on the part of such radically committed, dogmatically orthodox Christian groups as existed in British nonconformity, as we have seen, primarily among the Puritans of this period. In the Reformation generally a small but important group of Christian scholars gave to the study of Hebrew considerable attention. This interest grew rapidly apace in the face of highly esteemed opinions otherwise conconcerning its dubious value, as e.g., the expression that overmuch energy applied to Hebrew scholarship would mean a revival of Judaism among Christians which is attributed to none other than the great Erasmus.[1]

The motives which impelled a given group or scholar to emphasize Hebrew studies appear to have varied with the special interests of the day. The primary reason that Biblically oriented Christian students plunged into the study of the Old Testament, was, transparently and logically enough, to get at the foundations of Christian origins and literature. The Gospels' meaning "opened up" when one came to them with an apprehension of the Hebraic influences and sources which ramify all through them.

True, there are certain anomalous evidences to the contrary. Luther, with typical idiosyncracy, was willing on the one hand to bear the slur of his Papist enemies as a "Jewish-patron," "Half-Jew," "Judaizer" and even "Semi-Judaeus" because he used Rabinnical commentaries and sought individual Rabbinical opinions in revising his translation of the Bible (on more than one occasion he invited learned Jews and Jewish students into his home and to his table), and on the other hand he insisted that "not a knowledge of [Hebrew] grammar but of Holy Things is necessary to translate the Hebrew scriptures."[2] While Luther's early attitude toward Jews and things Jewish was ambivalent, his later feelings are notorious for their vitriol. Other students of Hebrew, as the great Reuchlin, Luther's contemporary, and even much earlier in the person of the Franciscan scholar of the thirteenth century, Roger Bacon, do not seem to have turned on their Jewish teachers after Luther's manner. Reuchlin, in particular, in the Pfefferkorn controversy, was upbraided by fellow Christians for not sufficiently hating the Jews.

Be this as it may, Hebraic studies took hold. In more recent times, this chief early impetus has borne much fruit in a scientific and academic interest in Hebrew as a language within the larger context of that family of languages and disciplines commonly called by the broader term "Semitics."

A second impetus to Hebrew studies was simply in the additional firepower and substance it made available for Christian polemicists and apologists to call upon in the religious arena. The arguments of Jewish controversialists who could cite at will the Hebrew text, interpret words, and even letters, in a manner contrary to accepted Christian doctrine, with not infrequent recourse to the abstruse esoterica of the Kabbalah, was a source of considerable embarrassment and consternation. Refutation of these evidences was simply impossible without access to the materials on the basis of first hand knowledge. The urgency of safeguarding one's reputation, position and religious views lent energy and passion to the pursuit of this new sector of information. Substantiation of the truth of religion was a matter of particularly great moment.

Side by side the fervid apologetic drive and the disinterested, purely scientific-linguistic motives, there was the nearly overweening strength of steadily growing evangelical temperament. We misunderstand the piety of the day entirely if we underestimate the tremendous power of the desire to make converts. The supreme goal was to convert Jews. The consummation of mundane history, as many Christians saw it, was to be ushered in by massive Jewish conversion. By demonstrating the parallelism, and in as many cases as possible, the identity, of Christian and Jewish teaching, great hopes were nourished of a soon approaching climax in nothing less than Jewish national conversion.

It is true that these underlying reasons to the "why?" of Hebrew studies as sketched here are oversimplified, are certainly not mutually exclusive of one another nor can they be traced to a precise kind of logical or historical continuity. There is good evidence, however, that they were universally felt and active, if in widely variant degrees of application, times and places. Moreover, they give us the major clues for understanding the motives behind the voluminous Old Testament and Hebrew studies of the primary Reformers, Luther, Calvin and Zwingli.[3] Matters theological were, we recall, the most ardently courted objects of affection of the age, a fever which spread comprehensively across northern Europe. That the atmosphere of the debates which ensued was often as acrimonious as it was arid, does not seem to have blurred its contagious influence.

The community marriage in England of unprecedented biblical zeal, of high eschatological expectations, and of the specifically British nonconformist desire to fuse Christian prophetic-apocalyptic visions with the nation of Israel, seems by natural propagation to have issued in the infant movement for Jewish restorationism which we have met already.[4]

With these facts in mind, we are not unduly surprised to find Puritans in England (and America)[5] seeking to restore to prominence and practice, in life and principle, literal observance of Old Testament precepts, sometimes going so far as to supplement them with Rabbinical injunctions. The Sabbatarian groups and emphases which we have observed in the research are an explicit example of the outworking of these forces.

While it is historically necessary, in the present writer's judgment, to distinguish between the religion of the Old Testament and what is known as Judaism, it is also necessary to say quite frankly that Christianity has since its birth contained strong, strictly Jewish elements. Direct influences and shaping from the Jewish person and from Jewish literature have played leading roles in this organic process—incidently, one which appears in our own day to be receiving fresh, reciprocal impetus and attention.

This basic fact of our study is virtually uncontested however much resented or suspected of sinister overtones on the part of some.[6] Luther, Calvin and Zwingli each had Jewish "acquaintances" from whom they learned.[7]

In England, however, with a very few exceptions, Jews in-the-flesh were almost unknown in the period of our study. Newman tells us that "the number of English Hebraists contemporary with and after Roger Bacon is not large."[8] We note that Bacon died in the same decade as the decree banishing Jews from England (1290). Three hundred years stands between Bacon and the front chronological borders of the present investigation. We are forced to look elsewhere for an explanation, therefore, than to the handful of Maranno families or the few converted Jews in the universities which dotted the scene.

The Hebraic ethos, in terms of its immense impact in England, was indeed greater for a sustained period of time than anywhere else, but its strength, in the main, lay in the genius and spirit of its literature, especially the power of the writing prophets, as these fit the eschatological-apocalyptic character of the day. Confirmation of the high but uniquely literary thrust to British Hebraism is represented in Richard de Bury, Bishop of Durham, in his famous *Philobiblion* (1345), where he expresses "uncommon regret" at the ignorance of Hebrew grammar which prevailed among his peers—especially the clergy.[9]

Moreover, the prominence attained in Britain by the Christian doctrine of the end of the world amidst a people positively transformed by the Bible, mixed with unquenchable faith in the miracle of the new birth[10] produced a unique belief in a special spiritual destiny for England. This is unanimously recognized by historians. George Macaulay Trevelyan—his voice but one among many—does not hesitate to say that the effect of continual domestic study of the Bible on the national character, imagination and intelligence was greater than any literary movement in England's annals or any religious movement since the life and work of Saint Augustine.[11]

When Cromwell, struggling in the ideological and physical warfare of the Interregnum, likened himself to Joshua or Gideon, his heart had been worked upon by the spirit of the Old Testament, not by the enervating, nitpicking casuistry of the Christian Scholasticism of his time. When his troops were animated, as Cromwell reports, by marching into battle singing Psalms, they had become the host of God. The numerous pamphlets and sermons which proclaimed variations on the theme of England and Israel paralleled, and the immense popularity of biblical names merely expressed the universality of the public's permeation with the great themes of the Old Testament. What to us now is only a curiosity or humorous footnote on this non play-it-cool, uncharacteristic non-phlegmatic episode in England's past, was deadly in earnest then — to the point of searching for and seriously using in several instances the remote biblical names of "Shear-Yashub" and "Maher-Shalal-hash-baz," for children.

Cromwell and Milton among many others were great lovers of the Old Testament. Puritan theology was guided in the whole by a fierce reliance upon the inspiration of the Bible. To the Puritan, the Bible was not only complete but also a final communication from God to man. We see this clearly in the Westminster Confession:

> The whole Council of God concerning all things necessary for his own Glory, Man's Salvation, Faith, Life, is either expressly set down in Scripture, or by good and necessary Consequence may be deduced from Scripture. Unto which nothing at any time is to be added, whether by new Revelation of the Spirit or Traditions of Men.[12]

The Puritans saw their revolt as akin to the Maccabean uprising, as the Waldensians and Hussites had before them. Laud's persecution in the machinery of the High Commission was paralleled to Jewish sufferings under Antiochus Epiphanes.

That Puritan England had also shared in the general revival of Hebrew letters which accompanied the Reformation across the channel on the Continent we have already seen. From the late years of the sixteenth century to the middle decade of the seventeenth century, Hebraic studies flourished greatly:

> During no period of equal length since the Revival of Letters has the knowledge of the Hebrew language apparently been so much diffused throughout the literary world as this.[13]

The Mosaic Code was frequently introduced in attempts to make it the fundamental law of the land. Some of Cromwell's officers suggested to him that he appoint seventy members of his Privy Council to accord with the composition of the old Jewish Sanhedrin. The Leveller sect announced its descent from the "Jewish race," called their opponents "Amalekites" and "Philistines." In sum, public life was so deeply flavored of Hebraic influence that one writer comments, "if only in Parliament speeches had been made in Hebrew, you might have believed yourself in Palestine."[14]

From the cumulative effect of this outlook on life, these spiritual and emotional foundations, these kinds of scholarly, social, religious and political institutions, to say that Puritan England had many points in common with the old Hebrews — whom they strived so strenuously to emulate — is to practice the art of understatement. The taking over by Englishmen to themselves of the Divine promises and prophecies bearing on the regathering of the children of Israel is predictable. Their own future appeard to them in the reflection of these ancient aspirations. Their vision was of the New Jerusalem as the supreme goal of their special struggle and pilgrimage. Zion thus became the symbol and image of their national future. John Milton has put it best and in its essence:

> Why else was this Nation chos'n before any other, that out of her as out of *Sion* should be proclaim'd and sounded forth the first tidings and trumpet of Reformation to all *Europ*.[15]

This notion of a spiritual destiny in the New Jerusalem appears best explained on the basis of this deeply anchored, profound reverence for the Word of God reinforced by the doctrine of predestination as expounded in the prevailing Calvinistic theology. The eager anticipation of this coming Zion cannot be explained on the basis of an allegorical or intellectual-philosophical ideal. Rather, it was to them, as to the early Christians, a cherished conviction in concrete geographical reality. Only this would satisfy their view of theodicy. The New Jerusalem was to bear out the prophecies, taking the place of Rome, as a spiritual reality in men's hearts and an earthly realm where the Messiah would reign in righteousness, justice and peace.

In retrospect, however, where the human equation is involved, as here, the laws of cause and effect, sufficient reason, etc. are difficult fully to satisfy. This is particularly true where the facts of one's religious convictions (or today, the suspicion of same) are such major factors in the equation. The "mystery" of the new birth in Christian faith and the concomitant doctrines of spiritual appropriation of the promises of God in the person and life of the individual through the indwelling power of the Holy Ghost, have, from time to time, led to heroics on the part of believers which would otherwise be inexplicable. The Old Testament Prophets themselves, as observed by the nonconformist, were very emphatic about God's activity in the realm of space-time history. Not all that occurs in man's worldly affairs, they maintained, is explainable on the basis of natural cause and effect, that is, on the basis of economic, military, psychological and kindred forces. Secular man, and most modern men, explain all of history this way, but the Bible does not. The Puritan saw that the Bible spoke of a true, space-time history which God has made. A history in which the interplay of cultural thought, military power, economic forces, and so forth, God worked in and through for His own good pleasure: Judgment in some cases, blessing and reward in others. Jeremiah, for one, pictured in vivid detail the strong forces of contemporary Egypt and Babylon and tremendous internal forces within his own nation as the handmaids of God's eternal purposes, one of which was immediately pending punishment upon Judah. The pious Scripturalists of England were similarly convinced: A holy and loving God really exists, and He works into the significant history which exists. He works on the basis of His character and the obedience of the elect. He is working in the events of our day. He is working in me (us). We have a special destiny to fulfill. God plus one (me) makes a majority. The cause is right; righteousness depends upon its accomplishment; God has specially endowed this nation (me) to act to this (God's) end. It will (must) come to pass. We shall bring it to pass. We are God's elect. Our faith makes us so and recent history demonstrates that we are.

Whether or not the men of our study were thus constrained and propelled, or were merely actors moving to a script written by natural forces in the continuing drama of human history is a conclusion, of course, which the reader will make for himself. But before we dismiss such a conception as impossibly unscientific, if not downright obscurantist, we do well to recall the enormous impact of the Jew himself, and his Christian antitype, the Puritan, on the civilization in which we presently live. Both groups were (and their descendants continue to be) minuscule in proportion to the mass of the rest of the resident population, are equally small in power of a real or concrete sort, in all, are truly minute, except in the abiding power of their spiritual and ethical and specifically religious preachment and practicum.

Summary Statement

Unique forces in Elizabethan and Stuart England (specifically here 1585-1640) prepared the way for the birth and early development of the idea of Jewish national restoration. Chiefly in the context of biblical exposition and theological discussion.   Throughout the period Bible based themes became more and more an endemic part of the culture, outlook and language of the people of Great Britain.

The rise of nonconformist parties, particularly the Puritans, was marked by increasingly greater stress upon the notion of the absolute truth of Scriptural teaching. This stood in opposition to the central principle of expediency, the moral myopia, the doctrinal broadness and laxity in the episcopacy of the established Anglican Church. Using historico-grammatical exegesis, the struggle for reform fastened its attention on prophetic content to the point of identification with the Old Testament nation of Israel. The apocalyptic character of the times pressed into the forefront God's promises of certain victory to the faithful, punishment on the wicked and a cosmic consumation of His eternal, Divine, immutable decrees (Calvin) in the Kingdom of Christ.

To these pious Scripturalists, the prophet's vision of a revivified Jerusalem where justice and righteousness reigned supreme in the millennial Kingdom of Christ was more than a blessed hope; it was something concrete and immediately pending. Its realization was the sublime duty of every genuine believer to strive to usher in. Nothing, therefore, touching this Biblical doctrine could be spiritualized away.

The despised *Opiniones Judicae* regarding Jewish restoration, of hermeneutic necessity, were revived from long burial and ecclesiastical disapproval.

In the literature under study the idea is broached in the course of a tract by Francis Kett (d. 1589) which covers the whole of systematic theology. The notion of Jewish restoration appears in his discussion of God's attributes (moving hence to the necessity of keeping prophetic promises). Opposition was immediate and vitriolic. Distinguished theologian and Anglican divine Andrew Willett (d. 1621), attacks the idea and Kett as one. The next stage is achieved in Thomas Draxe (d. 1618) who answers Willett and defends Kett on the ground that God *must* restore Israel to vindicate the integrity of His covenant and the majesty of His name otherwise sullied by man's sin. Draxe was also an advocate of toleration for Jews and their readmission to England. Systematic treatment is acheived in the writings of Thomas Brightman (1552-1607). He documents the idea massively and is thereafter referred to by successive authors on the topic.

Development is extended by the works of Giles Fletcher (1549-1611), ambassador to Russia, in the publication of them by Samuel Lee (1625-1691) in 1677, more than sixty years after the death of the author. Fletcher sees the Ten Lost Tribes as involved in the coming national restoration and speculates on their identity. Lee catalogues proof texts, quotes the classics of Jewish writers, Church fathers, natural history and geography in support. An anonymous tract *Newes from Rome etc.* (1606-7), translated out of Italian, speaks ominously of calamitous events soon to transpire and of a great army of Hebrew warriors about to retake their ancient home. Its unknown author confirms the participation of the ten lost tribes in the restoration.

Contiguous with this development is the life and writing of Sir Henry Finch (1558-1625). In his *The World's Great Restauration* he treats all aspects of the notion and refers specifically to preceding works. Joseph Mede (1586-1638) the eminent biblical scholar commends and confirms Finch's work in his private correspondence and his *Clavis Apocalyptica* (1627).

In the meanwhile, Oxford theologian John Prideaux in his inaugural address (1621), Archbishop William Laud in a sermon (1621) before King James, and Sir Edward Cook *et al.*, in House of Commons debates (May 1621) on a bill regarding the Sabbath, deride the idea and heap contumely on Finch. But instead of writing an epilogue, these prominent opponents, by their unjust derision, give the idea publicity and a highly visible martyr. In the same years, Johann Alsted (1588-1638) publishes in Latin his *Diatribe mille annis Apocalypticis* (1627) referring with approval to previous writers and recording corroborative evidence from the earliest Biblical commentators as well as those more recent.

Sir Francis Bacon (1581-1626), a former colleague of Finch, reflects the idea and its millenial dimensions in his Utopian essay *The New Atlantis* (written ca. 1614-1617). As late as 1650 the great historian Thomas Fuller refers to Finch, Finch's difficulties and, to him, the foolishness of the doctrine.

But the idea would not die. It went on to gain increasingly wide support in substantially the same forms we have thus far seen develop among succeeding generations of learned divines, *literati*, statesmen, men of affairs, etc., ultimately to blossom and come to fruition in frank Zionism of the kind seen in Lord Balfour.

Herzl and Zionism

When Theodor Herzl stepped into the foreground there already existed a 300 year history of Jewish restoration in Great Britain. Biblical exegetes represented in the persons of such Pastors as Alexander McCaul and Edward Bickersteth, the most notable of a very long list, had continued writing voluminously on the topic. No less creative figures than Robert Browning and George Eliot had spoken out with considerable passion on the idea, Browning poetically in his *Holy Cross Day* and Eliot in her novel *Daniel Deronda*, the latter a pinnacle of British sentiment for Jewish Restoration.

But now, even though the evidence before us is admittedly brief as an economy of representative facts, it is no longer in the light of accident that we find Herzl expressing himself in this connection by calling England the "Archimedian Point," nor that he met the Chaplain to the British Embassy in Vienna, an ardent restorationist, the Reverend William H. Hechler, during the first fateful congress there (1896), when the Zionist movement was born in that city. Hechler assured Herzl that "devout Christians would help the Jews return to

Palestine," and substantiated it with introductions to Kaiser Wilhelm II, arranged numerous meetings for Herzl in Christian circles, accompanied him to the Congress in Basle (1897), and travelled with him on Herzl's historic visit to Palestine. When Herzl recorded these words about Hechler16 in his diary, he signified the predestined crossroads of the British movement for Jewish national restoration and Jewish Zionism.

Notes

1 G. H. Box, "Hebrew Studies in the Reformation Period," *The Legacy of Israel* (Oxford: The Clarendon Press, 1953), pp. 315-375. Erasmus, however, the above sentiment to the contrary, was the perfect embodiment of the Renaissance spirit, but in his case distinctly allied to sincere moral purpose. As one of the fathers of the modern science of textual criticism he brought a great desire to ascertain the literal and original meaning of the Bible's writers, sans the abhorrent *a priori* allegory and mystic gobbledy-gook so long forwarded by the schoolmen. He frankly declares that the real meaning of the text can be had only in study of the original language. He points out that the theologian is not above the laws of grammar. Interpretation depends a great deal more on sober application of accepted principals in syntax, grammar, knowledge of metaphor, etymology, etc., than the inspiration of the divine doing the exegesis.

2 Louis Israel Newman, *Jewish Influence on Christian Reform Movements* (New York: Abraham's Magazine Service Press, 1966), p. 623. A fuller savoring of Luther's ambivalent attitude comes from his *Table Talks*, edited by Preserved Smith (New York: The Pilgrim Press, 1915), p. 249:

> "The Hebrew tongue is altogether despised because of impiety or perhaps people despair of learning it. Without this language there can be no understanding of the Scriptures, for the New Testament is full of Hebraisms; it is rightfully said that the Hebrews drink from the fountains; the Greeks from the streams, and the Latins from the pools. I am no Hebrew grammarian, nor do I wish to be; for I cannot bear to be hampered by rules, but I am quite at ease in the language; for whoever has the gift of tongues . . . has a wonderful gift of God. The translators of the Septuagint were unskilled in Hebrew; and their version is poor even though literal.

3 The reader is referred to the weighty work of Newman's cited above for thorough source documentation of Jewish influence in the continental Reformation, especially in the lives and work of the three "mainliners," Luther, Calvin and Zwingli. It is a superb work.

4 For a fuller explanation of the special outworkings of these forces and the unique way they seemed to combine and apply all at once in British nonconformity rather than in the fits and starts fashion common in

various Reform and Lutheran communities on the continent—consult again chapter three.

5   William Edward Hartpole Lecky, *Democracy and Liberty* (New York: Longmans, Green and Company, 1896), I, p. 67. Lecky's often quoted statement, "Hebraic mortar cemented the foundations of American democracy" is a significant tribute.

6   Lamentably, there are modern day descendants of the old Marcionites.

7   Jewish "teachers" is too strong a term for some Christians to accept.

8   Newman, *Jewish Influence on Christian Reform Movements*, p. 89. Newman traces significant Jewish influence in England back to the large settlement of Jews who had come to England through the invitation of William the Conqueror (reigned 1066-87).

9   Richard de Bury, *Philobiblion* (Los Angeles: University of California Press, 1948), p. 35. The present writer was introduced to de Bury's *Love of Books* in his undergraduate encounter with Greek. De Bury's passion for grammar went to the length of great personal expense in providing both Greek and Hebrew grammars for his students and in the bequest he left to the Oxford University Library.

10 The new birth, or regeneration, is the doctrine which teaches an inner-creating of fallen human nature by the gracious sovereign action of the Holy Ghost (John 3:5-8). The Bible conceives salvation as the redemptive renewal of man on the basis of a restored relationship with God in Christ, and presents it as involving a radical and complete transformation wrought in the soul (Romans 12:2, Ephesians 4:23) by God the Holy Ghost (Titus 3:5, Ephesians 4:24), by virtue of which we become "new men" (Ephesians 4:24, Colossians 3:10), no longer conformed to this world (Romans 12:2, Ephesians 4:22, Colossians 9), but in knowledge and holiness of the truth created after the image of God (Romans 12:2, Ephesians 4:24, Colossians 3:10).   James I. Packer, "Regeneration," *The Baker Dictionary of Theology* (Grand Rapids: Baker Book House, 1966), p. 440.

11 George Macaulay Trevelyan, *England Under the Stuarts* (New York: G. P. Putnam's Sons, 1933), p. 60. He adds, significantly, "While other literary movements, however noble in quality, affected only a few, the study of the Bible was becoming the national education" (p. 61).

12 *The Westminster Confession of Faith* (Edinburgh: Watson, 1719), I, paragraph vi, p. 6.

13 Henry Hallam, *The Literature of Europe* (London: John Murray, 1847), pp. iii, 444.

14 Werner Sombart, *Jews and Modern Capitalism* (New York: G. P. Putnam's Sons, 1913), p. 250.

15 John Milton, *Areopagitica* in *Works of John Milton* (New York: Columbia University Press, 1931), III, p. 341.

16 There seems little doubt that Hechler is the man glorified by Herzl in his *Altneuland* as the tolerant English preacher Hopkins. Incidently, Hechler survived Herzl, the man whose prophet he was. Living in London on a small pension, Hechler witnessed in his old age the consummation of that alliance between British restorationism and Jewish Zionism of which he had been one of the architects. The Balfour declaration is partly, hence, a monument to the Reverend William H. Hechler and a belated tribute to the pioneers and martyrs of the idea of Jewish national restoration whom we met in our study.

Appendix I

A Glossary

The following terms are defined in general conformity to standard dictionary[1] usage within the present field of study. In any case, the definitions below apply throughout the investigation. Items are listed alphabetically.

ANTICHRIST. The prince of Christ's enemies. In the New Testament he is referred to by name only in I John 2:18, 22; 4:3 and II John 7 (where he is identified with those who deny the Incarnation). Many see him, however, in the strange beasts of Revelation, and in the "man of sin" of II Thessalonians 2:3-10 who will appear after a great apostasy before "the day of the Lord" and sin in God's sanctuary, claiming to be God. In this latter sense he is frequently found in the literature of Nonconformity often with the further identification as the Roman Pope.

CHILIASM. (χίλοι, 'a thousand'). Another name for Millenarianism (q.v.), the theory the Christ will return to earth and reign here for a thousand years before the final consummation of all things. The doctrinal basis for this belief is derived chiefly from Daniel and Revelation (especially from the use of the term in Revelation 20).

ESCHATOLOGY. (from ἐσκατος, 'last', and λόγος, 'discourse'). As used here the term applies to the doctrine of last things. In all probability the term does not appear to have been used in England before the nineteenth century. It connotes that part of systematic theology which deals with the final destiny both of the individual soul and mankind generally. In the Old Testament eschatological teaching is closely bound up with the Messianic hope (q.v.), especially in Daniel, but also in many of the prophets, e.g., Isaiah, Ezekiel, Zechariah, and some of the Psalms (e.g. 49 and 73), and in the latter chapters of Job. In the New Testament it is the subject of many of Jesus' Parables (tares among the wheat, the drag net etc.). In Mark 13 and Matthew 24 it is the dominant theme. St. Paul often treats of it, especially in I and II Thessalonians, where it is portrayed in vivid imagery. Eschatology in this sense is also the main subject of the book of Revelation. The use of the term in modern theology to signify the incursion of the supernatural into man's mundane predicament in a crisis encounter with God is a radically different denotation. This use in the dialectical theology of Karl Barth, Emil Brunner, the New Testament "demythologizing" of Bultmann *et al.* is constantly being reformulated, and is sometimes given yet more distinctive sense as realized eschatology, i.e., man though living in time and history can participate existentially in the "Eschaton" inwardly in the soul.

HERMENEUTIC(S). (from ἑρμηνεύω, 'to interpret'). The science of the methods of the right interpretation of Scripture. It is a preliminary to Exegesis, which applies the rules found by hermeneutics. Its first object is to establish the way by which the reader arrives at the true meaning expressed in the words of the Bible. For finding the true sense there exist many natural aids to interpretation, such as textual, linguistic, cultural, historical, and even psychological, studies. The older orthodox exegetes, both Roman Catholic and Protestant, considered themselves bound in application of these means by a strict doctrine of Scriptural inspiration, which was held to imply that no statement made by an inspired author could contain a falsehood, while Roman Catholic hermeneutics was, and is, further controlled by the consent of the Fathers and the analogy of faith, according to which no biblical statement can contradict a doctrine of the Church. In Christian antiquity the science of hermeneutics hardly existed, though rules for the interpretation of Scripture were framed during the controversy between the Alexandrian and Antiochene

Schools, especially by Origen and elaborated by Tychonius and in St. Augustine's *De Doctrina Christiana*.

JUDGEMENT. In Christian theology, the final judgement on mankind after the Resurrection of the Dead at the Second Coming of Christ. The occasion of God's final sentence on humanity as a whole, as well as His verdict on both the soul and body of each individual.

KINGDOM OF GOD/CHRIST. The roots of the conception of the Kingdom of Christ or God (ἡβασιλεία τοῦ θεου) in Christ's teaching and elsewhere in the New Testament lie in Hebrew thought, according to which the word translated 'Kingdom' (χιςδυ) means rather the possession or exercise, rather than the sphere of kingship. God was eternally king (Psalms 97, 99, etc.) in heaven. But owing to the existence of godless heathen empires His kingship was not visibly and outwardly effective on earth, though it would become so at the 'Day of the Lord' or the Day of Final Judgement. Its establishment would involve the punishing of the wicked, especially the overthrow of heathen political powers and the transference of power to the 'saints,' i.e., Israel (understood in both literal and spiritual fashion, literally as a restored nation of Israel and typically, or spiritually, as the Church, of which, Old Testament Israel was the prefigurement), who would henceforth be ruled by God himself, or by God's Anointed One, the Messiah (Christ).

MILLENARIANISM. The belief in a future 'millennium', or in a thousand years associated with the Second Coming (q.v.) of Christ, during which He will reign upon earth in a kingdom of His saints and at its conclusion take them with Him into heaven. Its biblical bases are found principally in the books of Daniel and Revelation but also by inference in other scattered texts. It has had orthodox and heretical proponents, among the former Irenaeus, Justin Martyr, and Hippolytus of Rome, among the latter, the Gnostics and the Montanists. It received what was almost a death blow from Origen, chiefly in his spiritualizing hermeneutic, and was not extant through the Medieval epoch except among various persecuted groups as the Waldenses and Cathari. At the Reformation and following in growing number since, the Anabaptists, Moravians *et al.* reinitiated millennial doctrine and it swelled into a strong chorus among various of the Nonconformists in the late sixteenth century and first half of the seventeenth century in England.

NONCONFORMITY. Refusal to conform to the doctrines, polity or discipline of any Established Church. Originally in the seventeenth century, and in this investigation specifically, used of those who agreed with the doctrines of the Church of England as comprised in the 39 Articles but refused to conform to its discipline and practice, particularly in matters of ceremony. The term as generally applied since, as well as in the period of its origin, has come to be applied to all dissenters of Protestant sympathy in a generic sense, e.g., Independents, Puritans, Presbyterians, Congregationalists, the Ranters, Quakers, Levellers, etc., including groups that have become mainline denominations as Methodists, Baptists, etc., etc. The term "recusants" is reserved to Roman Catholic dissenters from the Established Church of England.

PRAEMUNIRE. The title of statutes (first passed in 1353, 1365 and 1393) which were designed to protect rights claimed by the English crown against encroachment by the Papacy. The name can denote the statutes, the offence, the writ, and the punishment. The statute of 1353 forbade the withdrawal from England of cases which should be decided in the king's courts, and the penalties prescribed in 1393 stiffened and extended to any who should promote any Papal bull or excommunication. In consequence, appeals to Rome dwindled. In 1529 Henry VIII claimed that T. Wolsey's activities as Papal legate infringed this statute, and, alleging that the acquiescent clergy were no less guilty, in 1531 blackmailed them into submitting to the Royal Supremacy. Elizabeth used Praemunire to deal with purely civil offences and with Roman Catholic recusants; and James I's judges used it to assist the encroachments of temporal upon ecclesiastical courts. A peer charged with Praemunire cannot claim to be tried by his peers, but must submit to trial by jury.

PURITAN(S). The more extreme English Protestant or Nonconformist who, dissatisfied with the Elizabethan Settlement (*vide infra* THIRTY-NINE ARTICLES), sought a further purification of the Church more along lines of the Genevan model from supposedly unscriptural and corrupt forms. Although never in the majority numerically, they were powerful and influential, especially among the mercantile classes of the last years of the sixteenth century and first several decades of the seventeenth century. They demanded express Scriptural warrant for all details of public worship, believing that all other forms were popish, superstitious, idolatrous and anti-Christian. They attacked church ornaments, vestments, surplices, rochets, organs, the sign of the cross, prelacy, ecclesiastical courts, and put corresponding emphasis on preaching, Sunday observance, Church government by presbyters, and the 'tablewise' position of the altar. The term itself, never had a precise use and ceased to be applicable after 1660.

RESURRECTION. The doctrine that at the Parousia or Second Coming (q.v.) of Christ, departed souls will be restored to a bodily life and the saved will enter in glorified bodies upon the life of Heaven. According to St. Paul in I Corinthians 15 and always in the teaching of believers, the doctrine of resurrection in this sense is the most rudimentary element in Christianity. Without it the entire Scripture and faith informed thereby is invalid.

SECOND COMING/ADVENT OF PAROUSIA OF CHRIST. ($\pi\alpha\rho\text{ου}\sigma\acute{\iota}\alpha$) 'presence' or 'arrival'). In its English form, parousia, the term is employed (following New Testament usage) to denote particularly the future return of Christ in glory ('the Second Coming') to judge the living and the dead, and to terminate the present world order. Primitive Christianity believed the event to be imminent and this belief has been revived from time to time throughout the history of the Church. The prevailing Christian testimony has been to maintain the certainty of Christ's return to end the present order, and mark the entry of redeemed men into resurrection-life in Heaven but also to oppose speculation as to exact time and manner of the Advent. In the Judgment humanity will be confronted by the risen and glorified Christ. The notion of a period of millennial reign on earth of Christ and His believers when He returned, was in early Christian circles associated with this theme and has continued among piestic and evangelical groups.

THEOLOGY. (θεολογία), literally, the 'Science of God'. In its Christian sense it is the science of the Divinely revealed religious truths. Its theme is the Being and Nature of God and His Creatures and the whole complex of the Divine dispensation from the Fall of Adam to the redemption through Christ and its mediation to men by His Church, including the so-called natural truths of God, the soul, the moral Law, etc., which are accessible to mere reason. Its purpose is the investigation of the contents of belief by means of reason enlightened by faith (*fides quaereus intellectum*) and the promotion of its deeper understanding. Catholic theology differs from Protestant theology in that it also admits the authority of tradition, the utterances of which are accounted binding, whereas Protestant theology, in so far as it is conservative, is circumscribed by the biblical revelation. Liberal Protestant theologians, however, recognize the existence of no revelation except in so far as it is confirmed by the conscience and reason of the believer. In the course of time, theology has developed into several branches, among them dogmatic, historical, and practical theology. The methods of classification of the sub-disciplines, however, fluctuate in different theological systems.

THIRTY-NINE ARTICLES. The set of doctrinal formulae finally accepted by the Church of England in its attempt to define its dogmatic in relation to the controversies of the sixteenth century. The earlier stages were the Ten Articles (1536), the King's Book (1543), and the Forty-Two Articles (1553). In 1563, Convocation (official council of bishops in the Church of England) issued the first text of the Thirty-Nine

Articles. In their final form (1571) the Articles gained synodical approval through Convocation. The Articles are not a statement of Christian doctrine in the form of a creed, nor mere exposition of a creed already accepted. They are, rather, short summaries of dogmatic tenets, each article dealing with some point raised in current controversies and laying down in general terms the Anglican view.

Notes

1 Perhaps the most recognized and widely used is *The Oxford Dictionary of the Christian Church*, edited by F. L. Cross (London: Oxford University Press, 1957).

Appendix II

Important Bibliographical Tools

Bibliography of British History: *Tudor period 1485-1603, Stuart period 1603-1714.* Issued under the direction of the American Historical Association and the Royal Historical Society of Great Britain. Oxford: University Press, 1928-33. Two volumes. Tudor period, 1485-1603, edited by Conyers Read. 1933. 467 pages; Stuart period, 1603-1714, edited by Godfrey Davies. 1928. 459 pages. In 1909 the Royal Historical Society and the American Historical Association undertook the compilation of a bibliography of British history from 1485. A joint committee of the two societies had the bibliography in hand for many years and the Tudor and Stuart volumes are the results of their long, intensive work. Each of these two volumes is alike in general plan with a select classified subject list, with author indexes, of book, pamphlet and document material in the field, with a liberal inclusion of articles in periodicals and society transactions. They are useful as the most satisfactory bibliography of the periods yet produced but do have inaccuracies in titles, a number of misprints, some of which are serious enough to be misleading. Some corrections are listed in the London University Institute of Historical Research *Bulletin* 11:80-84, 1933.

Bishop, William Warner. *A Checklist of American Copies of "Short-Title Catalogue" Books.* Second edition. Ann Arbor: University of Michigan Press, 1950. 203 pages. Compiled as a convenient guide to the location of Pollard, Regrave's, *Short-Title Catalogue of Books Printed in England, Scotland and Ireland, and of English Books Printed Abroad, 1475-1640*[1] titles in American libraries. It uses STC numbers to indicate holdings in some 110 libraries and collections. The second edition includes corrections and additions to the list in the first edition published in 1944 and records the holdings of ten more libraries.

Catalogue of Books in the Library of the British Museum Printed in England, Scotland, and Ireland, and of Books in English Printed Abroad to the Year 1640 by the Department of Printed Books of the British Museum. London: British Museum, 1884. Three volumes.

Williams Library, London, Early Nonconformity 1566-1800. 12 volumes. Boston: G. K. Hall, 1968. The Dr. Williams' library was opened in 1729. Dr. Daniel Williams (c. 1643-1717) was a Presbyterian minister, first in Ireland and then in London. In his will Williams had given detailed instructions for the charitable use of his fortune, and almost as an afterthought left his books as a public library. It was the early trustees' perspicacity that led them to realize its future possibilities, so that now the Library possesses some 112,000 volumes including a copious collection of manuscripts, pamphlets and periodicals. The Library has long specialized in the fields of theology, ecclesiastical history and philosophy. As the origins and age of the Library might suggest its central concern is the collection of books and pamphlets printed in and concerned with the early period of English Nonconformity. The 12 volumes of the published bibliography consists of a shelf list of books in the library printed in English between 1566 and 1800, together with related works from Scotland, Ireland, Wales and New England, which include the works of nonconformist divines, whether theological or not, those by laymen where relevant, those of Anglican and Roman Catholic writers where relevant, and works of a general historical or philosophical nature where bearing on Nonconformity. The Catalogue, published in 12 volumes, is in three parts, entries are under author, subject and date, with cross references and identifications of many authors, editors and writers of prefaces, etc., hitherto anonymous. This last feature affords a particularly fine bibliographical tool in screening for and locating materials on the topic at hand.

Early English Printed Books in the University Library, 1475-1640 by the Cambridge University Library. Cambridge: University Press, 1900-07. Four volumes. Includes 7750 titles, arranged by presses, with full indexes of authors and titles, printers and stationers, engravers and painters, towns, portraits, music.

Halkett, Samuel and Laing, John. *Dictionary of Anonymous and Pseudonymous Literature.* New and enlarged edition by James Kennedy, W. A. Smith and A. F. Johnson. Edinburgh: Oliver and Boyd, 1926-34. Seven volumes. A comprehensive list, arranged alphabetically by first word of title not an article, giving for each item listed: title (sometimes shortened), size, paging, place, date, author's name and (in some cases) the authority for attribution of authorship. The best for English works, always to be used as a first aid.[2]

Catalogue of the McAlpin Collection of British History and Theology. Union Theological Seminary, New York City. Compiled and edited by Charles Ripley Gillett, 1927-30. Five volumes. Valuable for historical, theological material published from 1500-1700. Arranged chronologically with alphabetical author and title index.

Dictionary of National Biography. Edited by Leslie Stephen and Sidney Lee. London: Smith and Elder, 1908-09. Reissued 1938. Sixty three volumes. With period volumes of supplements, Eratta and indices. Constitutes the most important reference work for English biography, containing signed articles by specialists, and excellent bibliographies. Articles are adequate, i.e., important names are treated at great length, minor names more briefly, and are generally reliable and scholarly. Scope includes all noteworthy inhabitants of the British Isles and the Colonies, exclusive of living persons; includes noteworthy Americans of the Colonial period. The supplements bring the record down to 1940 together with some additions and insertions to earlier volumes.

Pollard, Alfred William and Redgrave, G. R. *Short-Title Catalogue of Books Printed in England, Scotland and Ireland, and of*

English Books Printed Abroad, 1475-1640. Compiled with the help of G. F. Borwich *et al.* London: London Bible Society, 1926. 607 pages. Frequently cited as STC. The most comprehensive record of English books for this period including approximately 26,500 editions. Arranged alphabetically by authors and other main entries; gives, for each item, author, brief title, except for reasons of space, size, printer, date, reference to entry of the book in the Stationer's registers, and indication of the libraries possessing copies. This last important feature aims to record all known copies of very rare items and in case of commoner books a selection in representative British and American libraries and collections. The total number of libraries referred to is 148 (133 British, 15 American).

Roth, Cecil. *Magna Bibliotheca Anglo-Judaica; A Bibliographical Guide to Anglo-Jewish History.* New edition, revised and enlarged. London: Jewish Historical Society of England, University College, 1937. 464 pages. Classified by topic. A revised edition of *Bibliotheca Anglo-Judaica* compiled by Joseph Jacobs and Lucien Wolf (London, 1888). In two parts: part 1, "Histories" consisting largely of secondary works; part 2, "Historical material" listing primary sources usually up to the year 1837, though material on the reform movement is extended to 1842 and on Jewish emancipation to 1858. Includes the material on the study of Anglo-Jewish history in the Mocatta Library and the allied collections housed in University College, London.

Transcript of the Registers of the Company of Stationers of London 1554-1640. London Stationer's Company. Edited by Edward Arber. London: privately printed, 1875-77; Birmingham, 1894. Five volumes.

Whitley, William Thomas. *A Baptist Bibliography.* A register of the chief materials for Baptist history, whether in manuscript or in print, preserved in Great Britain, Ireland and the Colonies. Compiled for the Baptist Union of Great

Britain and Ireland. London: Kingsgate Press, 1916-22. Two volumes. Locates copies in 31 libraries, mainly British.

Winchell, Constance M. *Guide to Reference Books*. Seventh edition. New York: Columbia University Press, 1951. With four supplements 1950-52, 1953-55, 1956-58, 1959-62. A bibliography of bibliographies by category with author-title index. Each entry gives descriptive and functional details. A continuation of *Guide to the Study and Use of Reference Books* (1902) by Alice Bertha Kroeger in turn revised, enlarged and reissued as *Guide to Reference Books* by Isadore Gilbert Mudge (1917, 1928, 1929, 1936). *The Guide to Reference Books*, eighth edition is a newly reissued continuation of Constance M. Winchell's work under guidance of Eugene P. Sheehy. Greatly enlarged, revised, incorporating supplements of the 7th edition, 1964; First Supplement (1965-66) issue of 1968. Chicago: American Library Association.

Wing, Donald Goddard. *Short-Title Catalogue of Books printed in England, Scotland, Ireland, Wales and British America and of English Books Printed in Other Countries, 1641-1700*. New York: Printed for the Index Society by the Columbia University Press, 1945-46. Three two-part volumes. Published as a continuation of Polland and Redgrave's *Short-Title Catalogue . . . 1475-1640*. Items are located in more than 200 libraries; relatively common books are given five locations in Great Britain and five in the United States in as varied geographical areas as possible in order to provide convenient locations for scholars in various parts of the country. It is not a census of copies and it is only when less than five copies are located in either British or American libraries that any deduction can be drawn that copies mentioned are all that are to be found. Location symbols are not those used by STC nor the Union Catalogue, but follow a system devised by Mr. Wing. The scope and method of selection and entry are described in the preface which should be carefully read before the book is used in order not to misinterpret or misunderstand the information given. There are a few errors and omissions, but if used with the caution that Mr. Wing himself advises, the work should prove an invaluable addition to the bibliographical apparatus of English publications, as it covers a period for which there has been no adequate bibliography.

Notes

1 Hereafter abbreviated per standard reference use as STC.

2 It should be observed further that there are many reference books on the supposed authorship of anonymous and pseudonymous works. They differ considerably in function and authority, which value depends upon comprehensiveness within a given field or discipline, the quality (as well as quantity) of research that was invested in their manufacture, especially upon the listing of authorities for author attribution. This last element is of particular import for questions of authorship are frequently a matter of keen dispute and more often very difficult to establish. Where reasonable doubt exists listed sources ought to be checked before a decision is reached. For a discussion of a selected list of such reference books *vide* "Anonyms and Pseudonyms, An Annotated List," by Adah V. Morris, *Library Quarterly*, 3:354-72, October 1933.

Bibliography

Articles

Allum, J. A. C. "Interim Report of the International Christian Conference for Palestine," *New Zealand Jewish Chronicle*, (November 1945), 56-57.

American Bible Society. "A Distribution Comparison of English Versions by the American Bible Society." National Distribution Minutes. New York: American Bible Society, February 25, 1969.

Atkinson, Henry A. "The Christian Conscience; a Christian Leader in Entire Awareness of All Factors Expresses His Group's Adherence to the Jewish State," *New Palestine*, (August 17, 1945), 266-68.

Atkinson, Henry A. "The Jewish Problem is a Christian Problem," *Christianity and Crisis*, (June 28, 1943), 3-4.

Batshaw, Harry. "Canada Supports Free Jewish Palestine," *Canadian Zionist*, (November 24, 1944).

Bentwich, Norman. "Jewry's Magna Charta," *Palestine and Middle East* (Tel Aviv), October 1943.

Bickerman, Elias J. "The Historical Foundations of Post-biblical Judaism," In volume one of *The Jews, Their History, Culture and Religion*. Edited by Louis Finkelstein. New York: Harper and Row Publishers, 1960.

Bickley, A. C. "Holmes, Nathaniel." *Dictionary of National Biography*. Volume XXVII. Oxford: University Press, 1960.

Carlyle, E. Irving. "Tremellius, John Immanuel." *Dictionary of National Biography*. Volume LVII. Edited by Sir Leslie Stephen and Sir Sydney Lee. Oxford: University Press, 1960.

Chafer, Lewish Sperry. "An Introduction to the Study of Prophecy," *Bibliotheca Socia*, January-March, 1943.

"Christians Speak on Palestine," *Ivriah Journal*, (July 1947), 7-15.

Clouse, Robert. "The Apocalyptic Interpretation of Thomas Brightman and Joseph Mede," *Bulletin of the Evangelical Theological Society*, Volume eleven. No. 4, Fall 1968, pp. 181-194.

Cooper, Thompson. "Fletcher, Giles." *Dictionary of National Biography*. Volume XIX. Edited by Sir Leslie Stephen and Sir Sydney Lee. Oxford: University Press, 1960.

Coulton, G. G. "Reformation," *Encyclopaedia Brittanica*, XIX, 11th Edition. Cambridge: University Press, 1910.

Crawford, John Oliver. "The Impact of Puritanism on Education." Unpublished Ph.D. thesis, University of Colorado, 1956.

Deedes, Sir Wyndam. "Balfour vs. Hitler: Democracy's Solution to the Jewish Problem — England's Pledge," *Palestine and Middle East* (Tel Aviv). October 1943.

Fowler, Reverend Professor. "Bacon, Sir Francis." *Dictionary of National Biography*. Volume II. Oxford: University Press, 1960.

Freeman, D. "Forerunners of Balfour," *Palestine and Middle East*. October 1943, 145-46.

Gardner, Edmund G. "Joachim of Flora," *The New Catholic Encyclopedia*. New York: McGraw-Hill Book Company, 1967.

Gardiner, Samuel R. "James I." *Dictionary of National Biography*. Volume XXIX. Oxford: University Press, 1960.

Gilson, Etienne. "Foreward." in the Image Book edition of Saint Augustine's *The City of God*. Garden City: Doubleday, 1962.

Goldin, Judah. "The Period of the Talmud," In volume one of *The Jews, Their History, Culture and Religion*. Edited by Louis Finkelstein. New York: Harper and Row Publishers, 1960.

Goodwin, Alfred. "Kett or Ket, Francis." *Dictionary of National Biography*. Volume XI. Edited by Sir Leslie Stephen and Sir Sydney Lee. Oxford: University Press, 1960.

Gordon, Reverend Alexander. "Gouge, William." *Dictionary of National Biography*. Volume XXII. Oxford: University Press, 1960.

Gordon, Reverend Alexander. "Jessey or Jacie, Henry." *Dictionary of National Biography*. Volume XXIX. Edited by Sir Leslie Stephen and Sir Sydney Lee. Oxford: University Press, 1960.

Gottheil, Richard. "Zionism," *The Jewish Encyclopedia*. Volume XII. New York: Funk and Wagnalls, 1906. p. 666-686.

Haller, William. "John Foxe and the Puritan Revolution," *The Seventeenth Century: Studies in the History of English Thought and Literature from Bacon to Pope*. By John Foster Jones *et al*. Stanford, California: Stanford University Press, 1951.

Heppe, A. "Alsted, Johann Heinrich." *A'llgemeine Deutsche Biographie*. Volume I. Berlin: Duncker and Humblot, 1967.

Herzog, Johann Jakob. "Calvin Latinized form of *Cauvin* or *Caulvin*), John," *The Schaff-Herzog Encyclopaedia of Religious Knowledge*. New York: Funk and Wagnalls Company, 1882, pp. 365-369.

Herzog, Johann Jakob. "Waldenses," *The Schaff-Herzog Ency-clopaedia of Religious Knowledge.* New York: Funk and Wagnalls, 1891.

Hawke, E. G. "Prideaux, John." *Dictionary of National Biography.* Volume LXVI. Oxford: University Press, 1960.

Kobler, Franz. "Sir Henry Finch (1558-1625) and the First English Advocates of the Restoration of the Jews to Palestine," *Transactions of the Jewish Historical Society of England 1945-1951,* Volume XVI, pp. 101-120. (Being the fourth Lady Magnus Memorial Lecture, delivered before the Jewish Historical Society of England on April 27, 1944.)

Kolde, H. "Laud, William." *The New Schaff-Herzog Religious Encyclopedia.* Volume VI. New York: Funk and Wagnalls, 1891.

Laughlin, M. F. "Joachim of Fiore (Flora, Floris)." *The Catholic Encyclopedia.* Volume VII. New York: McGraw-Hill Book Company, 1967.

Macdonell, G. P. "Coke, Sir Edward," *Dictionary of National Biography.* Edited by Sir Leslie Stephen and Sir Sydney Lee. Oxford: University Press. Volume II, pp. 229-243.

McCaul, Alexander. "The Claim of the Jew." *The Pulpit.* Vol. LXXI. No. 1900. April 23, 1857.

McCaul, Alexander. "Jesus of Nazareth the True Messiah, the Co-equal and Eternal Son of God." *The Pulpit.* Vol. XXXII. No. 812.

McClain, Alva J. "A Premillennial Philosophy of History." *Bibliotheca Sacra.* Volume 113 (April 1956), pp. 111-116.

Mew, James. "Brightman, Thomas." *Dictionary of National Biography.* Volume II. Edited by Sir Leslie Stephen and Sir Sydney Lee. Oxford: University Press, 1960.

Moore, George Foot. "Christian Writers of Judaism," *Harvard Theological Review*, (July 1921), 197-254.

Mosse, George L. "Calvin, John." *World Book Encyclopedia.* Chicago: Field Enterprises, 1964.

Porter, Miss B. "Lee, Samuel." *Dictionary of National Biography.* Volume XXXII. Edited by Sir Leslie Stephen and Sir Sydney Lee. Oxford: University Press, 1960.

Rigg, James McMullen. "Finch, Henry." *Dictionary of National Biography.* Oxford: University Press, 1960.

Roth, Cecil. "The Challenge to Jewish History," *Transactions of the Jewish Historical Society of England 1935-1939.* Volume XIV, pp. 1-38. (Presidential Addresses delivered before the Jewish Historical Society of England, October 20, 1936, and January 11, 1938.)

John of Salisbury. "The Nature of a True Prince." *The Portable Medieval Reader.* Edited by James Bruce Ross and Mary Martin McLaughlin. New York: Viking Press, 1964.

Schmidt, Carl Wilhelm Adolf. "Albigenses," *The Schaff-Herzog Encyclopaedia of Religious Knowledge.* New York: Funk and Wagnalls, 1891.

Selbie, W. M. "The Influence of the Old Testament." In Bevan, Edwyn R. and Singer, Charles. *The Legacy of Israel.* Oxford: Clarendon Press, 1953.

Smith, Wilbur M. "Prophetic Literature of Colonial America," *Bibliotheca Sacra.* January-March, 1943.

Southgate, W. M. "James I of England." *World Book Encyclopedia.* Chicago: Field Enterprises, 1964.

Van Paassen, Pierre. "The Honor of Protestant England," *The Protestant.* May 1944, 15-18.

West, Nathanial. "History of the Pre-Millennial Doctrine." *Second Coming of Christ, Premillinial Essays.* Chicago: Fleming H. Revell, 1879.

Wolf, Lucien. "Zionism," *Encyclopaedia Brittanica.* Volume 23. London: Encyclopaedia Brittanica, Inc., 1952.

Wood, H. B. "Puritanism." *Hastings Encyclopaedia of Religion and Ethics.* Volume Ten. New York: Chas. Scribner's Sons, 1919.

Reference Works and Books of Introductory and Background Nature

Albright, Wm. F. *History, Archaelogy and Christian Humanism.* New York: McGraw-Hill Book Company, 1964.

Allen, John William. *A History of Political Thought in the Sixteenth Century.* London: Methuen and Co., 1957.

Allis, Oswald L. *Prophecy and the Church.* Philadelphia: Presbyterian and Reformed Publishing Co., 1945.

Arndt, Wm. F. and Gingrich. *A Greek-English Lexicon of the New Testament.* Chicago: University of Chicago Press, 1957.

Bain, Robert Nishet and Dyboski, Roman. "Poland: The Reformation to the Partitions," *Encyclopaedia Brittanica*, Vol. 18, 11th Edition. Cambridge: University Press, 1910.

Bainton, Roland H. *The Age of the Reformation.* Princeton: D. Van Nostrand, 1956.

Bainton, Roland H. *Here I Stand.* New York: Abingdon-Cokesbury, 1950.

Bainton, Roland H. *The Reformation of the Sixteenth Century.* Boston: Beacon Press, 1952.

Bainton, Roland H. *Studies in the Reformation.* Boston: Beacon Press, 1963.

Bandrillart, Alfred. *The Catholic Church, the Renaissance and Protestantism.* Translated by Mrs. Philip Gibbs. London: Kegan Paul, Trench, Grübner and Co., 1908.

Beecher, Willis J. *The Prophets and the Promise.* Grand Rapids: Baker Book House, 1963.

Belloc, Hilaire. *Characters of the Reformation.* New York: Image Books, 1958.

Bethune-Baker, James Franklin. *An Introduction to the Early History of Christian Doctrine.* London: Methuen and Co., 1923.

Blunt, John Henry (ed.). *Dictionary of Sects, Heresies, Ecclesiastical Parties, and Schools of Religious Thought,* Philadelphia: Lippincott and Co., 1874.

Bodensieck, Julius (ed.). *The Encyclopedia of the Lutherand Church.* Three volumes. Minneapolis: Augsburg Publishing House, 1965.

Böhmer, Heinrich. *Luther in the Light of Recent Research.* Translated by C. F. Huth, Jr. New York: The Christian Herald, 1916.

Brandes, Friedrich. *John Knox, der Reformator Schottlands.* Elberfeld: R. L. Fridericks, 1862.

Bright, John. *A History of Israel.* Philadelphia: Westminster Press, 1959.

British and Foreign Bible Society. *Historical Catalogue of Printed Editions of Holy Scripture.* London: The Bible House, 1903-11.

Brown, F., Driver, S. R., and Briggs, C. A. *A Hebrew and English Lexicon of the Old Testament.* Oxford: Clarendon Press, 1962.

Brown, P. Hume. *John Knox, A Biography.* London: Adam and Charles Black, 1895.

Browne, E. H. *An Exposition of the Thirty-nine Articles, Historical and Doctrinal.* Two volumes. London: John M. Parker, 1850-1853.

Buchan, David Stewart and Minto, Walter. *An Account of the Life, Writings and Inventions of John Napier of Merchiston.* Perth: R. Morrison and Co., 1787.

Buchberger, T. Alois. *Lexikon für Theologie und Kirche.* Ten volumes. Freiberg im Breisgan: Herder and Company, 1930-38.

Burk, Johann C. F. *A Memoir of the Life and Writings of John Abert Bengel.* London: William Bull, 1837.

Buttrick, George A. (ed.). *Interpreter's Dictionary of the Bible.* 4 vols. Nashville: Abingdon Press, 1962.

Campbell, M. E. *Erasmus, Tyndale and Moore.* London: Eyre and Spottiswoode, 1949.

Case, Shirley Jackson. *The Millennial Hope.* Chicago: University of Chicago Press, 1968.

Cassirer, Ernst. *The Platonic Renaissance in England.* Translated by James P. Pettegrove. Austin: University of Texas, 1953.

Century Cyclopedia of Names. New York: The Century Co., 1906.

Chauncy, M. Snell. *Dissertations on Unaccomplished Prophecy.* London: J. Nisbet, 1838.

Cheyney, E. P. (ed). *The Early Reformation in England.* London: P. S. King and Son, 1895.

Clarke, Wm. N. *The Use of the Scriptures in Theology.* New York: Chas. Scribner's Sons, 1905.

Clark, Henry M. *History of English Non-Conformity.* Two Volumes. London: Chapman and Hall, 1911.

Clayton, Joseph. *The Protestant Reformation in Great Britain.* London: Burns Oates and Washbourne, 1934.

Cohen, Israel (editor). *Lord Balfour's Speeches on Zionism.* London: J. W. Arrowsmith, 1928.

Constant, G. *The Reformation in England: Edward VI.* Translated by E. I. Watkin. New York: Sheed and Ward, 1942.

Cooper, Charles Henry and Cooper, Thompson. *Athenal Cantabrigiensis.* Cambridge: The Macmillen Co., 1861.

Cornfield, Gaalyalm. *The Pictorial Biblical Encyclopedia.* The Macmillan Co., 1964.

Cox, Francis A. *The Life of Philip Melancthon.* Boston: Gould, Kendall and Lincoln, 1835.

Cross, Arthur L. *A Shorter History of England and Greater Britain.* New York: The Macmillan Co., 1920.

Cross, F. L. (editor). *The Oxford Dictionary of the Christian Church.* London: Oxford University Press, 1957.

DeVaux, Roland. *Ancient Israel.* New York: McGraw Hill, 1961.

Dickens, A. G. *The English Reformation.* New York: Schocken Books, 1964.

Dickens, A. G. *Thomas Cromwell and the English Reformation.* London: English University's Press, 1959.

Dillenberger, John and Welch, Claude. *Protestant Christianity Interpreted Through Its Development.* New York: Chas. Scribner's Sons, 1954.

Döllinger, Johann J. *Prophecies and the Prophetic Spirit in the Christian Era.* London: Rivingtons, 1873.

Dorner, J. A. *History of Protestant Theology.* Translated by G. Robson. Edinburgh: T. and T. Clark, 1871.

Dorner, J. A. *History of Protestant Theology.* Translated by G. Robson. Edinburgh: T. and T. Clark, 1908.

Drysdale, Albert. *History of the Presbyterians in England: Their Rise, Decline and Revival.* London: Publication Committee of the Presbyterian Church of England, 1889.

Dunkley, E. H. *The Reformation in Denmark.* London: S.P.C.K., 1948.

Elliott-Binns, L. *The Reformation in England.* London: Duckworth, 1937.

Encyclopaedia Brittanica, 11th edition. Cambridge: Cambridge Cambridge University Press, 1910.

Epstein, Isidore. *Judaism.* Baltimore: Penguin Books, 1966.

Flick, Alexander Clarence. *The Rise of the Medieval Church.* New York: G. P. Putnam's Sons, 1909.

Fisher, G. P. *History of Christian Doctrine.* Edinburgh: T. and T. Clark, 1908.

Frank, A. H. *A Guide to the Reading and Study of the Scriptures.* Philadelphia: David Hogan, 1823.

Froom, L. E. *The Prophetic Faith of Our Fathers.* Four volumes. Washington, D.C.: Review and Herald Publishing Co., 1946-54.

Gairdner, J. *The English Church in the Sixteenth Century from the Accession of Henry VIII to the Death of Mary.* London: Macmillan, 1902.

Gardiner, S. R. *History of England from the Accession of James I to the Outbreak of Civil War, 1603-1642.* Ten volumes. London: Longmans, Green and Co., 1883-84.

Goldschmidt, E. D. *The Passover Haggadah.* New York: Schocken Books, 1969.

Gratez, Heinrich H. *History of the Jews.* Six volumes. Philadelphia: Jewish Publication Society of America, 1940.

Green, John Richard. *Short History of the English Speaking People.* Four volumes. New York: Harper and Brothers, 1893-1895.

Grill, P. Severinus. *Hermeneutik Des Alten Testaments.* Horn, N. Ö. West Germany: Ferninand Berger and Söhne, 1965.

Grimm, H. J. *The Reformation Era 1500-1650.* New York: Macmillan, 1954.

Grünberg, Paul. *Philipp Jacob Spener.* Gottingen: Vandenhoeck and Ruprecht, 1893.

Guinness, H. Grattan. *History Unveiling Prophecy or Time as an Interpreter.* New York: Fleming H. Revell Co., 1905.

Harbison, E. H. *The Christian Scholar in the Age of the Reformation.* New York: Scribner, 1956.

Hardwick, C. *A History of the Articles of Religion.* London: G. Bell and Sons, 1890.

Harnack, Adolph. *History of Dogma.* Translated from the third German edition by Neil Buchanan. Boston: Little, Brown and Company, 1895-99.

Harrison, Everett F. (ed.). *Baker's Dictionary of Theology.* Grand Rapids: Baker Book House, 1966.

Hastings, James (ed.). *Encyclopaedia of Religion and Ethics.* 12 vols. New York: Chas. Scribner's Sons, n.d.

Herbermann, Chas. G. *et al.* (eds.). *The Catholic Encyclopedia.* Fifteen volumes. New York: Robert Appleton Co., 1907.

Hopf, Constantin. *Martin Bucer and the English Reformation.* Oxford: B. Blackwell, 1946.

Hunt, John. *Religious Thought in England from the Reformation to the End of the Last Century*. Three volumes. London: Strahan and Company, 1870-1873.

Hutchinson, Francis E. *Cranmer and the English Reformation*. London: English Universities Press, 1951.

Interpreters Bible. Ten volumes. New York: Abingdon-Cokesbury, 1950-53.

Jackson, Samuel Macauley. *The New Schaff-Herzog Encyclopedia of Religious Knowledge*. Twelve volumes. Grand Rapids: Baker Book House.

Jewish Encyclopedia. New York: Funk and Wagnalls Co., 1925.

Jordan, W. K. *The Development of Religious Toleration in England from the Beginning of the English Reformation to the Death of Queen Elizabeth*. London: G. Allen and Unwin, Ltd., 1932.

Kent, Adolphus. *An Address to the Children of Israel*. London: J. Nisbet, 1891.

Kittel, Rd. (ed.). *Biblia Hebraica*. Stuttgart: Privileg. Württ. Bibelanstalt. Published for the American Bible Society.

Kraus, H. J. *The People of God in the Old Testament*. New York: Association Press, 1958.

Kurtz, Johann Heinrich. *Church History*. Three volumes. New York: Funk and Wagnalls, 1889-90.

Latourette, Kenneth Scott. *A History of Christianity*. New York: Harper and Row, 1953.

Latourette, Kenneth Scott. *A History of the Expansion of Christianity*. Seven volumes. New York: Harper, 1937-45.

Lecler, Joseph. *Toleration and the Reformation*. New York: Association Press, 1960.

Liliencron, R. V. (ed.). *Allegemeine Deutsche Biographie.* Fifty-six volumes. Leipzig: Duncker and Humblot, 1875-1912.

Loane, M. L. *Masters of the English Reformation.* London: Church Book Room Press, 1954.

London Parker Society. *The Works and Early Writers of the Reformed English Church.* Fifty-one volumes. Cambridge: University Press, 1841-55.

Mann, G. and Nitschke, A. (eds.). *Propyläen Weltgeschichte Von der Reformation zur Revolution.* Volume seven of eleven volumes. Berlin: Propyläen Verlag, 1964.

M'Clintock, John and Strong, James. *Cyclopaedia of Biblical, Theological and Ecclesiastical Literature.* Ten volumes. New York: Harper and Brothers, 1867-1883.

The Mennonite Encyclopedia. Mennonite Publishing House, 1955.

Neher, Andre. *Moses and the Vocation of the Jewish People.* Translated by Irene Marinoff. New York: Harper Torchbooks, 1959.

Neve, J. Ludwig. *History of Christian Thought.* Two volumes. Philadelphia: United Lutheran Publication House, 1943.

Newman, Albert Henry. *A Manual of Church History.* Philadelphia: American Baptist Publication Society, 1933.

Oehler, Gustave. *Theology of the Old Testament.* Grand Rapids: Zondervan, 1960.

Orr, James (ed.). *International Standard Bible Encyclopedia.* Five volumes. Grand Rapids: Wm. B. Erdmans, 1957.

Pollard, A. F. *Thomas Cranmer and the English Reformation.* G. P. Putnam's Sons, 1904.

Pollard, A. F. *Thomas Cranmer and the English Reformation.* London: Putnam's Sons, 1905.

Rambachii, Jacobi. *Institutiones Hermaneutical Sacrae.* Jenae: Iaon. Wilk. Hartungii, 1764.

Ritschl, Otto. *Dogmengeschichte des Protestantismus.* Leipzig: J. C. Henrichs'sche Buchhandlung, 1908.

Rosenberg, Edgar. *From Shylock to Svengali.* Stanford: Stanford University Press, 1960.

Sauer, Erich. *From Eternity to Eternity.* Grand Rapids: Wm. B. Erdmans Publishing Co., 1957.

Schaff, Philip. *The Creeds of Christendom.* Three volumes. New York: Harper, 1877-1884.

Schaff, Philip. *History of the Christian Church.* Seven volumes. New York: Chas. Scribner's Sons, 1894-1910.

Schaff, Philip (ed.). *Schaff-Herzog Encyclopaedia of Religious Knowledge.* Three volumes. New York: Funk and Wagnalls, 1882.

Smith, H. M. *Henry VIII and the Reformation.* London: Macmillan, 1948.

Smith, Sir Wm. and Wace, Henry. *Dictionary of Christian Biography, Literature, Sects, and Doctrines.* Four volumes. London: Murray, 1877-87.

Strack, Hermann L. and Billerbeck, Paul. *Kommentar zum Neuen Testament und Midrasch.* Five volumes. München: Ch. Beck'sche Verlags Buchandlung Oskarbwck, 1922-28.

Strong, A. H. *Systematic Theology.* Englewood Cliffs: Fleming H. Revell Co., 1907.

Strong, James. *Exhaustive Concordance of the Bible.* Nashville: Abingdon Press, 1955.

Walker, Williston. *A History of Christianity.* New York: Chas. Scribner's Sons, 1959.

Ward, A. W., Prothers, G. W. and Seathes, Stanley. (eds.). *The Cambridge Modern History.* Thirteen volumes. New York: Macmillan, 1934.

Whitney, Fredrick Lawson. *The Elements of Research.* Englewood-Cliffs: Prentice-Hall, 1964.

Whitney, J. P. *History of the Reformation.* London: S.P.C.K., 1940.

Williamson, Hugh Ross. *The Beginning of the English Reformation.* New York: Sheed and Ward, 1957.

Related Primary Materials

Alsted, Johann H. *Theologia Prophetica.* Hanoviae: Sumptibus Couradi Eifridi, 1622.

Amsdorf, Nicholas. *Fünff furnemliche und gewisse Zeichen aus gottlicher heiliger Schift.* Jena: Rödinger, 1554.

Archer, Henry. *The Personall Reign of Christ Upon Earth. In a Treatise Wherein Is Fully and Largely Laid Open and Proved, That Jesus Christ, Together With the Saints, Shall Visibly Possesse a Monarchicall State and Kingdome in this World.* London: Benjamin Allen, 1642.

Bale, John. *A Brefe Chronycle Concernyne the Eramynacyon and Death of the Blessed Martyr of Christ Syr Johan Oldecastell the Lord Cobham.* London: C. Davis, 1729.

Bale, John. *Select Works of John Bale. D.D., Bishop of Ossory. Containing the Examinations of Lord Cobhan, Wm. Thorpe, and Anne Askewe, and the Image of Both Churches.* Edited for the Puker Society by the Rev. Henry Christmas. Cambridge: University Press, 1849.

Barnes, Robert. *Workes of Doctour Barnes, in the Whole Workes of W. Lyndall, Iaon Frith and Doct. Barnes.* London: Ioan Daye, 1572.

Baronius, Caesar. *Annales Ecctesiastici.* 12 vols. Colonial Apgippinae: Sumptibus Joannis Gymnici and Antonij Hierati, 1609-13.

Becon, Thomas. *Works of Thomas Becon.* Edited for the Parker Society by John Ayre. Cambridge: University Press, 1843.

Becon, Thomas. *The Early Works of Thomas Becon.* Edited for the Parker Society by John Ayre, Cambridge: The University Press, 1843.

Becon, Thomas. *Prayers and Other Pieces of Thomas Becon.* Edited for the Parker Society by John Ayre. Cambridge: The University Press, 1844.

Bengel, Johann Albrecht. *Gnomon.* Edited by C. F. Werner. Ludwigsburg: Ferd, Riehm, 1860.

Beverley, Thomas. *An Appeal Most Humble, Yet Most Earnestly, by the Coming of Our Lord Jesus Christ, and Our Gathering Together Unto Him.* London: John Salusbury, 1691.

Beverley, Thomas. *The Catechism of the Kingdom of Our Lord Jesus Christ in the Thousand Years.* London: John Salusbury, 1690.

Beverley, Thomas. *The Prophetical History of Reformation.* n.p.: n.n., 1689.

Bibliander, Theodor. *An Ommium Ordinum Rupublicae Christianae Principes Viros, Populumque Christianum, Relatio Fidelis.* Basileae: Ex Officina J. Aporini, 1545.

Bradford, John. *Sermons, Meditations, Examinations, Letters, Treatises and Remains.* Edited for the Parker Society by Aubrey Townsend. Cambridge: The University Press, 1848-1853.

Brightman, Thomas. *The Workes of That Famous, Reverend, and Learned Divine, Mr. Tho. Brightman.* London: John Field for Samuel Cartwright, 1644.

Broughton, Hugh. *Daniel With a Brief Explication.* Hanaw: Daniel Aubri, 1607.

Brute, Walter. *Writings and Examinations of Brute, Thoyne, Cobham, Hilton, Pecock, Bileny and Others.* Philadelphia: Presbyterian Board of Publication, 1842.

Bullinger, Heinrich. *The Decades of Henry Bullinger, Minister of the Church of Zurich.* Edited for the Parker Society by the Rev. Thomas Harding. Cambridge: The University Press, 1849-52.

Bullinger, Heinrich. *Daniel Sapientissimus Dei Propheta.* Tiguri: C. Froschoverus, 1576.

Bullinger, Heinrich. *A Hundred Sermons Upon the Apocalips of Jesu Christe.* London: John Day, 1561.

Calvin, John. *Calvini Opera Omnia, Corpus Reformatorum.* vols. 29-87.

Calvin, John. *Commentaries on the Book of the Prophet Daniel.* Printed for and authorized by the Calvin Translation Society, 1851.

Calvin, John. *Institutes of the Christian Religion.* Translated by Ford Lewis Battles. Edited by John T. McNeill. Philadelphia: Westminster Press, 1960.

Calvin, John. *Tracts Relating to the Reformation.* 3 vols. Translated by H. Beveridge. Edinburgh: The Calvin Translation Society, 1844.

Church of England. *Certain Sermons or Homilies Appointed to Be Read in Churches in the Time of Queen Elizabeth of Famous Memory.* London: S.P.C.K., 1890.

Cocceius, Johannes. *Opera Omnia Theologica, Exegetica Didactica, Philologica.* 10 vols. Amstelodami: P. and J. Blaev, 1701.

Comenius, J. Amos. *The Bequest of the Unity of the Brethren.* Translated by Matthew Spinka. Chicago: National Union of Czechoslovak Protestants in America, 1940.

Conradus, Alfonsus. *In Apocolypsim D. Iaon. Apostoli Commentarius Alfonsi Conadi.* Basileae: Apud Petrum Pernam, 1560.

Cotton, John. *The Churches resurrection, or the opening of the fift and sixt verses of the 20th. Chap. of the Revelation.* London: R. O. and G. D. for H. Overton, 1642.

Coverdale, Miles. *Writings and Translations of Myles Coverdale, Bishop of Exeter.* Edited for the Parker Society by George Pearson. Cambridge: The University Press, 1844.

Coverdale, Miles. *Remains of Myles Coverdale, Bishop of Exeter.* Edited for the Parker Society by George Pearson. Cambridge: The University Press, 1846.

Cranmer, Thomas. *The Works of Thomas Cranmer.* Edited for the Parker Society by John E. Cox. Cambridge: The University Press, 1844.

Cranmer, Thomas. *Writings and Disputations.* Edited for the Parker Society by John E. Cox. Cambridge: The University Press, 1845.

Cranmer, Thomas. *Miscellaneous Writings and Letters.* Edited for the Parker Society by John E. Cox. Cambridge: The University Press, 1846.

Cromwell, Oliver. *Oliver Cromwell's Letters and Speeches.* Edited by Thomas Carlyle. London: Chapman and Hall, 1844.

The Day of the Lord Or, Israel's Retvrn, With an humble presentation of the Divine Characters whereby this Wonderfull Day may seem very neer approaching. London: T. W. for J. Crook, 1654.

Clemaus, R. *Hugh Latimer, a Biography.* London: Dalls, Lamar and Barton, n.d.

Flacius, Matthias. *Catalogus Testium Veritatis.* Lugdun.: Antonij Candidi, 1597.

Flacius, Matthias. *Ecclesiastic Historia.* 8 vols. Basle: n.n., 1560-74.

Geveren, Sheltco. *Of the Ende of This World, and Second Comming of Christ, a Comfortable and Necessary Discourse, for these Miserable and Dangerous Dayes.* London: Andrew Maunsell, 1577.

Held, Friedrich (ed.). *Dr. Martin Luther's Vorreden zur Heiligen Schrift.* Heibronn: E. Salzer, 1934.

Hooper, John. *Letters of Hooper to Ballinger.* Boston: Directors of the Old South Work, 1898.

Hooper, John. *Works.* Edited for the Parker Society by Samuel Carr. Cambridge: The University Press, 1843.

Hooper, John. *Early Writings of John Hooper.* Edited for the Parker Society by Samuel Carr. Cambridge: The University Press, 1847.

Hooper, John. *Later Writings of Bishop Hooper.* Edited for the Parker Society by Charles Nevinson. Cambridge: The University Press, 1852.

Joye, George. *The Exposycion of Daniel the Prophete, Gathered Out of Philip Melancthon, Johan Ecotapadius, Chonrade Pellicane and Out of John Draconite Ejc.* London: n.n., 1550.

Knox, John. *The Historie of the Reformation of Religioun Within the Realm of Scotland.* Edinburgh: Robert Fleming and Co., 1732.

Knox, John. *The Works of John Knox.* 6 vols. Edited by David Laing. Edinburgh: The Woodrow Society, 1846-96.

Latimer, Hugh. *Sermons.* Edited for the Parker Society by Elwes Corrie. Cambridge: The University Press, 1844.

Latimer, Hugh. *Sermons and Remains*. Edited for the Parker Society by Elwes Corrie. Cambridge: The University Press, 1845.

Lindsay, James L. *Bibliotheca Lindesiana. Collations and Notes No. 7; Catalogue of a Collection of Fifteen Hundred Tracts by Martin Luther and His Contemporaries 1511-1598.* Aberdeen: Privately Printed, 1903.

Luthers Werke. 58 vols. Kritische Gesammtausgabe. Weimar: Herman Böhlau, 1883.

Mede, Joseph. *Daniels Weeks*. London: M. F. for John Clark, 1643.

Mede, Joseph. *The Works of That Reverend, Judicious and Learned Divine, Mr. Joseph Meade Whereunto Are Added Sundry Discourses on Other Texts.* London: M. F. for John Clark, 1648.

Melanchthon, Philip. *Opera Quae Supersunt Omnia.* Edited by C. G. Bretschneider. Halis Saxonum: C. A. Schwtschke et Filium, 1834-60.

More, Henry. *A Plain and Continued Exposition of the Several Prophecies or Divine Visions of the Prophet Daniel.* London: M. F. for Walter Kettilby.

Musculus, Andreas. *Vom jüngsten Tage.* Erfurt: n.n., 1559.

Aecolampadius, Johann. *In Danielem Prophetam.* Genevae: E. Typographia Crispiniana, 1567.

Pelikan, Jaroslav. *Luther's Works.* St. Louis: Concordia Publishing House, 1958.

Philpot, John. *Examinations and Writings.* Edited for the Parker Society by Robert Eden. Cambridge: The University Press, 1842.

Pinchion, William. *The Jewes Synagogue: or, A Treatise Concerning The Ancient Orders and Manner of Worship used by the Jewes in Their Synagogue Assemblies.* London: John Bellamie, 1652.

Ridley, Nicholas. *Works of Nicholas Ridley, D.C., Sometime Lord Bishop of London, Martyr, 1555.* Edited for the Parker Society by Rev. Henry Christmas. Cambridge: The University Press, 1841.

Shager, John. *A discoverie of the world to come according to the Scripture wherein, 1. The doctrine of the world to come is propounded . . . 2. The doctrine of millenaries, touching a new Reformed Church in the latter times, whiich they call a new world is confuted.* London: J. Mosbek for L. Farne, 1650.

Sherwin, W. *. . . or The Saints First Revealed and Covenanted Mercies Shortly Approaching.* London: n.n., 1676.

Smith, Preserved. *Luther's Table Talk: a Critical Study.* New York: Columbia University Press, 1907.

Spener, Jacob. *Pia Desidina.* Frankfurt au Mayn: Johann David Zunner, 1676.

Tillenghast, John. *Knowledge of the Times.* London: R. I. for L. Chapman, 1654.

Translations and Reprints from the Original Sources of European History. 6 vols. Philadelphia: Dept. of History of the University of Pennsylvania, 1894-99.

Ussher, James. *Annales Veteris Testamenti.* London: Ex Officina J. Flesher, 1650.

Works of Martin Luther. Philadelphia Edition: Muhlenberg Press, 1943.

The Zurich Letters. Edited for the Parker Society by H. Robinson. Cambridge: University Press, 1842-45.

Zwingli, Hudrich. *Hanpschriften.* Edited by F. B. Pauke *et al.* Zurich: Zwingli Verlag, 1942.

Specific Primary Materials

"An Admonition to Parliament, 1572." In Haller, William. *Elizabeth I and the Puritans.* Ithaca, New York: Cornell University Press for the Folger Shakespeare Library, 1964, Page one.

Alsted, Johann Heinrich. *The Beloved City or, The Saints Reign on Earth a Thousand Yeares; Asserted, and Illustrated from LXV. places of Holy Scripture; Besides the judgement of Holy Learned men, both at home and abroad; and also Reason itselfe. Written in Latine by Ioan. Henr. Alsedius, Professor the University at Herborne. Faithfully Englished; With some occasionall Notes; And the Judgement herein [not only of Tycho Brahe, and Carolus Gallus; but also] of some of our owne famous Divines.* London: n.p. Printed in the yeare of the last expectation of the Saints. MDCXLIII.

Alsted, Johann Heinrich. *Diatribe de mille annis Apocalypticis.* Francofurti: Danielis and Johannis, 1627.

Archer, John. *The Personall Reigne of Christ upon the Earth.* London: Benjamin Allen, 1642.

Articles To Be Enqvired of within the Dioces of London in the first generall Visitation of the Reverend Father in God, Thomas Lord Bishop of London, 1607. London: Henry Bullard, 1607.

Saint Augustine. *The City of God.* Volume seven of fourteen. *Nicene and Post Nicene Fathers.* Book one. Edited by Philip Schaff. New York: Chas. Scribner's Sons, 1905-1917.

Augustine. *The City of God.* Garden City: Doubleday and Co., 1962.

Aylett, Robert. *A briefe chronologie of the Holie Scriptures according to the extent of the severall historicall bookes thereof.* London: J. Harison, 1600.

Bacon, Sir Francis. *The New Atlantis.* London: Joseph Rickerby, 1838.

Barbarossa, Frederick. "The Independence of the Temporal Authority." *The Portable Medieval Reader.* Edited by James Bruce Ross and Mary Martin McLaughlin. New York: Viking Press, 1964.

Baxter, Richard. *The glorious Kingdom of Christ, described and vindicated against the asserters of the 1000 years kingdom answering Mr. Tho. Beverly in his twelve principles and Catechisms.* London: T. Parkhurst, 1691.

Baxter, Richard. *A Reply to Mr. Tho. Beverley's Answer (A Thousandyears Kingdom . . .) to my reaons against his doctrine of the Thousand years Middle Kingdom, and of the conversion of the Jews.* London: T. Parkhurst, 1691.

Beverly, Thomas. *The Thousand years kingdom of Christ in its full Scriptural State, answering Mr. Baxter's new treatise The glorious kingdom of Christ in opposition to it.* London: n.p., 1691.

Brightmans Predictions and Prophecies: Written 46. years since; Concerning the three Churches of Germanie, England and Scotland. Foretelling the miserie of Germanie, the fall of the pride of Bishops in England by the assistance of the Scottish Kirk. All which should happen (as he foretold) between the years of 36. and 41. etc. London: n.p., 1641.

Brightman, Thomas. *Brightman Redivinus: Or The Post-Humian Of Spring of Mr. Thomas Brightman. In IIII Sermons 1. Of the Two Covenants 2. The danger of Scandals 3. Gods Commission to Christ to Preach the Gospell. 4. The Saints Securitie.* London: Printed for Peter Cole, and are to be sold at the Sign of the Printing Presse in Cornhill neer the Royall-Exchange, 1647.

Brightman, Thomas. *A Most Comfortable Exposition of the Last and Difficult Part of the Prophecies of Daniel — Wherein the restoring of the Jews and their calling to the faith of Christ, after the overthrow of their last enemies is Set Forth in Lively Colours.* London: n.p., 1635.

Brightman, Thomas. *A Commentary on the Canticles or the Song of Solomon. Wherein the Text is Analised, the Native signification of the Words Declared, the Allegories Explained, the Order of times whereunto they relate Observed.* London: Printed by Iohn Field, for Henry Overton, in Popes-head-Alley, 1644.

Brightman, Thomas. *A Revelation of the Revelation, that is, The Revelation of St. John Opened Clearly with a Logicall Resolution and Exposition Wherein the Sense is cleared, out of Scripture, the Event also of Thinges Foretold is Discussed of the Church Historyes.* Amsterdam: n.p., 1615.

Brightman, Thomas. *The Workes Of That Famous, Reverend, and Learned Divine, Mr. Tho. Brightman: Viz. A Revelation of the Apocalyps: Containing an Exposition of the whole book of the Revelation of Saint John, Illustrated with Analysis and Scholions. Where in the sense is opened by the Scripture, and the event of things foretold, shewed by History. Whereunto is added, A most comfortable Exposition of the last and most difficult part of the Prophesie of Daniel, wherein the restoring of the Jews, and their calling to the Faith of Christ, after the utter overthrow of their three last Enemies, is set forth in lively colours. Together with a Commentary on the whole Book of Canticles, or Song of Solomen.* London: Printed by John Field for Samuel Cartwright and are to be sold at the Hand and Bible in Ducklane, 1644.

Broughton, Hugh. *A Concent of Scripture.* London: n.p., 1590.

Broughton, Hugh. *Works of the Great Albionean Divine.* London: N. Ekins, 1662.

Burges, Cornelius. *A Sermon Preached to the Honourable House of Commons Assembled in Parliament at their Publique Fast, Novem. 17, 1640.* London: n.p.,

Carlton, George (Bishop). *A Thankful Remembrance of God's Mercy in an Historical Collection of the Great and Merciful Deliverances of the Church and State of England, Since the Gospel Began Here to Flourish, from the Beginning of Queen Elizabeth.* London: I. D. for Robert Mylbourne and Humphrey Robinson, 1624.

Calvin, Iohn. *A Commentary upon the Prophecie of Isaiah.* Translated ovt of the French into English: by C. C. London: Imprinted by Felix Kyngston, and are to be sold by William Cotton, dwelling in Paternoster Row, at the signe of the golden Lion, 1609.

Calvin, John. *Commentary on the Prophecie of Isaiah.* London: Felix Kingston, 1609.

Calvin, John. *Institutes of the Christian Religion.* Two volumes. Translated by Ford Lewis Battles. Edited by John T. McNeill. Philadelphia: Westminster Press, 1960.

Cooper, [Thomas]. *The blessing of Jophet, proving the gathering in of the Gentiles, and finall conversion of the Iewes. Expressed in divers profitable sermons.* n.p. n.p., 1615.

Cox, John. *A Millenarian's Answer of the Hope that is in Him; or, a brief Statement and Defense of the Doctrine of Christ's Pre-Millennial Advent and Personal Reign on Earth.* Philadelphia: Orrin Rogers, 1840.

Draxe, Thomas. *An Alarvm to the Last Ivdgment or An exact discourse of the second coming of Christ, and of the generall and remarkeable Signes and Fore-runners of it past, present, and to come; soundly and soberly handled, and wholesomely applyed, Wherein divers deep Mysteries are plainly expounded, and sundry curiosities are duely examined, answered and confuted.* London: Printed by Nicholas Okes for Matthew Law, 1615.

Draxe, Thomas. *The Churches Securitie, Togither with the Antidote or preservative of ever waking Faith. A treatise conteyning many fruitefull instructions, moralities and consolations fit for the time and age wherein wee live. Hereunto is annexed a sound and profitable treatise of the generall signes and forerunners of the last judgement.* London: Imprinted by George Eld, and to be sold by John Wright, 1608.

Draxe, Thomas. *The Earnest of Ovr Inheritance: Together With A Description Of The New Heaven and of the New earth, and a demonstration of the glorious Resurrection of the bodie in the same substance. Preached at Paul's Crosse the second day of August. 1612.* London: F. K. for George Norton, 1613.

Draxe, Thomas. *The Lambes Spouse.* London: n.p., 1608.

Draxe, Thomas. *The VVorldes Resvrrection, Or The generall calling of the Iewes. A familiar Commentary vpon the eleventh Chapter of Saint Paul to the Romaines, according to the sense of Scripture, and the consent of the most iudicious interpreters, wherein above fiftie notable questions are soundly answered, and the particular doctrines, reasons and uses of every verse, are profitably and plainly delivered.* London: Printed by G. Eld, for John Wright, 1608.

Eudaemon-Joannes, Andreas. *Castigatis Apocalypsis Apocalpseos Thomas Brightman Angli.* n.p.: A. J. Kinekium, 1613.

Fairclough, Samuel. *The Troublers Troubled, or Achan Condemned and Executed. A Sermon Preached before sundry of the Hon. House of Commons, Apr. 4, 1641.* London: Henry Brome, 1641.

Fenwiche, Sir John. *Zions Ioy in Her King Coming in His Glory.* London: Benjamin Allen, 1643.

[Finch, Henry]. *An Exposition of the Song of Solomon.* London: John Beale, 1615.

[Finch, Henry]. *The Sacred Doctrine of Divinitie, Gathered out of the Word of God.* London: [Published by William Gouge Esq.], 1599.

[Finch, Henry]. *The World's Resurrection or The Calling of the Jewes. A Present to Judah and the Children of Israel that*

Ioyned with Him, and to Ioseph (that valiant tribe of Ephraim) and all the House of Israel that Ioyned with Him. London: Edward Griffin for William Bladen, 1621.

Fletcher, Giles. *Israel Redux: or the Restauration of Israel; or the Restauration of Israel, exhibited in two short treatises. The first contains an essay on some probable grounds, that the present Tartars, near the Caspian Sea, are the posterity of the ten Tribes of Israel. By G. F., LL.D. The second, a dissertation concerning their ancient and successive state with some Scripture evidences of their future conversion and establishment in their own land. By S. L[ee]. or a superaddition to the Former dissertation, etc.* London: S. Streater for John Hancock, 1677.

Foxe, John. *The Acts and Monuments of John Foxe.* Edited by Stephen Reed Cattley. London: R. B. Seeley and W. Burnside, 1837.

Fuller, Andrew. *A Pisgah-Sight of Palestine and Confines Thereof, with the History of the Old and New Testament Acted Thereon.* London: J. F. for John Williams, 1650.

Goodwin, Thomas [Knollys, Hanserd]. *A Glympse of Syons Glory: or, The Churches Beautie Specified.* London: William Sarner, 1641.

Great Britain. *Cobbett's Parliamentary History of England, being the Parliamentary or Constitutional History of England from the Earliest Times to the Restoration of King Charles II, Collected from the Records, the Rolls of Parliament, the Journals of Both Houses, the Public Libraries, Original Manuscripts, Scarce Speeches and Tracts, All Compared with the Several Contemporary Writers and Connected Throughout with the History of the Times, by Several Hands.* Second Edition. Twenty-four volumes. London: J. and R. Tonson and A. Miller, 1761-63.

Great Britain. *The Parliamentary History of England from the Earliest Period to the Year 1803.* Volume I 1066-1625 [of 36 volumes], From Which Last Mentioned Epoch it is Continued Down in the Work Entitled *The Parliamentary*

Debates [775 volumes to 20 December 1968]. London: T. C. Hansard for Longman, Hurst, Rees, Orme and Browne; *et al.* 1806—.

Great Britain. *The Parliamentary or Constitutional History of England from the Earliest Times to the Restoration of King Charles II.* Twenty-four volumes. London: J. and R. Tonson, and A. Millar, 1761-63.

Great Britain. *Parliamentary Papers.* Crnd. 6019. "Palestine Statement of Policy." London: His Majesty's Stationery Office, 1939.

HaKohen, Joseph. *Emek HaBaka.* Cracav: n.p., 1895.

Hall, Thomas. *Chiliasto-mastrix redivivus, nive Homesus energatus. A confutation of the Millenarian opinion . . . where you also have many texts of Scripture vindicated from the vain glasses of one Dr. Homes, a great Millenarian . . . with a word to our Fifth Monarchy-men.* London: J. Starkey, 1657.

Hammon, George. *Syons Redemption and original sin vindicated.* London: C. Dawson, 1658.

Harrington, J. *The Act of Law-Giving.* London: J. C. for Henry Fletcher, 1659.

Hartlys, Samuel. *Clavis Apocalyptica: or, the Revelation revealed in which the great mysteries in the Revelation of St. John, and the Prophet Daniel are opened; it being made apparent that the prophetical numbers come to an end with the year of our Lord 1655. Written by a Germane D. D. translated out of High Dutch.* London: W. D. for T. Matthews, 1651.

Hayne, Thomas. *Christs Kingdome on Earth, Opend according to the Scriptures. Herein is examined, what Mr. Th. Brightman, Dr. J. Alstede, Mr. I. Mede, Mr. H. Archer, The Glympse of Sions Glory, and such as concurre in opinion with them, hold concerning the thousand years of the Saints Reign with Christ, And of Satans binding: Herein also their Arguments are answered.* London: Ric. Cotes for Stephen Bowtell, 1645.

Herzl, Theodor. *An Anthology of the Congress Addresses of Theodor Herzl.* New York: Theodor Herzl Institute, 1960.

Herzl, Theodor. *Complete Dairies.* Edited by Raphael Patai. Translated by Harry Zohn. New York: Herzl Press and Thomas Yoseloff, 1960.

Holland, Hezekiah. *An exposition or a short but full, plaine and perfect epitome of the most choice commentaries upon the Revelation of St. John.* London: T. R. and E. M. for C. Calvert, 1650.

Holmes, Nathaniel. *The New World.* London: T. P. and M. S. for W. Adderton, 1641.

Irenaeus. *Against Heresies. Ante-Nicene Fathers. Translations of the Writings of the Fathers Down to A.D. 325.* First volume of Ten. New York: Chas. Scribner's Sons, 1899-1926.

Israel, Manasseh ben. *Apology for the Honourable Nation of the Jews.* London: John Field, 1648.

Israel, Manasseh ben. *Hope of Israel.* London: R. I. for Hannah Allen, 1650.

Israel, Manasseh ben. *Precious Stone or the Image of Nebnchadnezzar, or the Fifth Monarchy.* London: n.p., 1655.

James I. *Workes of the Most High and Mightie Prince, James, King of Great Britaine.* Edited by Iames [Montague] Bishop of Winton. London: Robert Barker and Iohn Bill, 1616.

Saint Jerome. *Commentaria in Danielem.* In Migne, *Patristica Latina.* Volume 25. Chapter seven. Paris: J. P. Migne, 1841-86.

Saint Jerome. *Commentaria in Ezechielem.* In Migne, *Patristica Latina.* Volume 25. Chapter seven. Paris: J. P. Migne, 1841-86.

Joachim (of Floris). *Exposito Magni Prophete Abbatis Joachim in Apocalyssim.* Ventijs: In Edibus Francisci Bindoni ac Maphei Pasini Socii, 1527.

Kett, Francis, *The Glorious and beautiful Garland of Man's Glorification containing the godly misterie of heavenly Jerusalem.* London: Roger Ward, 1585.

Knollys, Hanserd. *Apocalyptical Mysteries.* n.p. n.p., printed 1667.

Knollys, Hanserd. *The Rudiments of Hebrew Grammar.* London: M. B., 1648.

Lactantius. *Epitome.* Chapter 72. *Ante-Nicene Fathers. Translation of the Writings of the Fathers Down to A.D. 325.* Volume VII. New York: Chas. Scribner's Sons, 1899-1926.

Lactantius. *Institutes.* Book seven. *Ante-Nicene Fathers. Translations of the Writings of the Fathers Down to A.D. 325.* Volume VII. New York: Chas. Scribner's Sons, 1899-1926.

Laud, William. *A Sermon Preached Before His Maiestie on Wednesday the fift of July, at Whitehall.* London: Printed for Richard Badger, 1626.

Laud, William (Archbishop). "Sermon Preached before His Majesty, on Tuesday the 19. of June, at Wanstead, Anno 1621. Psalm 122:6, 7: 'Pray for the Peace of Jerusalem; let them prosper within thy walls, and prosperity within thy palaces.'" *Seven Sermons Preached Upon several Occasions.* London: Printed for R. Lowndes, at the White Lion in S. Pauls Church-yard, 1651.

Lee, Samuel (editor and author of parts). *Israel Redux: or the Restauration of Israel; or the Restauration of Israel exhibited in two short treatises. The first contains an essay on some probable grounds that the present Tartars, near the Caspian Sea are the posterity of the ten Tribes of Israel. By G. F. L.L.D. The second a dissertation concerning their ancient and successive state, with some Scripture evidences of their future conversion and estab-*

lishment in their own land. London: S. Streater for John Hancock, 1677.

Luther, Martin. *Ein trosliche predigt von der zukunft Christi und den vorgehenden zeichen des Jüngesten Tags.* Wittenberg: Hans Luft, 1532.

Luther, Martin. *The Signs of Christs coming and of the last Day. Being the substance of a sermon preached by Martin Luther upon Luke 21, verses 25, 26 to verse 34 lately translated out of his narrations on the Gospels.* London: n.p., 1661.

Marshall, Stephen. *A Sermon Preached before the Honourable House of Commons, now assembled in Parliament, at their publique Fast, November 17, 1640.* London: n.p., 1641.

Martyr, Justin. *Dialogue with Trypho the Jew. Ante-Nicene Fathers. Translations of the Writings of the Fathers Down to A.D. 325.* Fifth volume of ten. New York: Chas. Scribner's Sons, 1899-1926.

Mather, Increase. *The Mystery of Israel's Salvation.* London: J. Allen, 1669.

Maton, Robert. *Israel's Redemption, Or, the Jewes generall and miraculous conversion to the faith of the Gospel: and return into their owne Land: And our Saviours personall Reigne on Earth, cleerly proved out of many plaine Prophecies of the Old and New Testaments.* London: Matthew Simons, 1642.

Maton, Robert. *Israel's Redemption Redeemed. Or, the Jewes generall and miraculous conversion to the faith of the Gospel: and returne into their owne Land: And our Saviours personall Reigne on Earth, cleerly proved out of many plaine Prophecies of the Old and New Testaments. And the chiefe Arguments that can be alleged against these Truths, fully answered: Of Purpose to satisfie all gainsayers; and in particular Mr. Alexander Petrie, Minister of the Scottish Church in Roterdam. By Robert Maton, the Author of Israel's Redemption. Divided into two Parts, whereof the first concernes the Jewes Restauration into a visible Kingdome in Judea: And the second, our Saviours visi-*

ble Reigne over them, and all other nations at his next appearing. Whereunto are annexed the Author's Reasons, for the literall and proper sense of the plagues contain'd under the Trumpets and Vialls. London: Printed by Matthew Simons, and are to be sold by George VVhittington at the blew Anchor neere the Royall-Exchange, 1696.

Mede, Joseph. *The Apostacy of the Latter Times.* London: Samuel Man, 1644.

Mede, Joseph. *Daniel's Weeks.* London: M. F. for John Clark, 1643.

Mede, Joseph. *The Key to the Revelation.* Dublin: M. Goodwin, 1831.

Mede, Joseph, 1586-1638. *The works of . . . Joseph Mede . . . Corrected and enlarged according to the author's own mss . . .* London: Printed by Robert Norton, for Richard Royston, 1677.

Newes from Rome. Of two mightie Armies, aswell footemen as horsmen: The first of the great Sophy, the other of an Hebrew people, till this time not discovered, comming from the Mountaines of Caspij, who pretend their warre is to recover the Land of Promise, & to expell the Turks out of Christendome. With their multitudes of Souldiers, & new invention of weapons. Also certain prophecies of a Iew serving to that Armie, called Caleb Shilocke, prognosticating many strange accidents, which shall happen the following yeere, 1607. Translated out of Italian into English, by W. W. London: Printed for I. R. for Henry Gosson, [and are to be sold in Pater Noster Rowe, 1607].

Newton, Sir Isaac. *Observations upon the Prophecies of Daniel and the Apocalypse of St. John.* London: J. Roberts, 1733.

Petrie, Alexander. *Chiliasto-Mastix, Or The Prophecies in the Old and New Testament Concerning the Kingdome of Our Saviour Jesus Christ Vindicated from the Misrepresentations of the Millenaries and Specially of Mr. Maton in his book called Israel's Redemption.* Roterdame: Isaac Voesbergen, 1644.

Prideaux, John. "De Judaeorum Vocatione." *Orationes Novem Inavrvgales, De Totidem, Theologiae Apicibus, scitui non indignis, pront promotione Doctorum, Oxionae publica proponebantus in Comitijs.* Oxioniae: Iohannes Lichfield, and Guilielmus Turner, 1626.

Spedding, James. *Life and Letters of Bacon.* Seven volumes. London: Longman, Green, Longman and Roberts, 1861-1874.

Tertullian. *Against Marcion. Ante-Nicene Fathers. Translations of the Writings of the Fathers Down to A.D. 325.* Third volume of ten. New York: Chas. Scribner's Sons, 1899-1926.

Tertullian. *An Answer to the Jews. Ante-Nicene Fathers. Translations of the Writings of the Fathers Down to A.D. 325.* Third volume of ten. New York: Chas. Scribner's Sons, 1899-1926.

Whitelock, Blustrode. *Memorials of English Affairs from the Beginning of the Reign of Charles the First to the Happy Restoration of King Charles the Second.* Four volumes. Oxford: University Press, 1853.

Willet, Andrew. *De Vniversali et Novissima Ivdaeorum Vocatione, Secundum Apertissimun, in vltimio hisce diebus praestandas Liker vnno.* Ex officina Johannis Legati Cantabrigiensis Typographi, 1590.

Wilson, Thomas. *David's Zeale for Zion: A Sermon Preached before Sundry of the Hon. House of Commons at St. Margarets at Westminster, April 4, 1641.* London: n.p., 1641.

Titles on Pertinent Aspects of the Topic

Anderson, William. *An Apology for Millennial Dcotrine in the Form in Which it was Entertained by the Primitive Church.* Philadelphia: Orrin Rogers, 1840.

Ashe, Geoffrey. *The Land and the Book.* London: Collins, 1965.

Authorized King James Version of the Holy Bible Containing Old and New Testaments and the Apocrypha. Oxford: University Press.

Aubrey, John. *'Brief Lives,' Chiefly of Contemporaries, Set Down by John Aubrey, Between the Years 1669 & 1696.* Edited by Andrew Clarke. Two volumes. Oxford: Clarendon Press, 1898.

Badi, Joseph. *The Government of the State of Israel.* New York: Twayne Publishers, 1963.

Bamberger, Bernard J. *The Story of Judaism.* New York: Schocken Paperback, 1967.

Baron, Joseph L. (ed.). *Stars and Sand.* Philadelphia: Jewish Publication Soceity, 1944.

Baron, Salo Wittmayer. *A Social and Religious History of the Jews.* Thirteen volumes. New York: Columbia University Press, 1966.

Beard, Charles. *The Reformation of the Sixteenth Century in Its Relation to Modern Thought and Knowledge.* New York: Constable and Company, 1927.

Beecher, Willis J. *The Prophets and the Promise.* Grand Rapids, Michigan: Baker Book House, 1963.

Begg, James A. *A Connected View of Some of the Scriptural Evidence of the Redeemer's Speedy Return and Reign on Earth with His Glorified Saints, During the Millennium; Israel's Restoration to Palestine; and the Destruction of Antichristian Nations.* London: J. Nisbet, 1831.

Bentwich, Norman. *Early English Zionists.* Tel Aviv: Lion the Printer for the Zionist Organization, Youth Department, n.d.

Bevan, Edwyn R. and Singer, Charles (editors). *The Legacy of Israel.* Oxford: Clarendon Press, 1953.

Beveridge, William. *Ecclesia Anglicana Ecclesia Catholica; or The Doctrine of the Church of England Consonant to Scripture, Reason, and Fathers: In a Discourse upon the Thirty-nine Articles Agreed Upon in the Convocation Held in London MDLXII. 2 vols.* Oxford: University Press, 1840.

Bicheno, James. *The Signs of the Times; or, The Dark Prophecies of the Scripture Illustrated by the Application of the Present Important Events.* West Springfield, England: Richard Davison, 1796.

Bickersteth, Edward. *A List of the Principle Books on the Subject of Prophecy.* Philadelphia: Orrin Rogers, 1841.

Bickersteth, Edward. *A Practical Guide to the Prophecies.* London: Seelys, 1852.

Bickersteth, Edward. *The Restoration of the Jews.* London: Seelys, 1852.

Bickersteth, Edward. *The Signs of the Times.* London: Seelys, 1852.

Bickley, A. C. "Holmes, Nathaniel." *Dictionary of National Biography.* Volume XXVI, pp. 193, 194.

Binns, L. Elliott. *The Reformation in England.* London: Duckworth, n.d.

Brook, Benjamin. *The Lines of the Puritans.* London: James Black, 1813.

Brooks, Joshua William. *Elements of Prophetical Interpretation.* Philadelphia: Orrin Rogers, 1841.

Brown, David. *The Restoration of the Jews.* London: Hamilton, Adams and Co., 1861.

Brown, John. *The English Puritans.* New York: G. P. Putnams, 1912.

Brown, Louise F. *The Political Activities of the Baptists and Fifth Monarchy Men in England During the Interregnum.* Washington, D.C.: American Historical Association, 191.2

Burnet, Thomas. *Archaeologiae philosophical: or The Ancient Doctrine Concerning the Originals of Things.* Translated by Thomas Foxton. London: E. Curll, 1729.

Burnet, Thomas. *De statu mortuorum et resurgentium liber. Accesserunt epistolae dual circa libellum de archaeologiis philosophicis.* London: n.p., 1723.

Burrage, Champlin. *The Early English Dissenters.* Two Volumes. Cambridge: University Press, 1912.

Bush, George. *The Valley of Vision; or, The Dry Bones of Israel Revived.* New York: Saxton and Miles, 1844.

Case, Shirley Jackson. *The Millennial Hope.* Chicago: University of Chicago Press, 1918.

Chamberlain, Walter. *The National Restoration and Conversion of the Twelve Tribes of Israel.* London: Wertheim and Macintosh, 1854.

Cohn, Norman. *Pursuit of the Millennium.* New York: Harper and Brothers, 1961.

Cohen, Alfred. "The Kingdom of God in Puritan Thought: A Study of the English Puritan Quest for the Fifth Monarch." Unpublished Ph.D. thesis. Indiana University, 1961.

Colley, Philip. *The Conversion and Restoration of the Jews.* Boston: Perkins & Marvin, 1836.

Collyer, William Bengo. *The Aspect of Prophecy Respecting the Present and Future State of the Jews.* London: n.p., 1829.

Culver, Robert D. *Daniel and the Latter Days.* Chicago: Moody Press, 1954.

Danielou, Jean. *The Theology of Jewish Christianity.* Translated by John A. Baker. Chicago: Henry Regnery Co., 1964.

The Destiny of the Jews. London: John Hatchard, 1841.

Elliott, Edward B. *Horae Apocalypticae; or, A Commentary on the Apocalypse, Critical and Historical.* Four volumes. London: Selley, Burnside and Seeley, 1847.

Faber, George Stanley. *A Dissertation on the Prophecies, That Have Been Fulfilled are now Fulfilling, or Will Hereafter Be Fulfilled, Relative to the Great Period of 1260 Years; the Papal and Mohammedan Apostacies; the Tyrannical Reign of Antichrist, or the Infidel Power; and the Restoration of the Jews.* Second Edition Revised and Corrected. London: F. C. and J. Rivington, 1807.

Faber, George Stanley. *A Dissertation on the Prophecies, that Have Been Fulfilled, are Now Fulfilling, or Will Hereafter be Fulfilled, Relative to the Great Period of 1260 Years; the Papal and Mohammedan Apostacies; the Tyrannical Reign of Antichrist, or the Infidel Power; and the Restoration of the Jews.* First American from the Second London Edition. Boston: Andrews and Cummings, 1808.

Faber, George Stanley. *A Dissertation on the Prophecies, That Have Been Fulfilled, are now Fulfilling, or Will Hereafter Be Fulfilled, Relative to the Great Period of 1260 Years; the Papal and Mohammedan Apostacies; the Tyrannical Reign of Antichrist, the Infidel Power; and the Restoration of the Jews.* Second American from the Second London Edition. New York: M. and W. Ward, 1811.

Faber, George Stanley. *A Dissertation on the Prophecy Contained in Daniel IX. 24-27; Generally Denominated the Prophecy of the Seventy Weeks.* London: F. C. and J. Rivington, 1811.

Faber, George Stanley. *Eight Dissertations on Certain Connected Prophetical Passages of Holy Scripture, Bearing More or Less, Upon the Promise of a Mighty Deliverer.* London: Seely, Burnside and Seely, 1845.

Farrar, Frederic W. *History of Interpretation.* London: Macmillan and Co., 1886.

Fisch, Harold. *Albion and Jerusalem.* New York: Schocken Books, 1964.

Fixler, Michael. *Milton and the Kingdoms of God.* London: Faber and Faber, 1964.

Fletcher, Joseph. *The History of the Revival and Progress of Independency in England Since the Period of the Reformation.* Four volumes. London: John Snow, 1867.

Geismer, Alan. "Messianic and Millenarian Activity in Seventeenth Century England." Unpublished honors thesis, Harvard University, 1938.

Haller, William. *Elizabeth I and the Puritans.* Published for the Folger Shakespeare Library. Ithaca, New York: Cornell University Press, 1964.

Haller, William. *Foxe's Book of Martyrs and the Elect Nation.* London: J. Cape, 1963.

Haller, William (ed.). *The Leveller Tracts 1647-1653.* New York: Published by the Columbia University Press in cooperation with Henry E. Huntington Library and Art Gallery, 1944.

Haller, William. *Liberty and Reformation in the Puritan Revolution.* New York: Columbia University Press, 1953.

Haller, William. *Tracts on Liberty in the Puritan Revolution 1638-1647.* Three volumes. New York: Columbia University Press, 1934.

Hallilwell-Phillips, James Orchard. *Halliwell's Shakespeare.* Five volumes. London: The Halkyut Society, 1853.

Hanbury, Benjamin. *Historical Memorials Relating to the Independents or Congregationalists: From Their Rise to the*

Restoration of the Monarchy. London: The Congregational Union of England and Wales, 1839.

Henson, H. Hensley. *Puritanism in England.* London: Hodder and Stoughton, 1912.

Hertzberg, Arthur (ed.). *The Zionist Idea.* New York: Meridian Books, 1960.

Herzl, Theodor. *The Jewish State.* New York: Scopus Publishing Co., 1943.

Hess, Moses. *Rome and Jerusalem.* New York: Block, 1918.

Hughes, Philip Edgcumbe (ed.). *The Register of the Company of Pastors of Geneva in the Time of Calvin.* Grand Rapids, Michigan: William B. Eerdmans Publishing Company, 1966.

An Inquiry Concerning the Arguments which relate to Our Controversy With the Jews. Dublin: William Sleater, 1774.

Jastrow, Morris. *Zionism and the Future of Palestine.* New York: The Macmillan Company, 1919.

Jones, Richard Foster, *et al. The Seventeenth Century: Studies in the History of English Thought and Literature from Bacon to Pope.* Stanford, California: Stanford University Press, 1951.

Kac, Arthur W. *The Rebirth of the State of Israel.* Chicago: Moody Press, 1958.

Kellog, Samuel Henry. *The Jews; or, Prediction and Fulfillment: an Argument for the Times.* New York: A. D. F. Randolph and Co., 1883.

Kelly, John Norman Davidson. *Early Christian Doctrines.* New York: Harper and Brothers, 1958.

Klausner, Joseph. *The Messianic Idea in Israel.* Translated by M. F. Stinespring. New York: The Macmillan Co., 1955.

Kobler, Franz. *The Vision Was There*. London: World Jewish Congress, 1956.

Levensohn, Lotta. *Outline of Zionist History*. New York: Scopus Publishing Co., 1941.

Litvinoff, Barnet. *To the House of Their Fathers*. New York: Prager, 1965.

Lord, John. *Beacon Lights of History*. New York: Fords, Howard and Hulbert, 1884.

Lumsden, Carlos B. *The Dawn of Modern England*. London: Longmans, Green and Co., 1910.

Manuel, Frank E., ed. *Utopias and Utopian Thought*. Boston: Houghton Mifflin Co., 1966.

Marcus, Jacob R. *The Jew in the Medieval World, a Source Book, 315-1791*. Cincinnati: Union of American Hebrew Congregations, 1938.

Marcus, Jacob R. *The Jew in the Medieval World*. New York: Harper and Row, 1965.

Margolis, Max L. and Marx, Alexander. *A History of the Jewish People*. New York: Harper and Row, Harper Torchbooks, 1965.

Mason, Archibald. *A Scriptural View and Practical Improvement of the Divine Mystery Concerning the Jews' Blindness and Rejection*. London: T. Hamilton, 1825.

Masson, David. *The Life of John Milton*. Six volumes. London: Macmillan and Co., 1875.

Mattingly, Garrett. *Catherine of Aragon*. London: J. Cape, 1951.

Mattingly, Garrett. *The Armada*. Boston: Houghton Mifflin, 1959.

McCaul, Alexander. *The Conversion and Restoration of the Jews.* Second Edition. London: Benjamin Wertheim, 1838.

McCaul, Alexander. *The Old Paths; or, A comparison of the Principles and Doctrines of Modern Judaism with the Religion of Moses and the Prophets.* London: Duncan, 1837.

McClain, Alva J. *The Greatness of the Kingdom.* Grand Rapids: Zondervan Publishing House, 1959.

McNeile, Hugh. *Popular Lectures on the Prophecies Relative to the Jewish Nation.* London: J. Hatchard and Son, 1840.

Miller, Irving. *Israel, the Eternal Ideal.* New York: Farrar, Straus and Cudahy, 1955.

Newman, Louis Israel. *Jewish Influence on Christian Reform Movements.* New York: Abraham's Magazine Service Press, Inc., 1966.

Nott, Kathleen. *The Emperors Clothes.* Bloomington, Illinois: University of Illinois Press, 1958.

Observations on certain prophecies in the Book of Daniel and the Revelation of St. John, which relate to the second appearing of our Lord. London: n.p., 1787.

Olson, Arnold. *Inside Jerusalem.* Glendale, California: Regal Books, 1968.

One Hundred Selected Editorials From the Secular Press of America on the Zionist Movement. New York: Zionist Organization of America, 1918.

Parzen, Herbert. *A Short History of Zionism.* New York: Herzl Press, 1962.

Parker, T. H. L. (ed.). *English Reformers, Library of Christian Classics.* London: SCM Press, 1966.

Perry, Ralph Barton. *Puritanism and Democracy.* New York: The Vanguard Press, 1944.

Peters, George Nathaniel Henry. *The Theocratic Kingdom of Our Lord Jesus Christ.* Three volumes. Grand Rapids: Kregel Publications, 1957.

Pierce, W. *An Historical Introduction to the Marprelate Tracts.* London: Constable, 1908.

Pieters, Albertus. *The Seed of Abraham.* Grand Rapids: Wm. B. Eerdmans, 1950.

Plaut, M. Gunther. *The Case for the Chosen People.* Garden City: Doubleday, 1965.

Raab, Felix. *The English Face of Machiavelli.* London: Routledge and Kegan Paul, 1965.

Ramm, Bernard. *Protestant Biblical Interpretation.* Boston: W. A. Wilde Co., 1956.

Roth, Cecil. *History of the Jews.* New York: Schocken Paperback, 1966.

Roth, Cecil. *History of the Jews in England.* Oxford: Clarendon Press, 1941.

Roth, Cecil. *History of the Marranos.* New York: Harper and Row, 1966.

Rudavsky, David. *Emancipation and Adjustment.* New York: Diplomatic Press, Inc., 1967.

Russell, Charles Edward and Gordon, Hirsch Loeb. *Zionism and Prophecy.* Brooklyn: Dawn Publishers, 1936.

Sachar, Howard Morley. *The Course of Modern Jewish History.* New York: Dell Publishing Co., 1958.

Sampter, Jessie Ethel. *A Guide to Zionism.* New York: Zionist Organization of America, 1920.

Sarachek, Joseph. *The Doctrine of the Messiah in Medieval Jewish Literature.* New York: Jewish Theological Seminary, 1932.

Scarisbrick, J. *Henry VIII.* London: Eyre and Spottiswood, 1968.

Schauss, Hayyim. *Guide to Jewish Holy Days.* New York: Schocken Books, 1965.

Schauss, Hayyim. *Lifetime of a Jew.* New York: Union of American Hebrew Congregations, 1965.

Schenk, W. *The Concern for Social Justice in the Puritan Revolution.* New York: Longmans, Green and Co., 1948.

Seiss, Joseph A. *The Last Times, or Thoughts on Momentous Themes.* Philadelphia: J. B. Lippincott and Co., 1878.

Shimeall, R. C. *The Second Coming of Christ.* New York: Henry S. Goodspeed and Co., 1873.

Sibbes, Richard. *The Christian's Portion.* London: J. O. for Io. Rothwell, 1638.

Silver, Abba Hillel. *A History of Messianic Speculation in Israel from the First Through the Seventeenth Century.* New York: The Macmillan Co., 1927.

Simpkinson, C. H. Thomas Harrison. *Regicide and Major-General.* London: J. M. Dent and Co., 1905

Smith, Uriah. *The Prophecies of Daniel and Revelation.* Nashville: Southern Publishing Association, 1946.

Smith, Wilbur M. *Arab/Israeli Conflict and the Bible.* Glendale, California: Regal Books, 1967.

Sokolow, Nahum. *Hibbath Zion.* Jerusalem: L. Mayer, 1934.

Sokolow, Nahum. *History of Zionism.* Two volumes. New York: Longmans, Green and Co., 1919.

Sokolow, Nahum. *Zionism In The Bible.* New York: Longmans, Green and Co., 1919.

Stenographishes Protokoll der verhandungen des Fourth Zionisten Congresses London, 13, 14, 15, 16 August, 1900. Wien: World Zionist Organization, 1900.

Taylor, Daniel T. *The Voice of the Church on the Coming and Kingdom of the Redeemer: I A History of the Doctrine of the Reign of Christ on Earth.* Philadelphia: Lindsay and Balkiston, 1856.

Tillyard, Eustace Mandeville Wettenhall. *Studies in Milton: Private Correspondence.* London: Challo and Windus, 1951.

Torrance, Thomas F. *The Apocalypse Today.* Grand Rapids: William B. Eerdmans Publishing Co., 1959.

Torrey, Charles C. *The Apocalypse of John.* New Haven: Yale University Press, 1958.

Trevor-Roper, Hugh Redwald. *The Crisis of the Seventeenth Century.* New York: Harper and Row, 1968.

Waldegrave, Samuel. *New Testament Millenarianism: or The Kingdom and Coming of Christ.* London: Hamilton Adams and Co., 1855.

Wallbank, T. Walter and Taylor, Alastair M. *Civilization Past and Present.* Two volumes. New York: Scott, Foresman and Company, 1954.

Walvoord, John F. *The Millennial Kingdom.* Findlay, Ohio: Dunham Publishing Co., 1959.

Whitelock, Bulstrode. *Memorials of the English Affairs from the beginning of the Reign of Charles the First to the Happy Restoration of King Charles the Second.* Oxford: University Press, 1853.

White, Jeremiah. *The Restoration of all Things; or, A Vindication of the Goodness and Grace of God, Recovery of His Creation out of Their Fall.* Philadelphia: Gilson, Fairchild and Co., 1844.

Williams, George Huntson. *The Radical Reformation.* Philadelphia: Westminster Press, 1962.

Williams, Robert Folkestone. *The Court and Times of James the First.* Two volumes. London: H. Colburn, 1848.

Witherley, William. *Hints Humbly Submitted to Commentators, and More Especially to Such as Have Written Elaborate Dissertations on the Prophecies of Daniel and the Revelation of St. John.* London: n.p., 1821.

Woodhouse, Arthur Sutherland Pigott. *Puritanism and Liberty.* Chicago: University of Chicago Press, 1951.

Zangwill, Israel. *The Voice of Jerusalem.* New York: The Macmillan Company, 1921.

Tools of Research

Bainton, Roland H. *Bibliography of the Continental Reformation.* Chicago: American Society of Church History, 1935.

Barrow, John Graves. *A Bibliography of Bibliographies in Religion.* Ann Arbor: Edwards Bros., 1955.

Bishop, William Warner. *A Checklist of American Copies of "Short-Title Catalogue" Books.* Ann Arbor: University of Michigan Press, 1950.

British Museum General Catalogue of Printed Books. Photolithographic edition to 1955. London: Trustees of the British Museum, 1961.

Cambridge University Library. *Early English Printed Books in the University Library, 1475-1640.* Four volumes. Cambridge: University Press, n.d.

Case, Shirley Jackson, *et al. Bibliographical Guide to the History of Christianity.* Chicago: University of Chicago Press, 1931.

Catalogue of the Historical Library of Andrew Dickson White, First President of Cornell University: The Protestant Reformation and Its Forerunners. Ithaca: New York: The University Press, 1889.

Davies, Godfrey (editor). *Bibliography of British History: Stuart Period 1603-1714.* Oxford: University Press, 1928.

Department of Printed Books of the British Museum. Catalogue of Books in the Library of the British Museum Printed in England, Scotland, and Ireland, and of Books in English Printed Abroad to the Year 1640. Three volumes. British Museum, 1884.

Finkelstein, Louis (ed.). *The Jews, Their History, Culture and Religion.* Two volumes. New York: Harper and Row, 1960.

Froom, LeRoy Edwin. *Prophetic Faith of our Fathers.* Four volumes. Washington, D.C.: Review and Herald, 1946-1954.

Gee, H. and Hardy, W. J. *Documents Illustrative of English Church History Compiled from Original Sources.* London: Macmillan, 1896.

Gillett, Charles Ripley. *New York City Union Theological Seminary Library Catalogue of the McAlpin Collection of British History and Theology.* Five volumes. New York: Union Theological Seminary, 1927-30.

Gouge, Henry. *A General Index to the Publications of the Parker Society.* Cambridge: University Press, 1855.

Graetz, Heinrich. *History of the Jews.* Four Volumes. Philadelphia: Jewish Publication Society of America, 1891-95.

Gruber, L. Franklin. *Documentary Sketch of the Reformation.* St. Paul: Ernst Mussgang, 1917.

Halkett, Samuel and Laing, John. *Dictionary of Anonymous and Pseudonymous Literature.* Nine volumes. Edinburgh: Oliver and Boyd, 1926-34.

Index to Religious Periodical Literature, 1953-54. Chicago: American Theological Library Association, 1956.

Kauffman, Donald T. *The Dictionary of Religious Terms.* Westwood, New Jersey: Fleming H. Revell Company, 1967.

Kidd, B. J. *Documents Illustrative of the Continental Reformation.* Oxford: The Clarendon Press, 1911.

London Stationers' Company. *Transcript of the Registers of the Company of Stationers of London 1554-1640* London: privately printed, 1875-77.

Migne, Jacques Paul. *Patrologiae Cursus Completus, . . . Series Graeca.* 161 volumes. Paris: J. P. Migne, 1857-66.

Migne, Jacques Paul. *Patrologiae Cursus Completus, . . . Series Latina,* 221 volumes. Paris: J. P. Migne, 1841-86.

Modder, Montagu Frank. *The Jew in the Literature of England to the End of the Nineteenth Century.* Philadelphia: Jewish Publication Society of America, 1939.

Modder, Montagu Frank. *The Jew in the Literature of England to the end of the Nineteenth Century.* New York: Meridan, 1960.

The New Schaff-Herzog Encyclopedia of Religious Knowledge. Fourteen volumes. Edited by Samual Macauley Jackson. New York: Macmillan, 1899.

Miesel, Wilhelm. *Calvin-Bibliographie.* München: Chr. Kaiser Verlag, 1961.

O'Malley, C. D. (compiler). *Sutro Collection of Books and Pamphlets on the Protestant Reformation.* San Francisco: California State Library, 1940.

Pollard, Alfred William and Redgrave, G. R. *Short-Title Catalogue of Books Printed in England, Scotland and Ireland, and of English Books Printed Abroad, 1475-1640.* London: London Bible Society, 1926.

Read, Conyers (editor). *Bibliography of British History: Tudor Period 1485-1603*. Oxford: University Press, 1928-33.

Richardson, Ernest Cushing. *An Alphabetical Subject Index and Index Encyclopaedia of Periodical Articles on Religion, 1889-1899*. New York: Scribner, 1907-11.

Roth, Cecil. *Magna Bibliotheca Anglo-Judaica*. Two volumes. London: The Jewish Historical Society of England, 1937.

Schaff, Philip (ed.). *A Select Library of Nicene and Post Nicene Fathers*. Fourteen volumes. New York: Charles Scribner's Sons, 1905-1917.

Sheehy, Eugene P. *Guide to Reference Books*. Eighth Edition. First Supplement 1965-66. Chicago: American Library Association, 1968.

Shuriami, Schlomo. *Bibliography of Jewish Bibliographies*. Jerusalem: University Press, 1936.

Smith, Wilbur M. *A Preliminary Bibliography for the Study of Prophecy*. Boston: W. A. Wilde Co., 1952.

Stephen, Leslie and Lee, Sidney (eds.). *Dictionary of National Biography*. Sixty-three volumes. London: Smith and Elder, 1908-09.

Stephen, Sir Leslie and Lee, Sir Sidney (eds.). *The Dictionary of National Biography*. Sixty-nine volumes. Oxford: Oxford University Press, 1959-60.

Strack, Hermann L. and Billerbeck, Paul. *Kommentar zum Neuen Testament aus Talmud und Midrasch*. München: Ch. Back'sche Verlags Buchandlung Oskarbeck, 1922-28.

Twinn, Kenneth (editor). *Williams Library, London, Early Nonconformity 1566-1800*. Twelve volumes. Boston: G. K. Hall, 1968.

Verein fur Reformationsgeschichte. *Quellen und Forschungen zur Reformations geschichte.* Leipzig: Gütersloher Verlagshaus, G. Mohn, 1911.

Whitley, William Thomas. *A Baptist Bibliography for Great Britain, Ireland and the Colonies.* Two volumes. London: Kingsgate Press, 1916-22.

Winchell, Constance M. *Guide to Reference Books Fourth Supplement 1959-1962.* Chicago: American Library Association, 1963.

Winchell, Constance M. *Guide to Reference Books Third Supplement 1956-1958.* Chicago: American Library Association, 1960.

Winchell, Constance M. *Guide to Reference Books Second Supplement 1953-1955.* Chicago: American Library Association, 1956.

Winchell, Constance M. *Guide to Reference Books* Supplement 1950-52. Chicago: American Library Association, 1954.

Winchell, Constance M. *Guide to Reference Books.* Chicago: American Library Association, 1951.

Wing, Donald Goddard. *Short-Title Catalogue of Books printed in England, Scotland, Ireland, Wales and British America and of English Books Printed in Other Countries, 1641-1700.* Six volumes. New York: Columbia University Press, 1945-46.

Wordsworth, Christopher. *Ecclesiastical Biography; or, Lives of Eminent Men, Connected with the History of Religion in England; From the Commencement of the Reformation to the Revolution.* Four volumes. London: Francis and John Rivington, 1853.

World Zionist Organization. *Stenographisches Protokoll der verhandungen des IV. Zionisten Congresses in London 13, 14, 15, 16 August 1900.* Wien: World Zionist Organization, 1900.

Index